SEMANTIC ISSUES

SEMANTIC ISSUES

M. F. H. ROE

THE BRITANNIA PRESS
LONDON

First published in Great Britain in 1994
by The Britannia Press
8 Caledonia Street
London N1 9DZ

© 1994 M.F.H. Roe

ISBN 1 872571 02 6
Typeset in 10pt Baskerville by GCS
Printed in Great Britain

Semantic Issues

TABLE OF CONTENTS

Preface

The question is: What is the issue under study in this text? Put simply it is this: that philosophy's essential, not its only, role is to attend to what science, for a number of reasons, cannot properly undertake: namely *general* evaluation, when that refers to value as it accrues to all men, particularly in a social context. This may in part be interpreted as the study of priorities of importance, or, otherwise said, the values by which society most sanely lives – a matter of some significance today.

Two factors render this subject peculiarly difficult to consider. First, that there is no adequate discipline with which to proceed, since rationalistic methodologies developed to serve the cognitive interest specifically are plainly inapt when this is the concern, especially as value in general accrues in relation to the dynamic, interrelative complex that characterizes society as much as it does the natural order. And secondly, that a fitting vocabulary for dealing with such matters is scarcely available, since the terms that apply have been purloined to serve the dominant cognitive interest, so that they have lost the meanings they once had and must be redefined if they are to be used effectively. Hence, the first requirement is some clarification, to be followed in a later book, by discussion of appropriate procedures, an alternative organon.

That this thought is in some sense dependent on Chinese presuppositions – the most important of which is that the criterion for serious thinking is not truth but social need – is as it may be. I

1

then address Western thinkers with the idea that that is a matter that cannot be neglected. Indeed, it would be absurd to think that it is out of order to learn from sources which have something to teach us, in this case the importance of thought on social problems, which, with the idealist cult of the autonomous individual, have tended to be misinterpreted, in that they are not in strict sense amenable to cognitive engagement.

If the reader finds this unacceptable, as a challenge to current ideas, he can cast the book aside. But if the subject is serious, such matters as these, with their verbal connotations in the present text, should not be brushed aside, as if there were no occasion to reconsider what words mean in evaluative discourse.

M.F.H. Roe

London, 1992

Introduction

No language has a ready-made vocabulary for the needs of mental activity. They all borrow their vocabularies from words originally meant to correspond either to sense experience or to other experiences of normal life.

Arendt

There is a saying of Chuang Chou, which when put into English, may be rendered in various way. One, which may reflect the spirit in which he wrote, might be given such a form as this: "Once the meaning is grasped, the term may be thrown away", to which an alternative is: "When the idea is expressed, the language may be ignored".[1] Rationalists seem to find this statement incomprehensible, a piece of gratuitous nonsense. But, in the absence of prejudice, its import is by no means difficult to discern, and it calls for no great acumen to understand its bearing. For what it implies is simply this, which is surely plain enough: that meaning resides in need as that appertains to life, and not or not directly in some verbal formulation. And that sentence, to confirm this, could readily be framed, as it has been above, in different words without loss of its essential message. For words are, properly speaking, no more than signals projected to draw their hearer's attention to what immediately signifies in the conditions obtaining. And if that is questioned on the score of its vagueness – for 'what

3

immediately signifies' is a loose expression – it may yet, without recourse to rigorous definition, be shown to be comprehensible.

Even to translate from one related language into another, from French to English for instance, is not without its difficulties, as words in either language may not have precisely the same significance. And when it comes to the translation of a Chinese or Sanskrit text into some Western language, this difficulty is compounded, as may even be the case with the writings of antiquity. That it is possible to achieve such transfers as these at all is because the experiences that human beings have, at least on basic levels, common characteristics. 'I am hungry or thirsty', 'turn left', 'look sharp', 'take care', or 'let us meet tomorrow morning', are expressed in various ways in every human language, as are common relationships, 'parent', 'child', 'brother', and so on, which apply to normal living. Behind most words, of course, lie layers of further meanings, of meanings that are modified as ideas and cultures develop. This renders the translation of earlier texts more difficult than is the case with contemporary statements in kindred languages, behind which experiences in life in a broad sense are similar; and so much so that in normal concerns direct substitution of terms is possible, even easy. Conversely, to understand what was being said even in archaic forms of a familiar language sometimes leads to error in interpretation despite the use of similar terms, when what is receiving attention is something more complex and intricate than fundamental interests. If, then, we wish to study ancient or foreign texts, we must attempt to think as those who wrote them thought in order justly to grasp what their expressions signify. Indeed, it is often said with relation to current tongues that, to speak another language well, one should be able to think in it, that is, to share the experience of those reared under its influence. To translate, then, it is requisite to place oneself, in as far as one can, in the frame of mind of the thinker, which is plainly easier as languages have common roots and as those who use them are more or less contemporaries, who have been subjected to effectively similar influences in their conscious and subconscious lives. In so far, however, and this is the salient point, as all communication involves an exchange of ideas, it is the *meaning* to be conveyed that ultimately counts irrespective of the words chosen to convey it.

All this, however, is by the way and merely serves to show that this apparently dubious insight has substance and indeed some philosophical implications, for meaning is very surely a philosophical interest. So, let us turn to contemporary life and consider those in terms of everyday experience and the evident need for its communication, which cannot normally be sustained unless in special conditions – silent understanding – without some agreement on meanings. But this is not as straightforward as is at times supposed when clear and precise expression alone is taken into account. For, it was another Chinese thinker, whose name at once escapes me, who declared that four obstacles had to be overcome to secure clear communication. First, that the speaker had to form the idea he sought to express, and then to find suitable words with which to give it expression. Thirdly, the hearer had to interpret what was said, and finally had to formulate what was being conveyed into a clear idea within his own experience.[2] Normally, of course, this apparently complex process takes place with extreme rapidity, the more so as the idea expressed is free from complication or latent ambiguity. To respond to the order "Stand at ease" requires no great mental effort, and 'Beware' is a form of address that calls for no complicated analysis or indeed gives time for it, for debate or hesitation. But, as what is said is more intricate or suggestive or as the words in which it is framed are tinged with equivocation, obstacles to a ready grasp become increasingly formidable. The end, however, remains the same: that an adequate response to the message is evoked.

Thus far, the bias in this has tended to turn on words and their adequate conveyance, on expression that is to say, so that those who deal with verbal formulations, logicians and verbal analysts, may, despite these complications, find themselves in sympathy with the thoughts projected. For it is in reducing these obstacles to clear communication that formal logic finds its purpose and its warrant. A sentence with obscure or contradictory reference, for instance the Liar's Paradox, presents a peculiar challenge when this is the aim in view. As this has little relation to what is of moment in ordinary life, the difficulties encountered scarcely worry simple people. Put bluntly, problems of this type have no vital meaning, no relation to real needs, and are of interest only to those intrigued by such conundrums.[3] And real need is what language relates to when it is used to serve vital ends. There are times, of course, when words are not required, since what befits the occasion may be met in other ways. It is well-known, for instance, that sympathy is often best conveyed by silence, as if words were clumsy instruments with which to express the involvement: feeling which is sincere and which is mutually understood. But such relations are exceptional and do not call for any third-party intervention, which is otherwise to say that they are not the concern of philosophy, which should restrict itself to what can properly be generalized. Hence, the point that is really being made, which is one of some significance in a philosophical sense, is that meaning resides in the answering of some interest, the serving of some purpose which is more than merely personal, in which sense alone it has a general bearing. Need is the essential concern, and that carries this implication: that words used in philosophy have reference less to things than to basic requirements as those relate to the process of living. And that is what should condition their use in directed discourse, in which what is at issue are needs in the deepest sense, needs that can only be met in the complex of actuality, demanding that the terms employed are those to which the meanings are suited, properly suited to what signifies in life.

The process of living is, of course, permeated with meaning, from the infant's need for milk, which reflects all basic material needs, for food, for shelter, security, self-preservation, and so on – needs that men share on this plane with all other sentient beings – to needs which are, without hyperbole, rather thought of as 'spiritual', for sympathy, affection, justice, co-operation, to cite the most obvious among them. Even the need to answer some abtruse or difficult question of a type that might interest a scholar is something that gives a meaning to life, albeit that in such a case the interest is largely personal, unless his studies acquire a further justification by enhancing quality of life for others than himself. But need is more certainly present in the most ordinary aspects of life, indeed in the very notion of action, which is normally undertaken to serve some felt or overt requirement. Words in this sense are but means to some end, which end, to the broadest reading, is simply the end of living. Hence, meaning to this reading always has priority; and words, which allow it to be conveyed, more or less successfully, are subordinate to it, instrumental rather than significant in themselves. As instrumental, however, they must be used with care when the end is to refer to need in the deepest sense.

*

In so far as philosophers aim, when their thought is realistic, to attain to a better and deeper understanding of basic human needs - spiritual in their field, for it is the province of science to deal with those that are material - and of the forms in which they are met, it is a clear requirement that they should use words which relate to them in their most meaningful senses. For, an improper use of terms may lead to misunderstanding, notably as it is or seems to be forgotten that their vital meanings refer to what is of moment in life, the answering of such needs. Of these in their many varieties, verbal precision or rigour in statement is but one, with essential bearing only in exceptional circumstances, those in which the interests at stake - as in making decisions affecting the lives of others - demands careful deliberation. Thus, the use of more than one word to ensure that a meaning is clear constitutes a means of avoiding misunderstanding when words may be amenable to varied interpretations. Law affords an instance of this when it employs several words to cover any contingency that might be conceived, in implicit recognition that no single expression suffices to meet every eventuality. And in so far as what is of concern to philosophy when it attends to real issues is very much more complex than what is defined by law, care is especially needed to ensure that what is said shall have a meaning that is pertinent, however difficult it may be to ensure that it has that character when reference is to man's involvement with reality, the dynamic of becoming. It is pointed, then, to repeat that the meanings of words relate, when discourse takes this form, directly to exigences, so that, if their bearings are not considered properly, in real as opposed to ideal terms, their vital connotations may be lost or obscured. Thus, it is wholly proper to stress that meanings in this sense have absolute priority; and that no amount of strict linguistic analysis is to the point unless the meanings it considers are those directly related to life.

Although this is not entirely the case, the analysis of terms in latterday philosophy has tended to be confined to logical connectives or to words that are submissive to investigation logically. And this is the more regrettable in that that approach has been essentially idealistic, concerned, despite a dubious use of subjective generalization, with what is of interest to the conscious

7

individual or, rather more precisely, the rationalizing thinker. That needs at basic levels are not in strict sense definable, or are misrepresented if too strictly defined, that many needs are not brought clearly into consciousness, such that they cannot be subjected to 'analysis' or, better said, cognized, is so far forgotten that such needs are not discussed, with the consequence that they do not receive proper consideration. As was said by Searle, to give this confirmation: "It is not his job as a philosopher to tell people what they ought to do (to give thought to needs as they are met in the social complex), because such statements are evaluative, and thus cannot be strictly speaking true or false at all".[4] And though this citation is scarcely fair to analysts in general, it shows that an idealistic or, rather more decisively, a cognitive approach is ill-fitted to deal with vital meanings or needs. For, in any realistic sense, needs are always evaluative.

It seems to be the case that a preoccupation with cognitive enquiry so far rules the current scene that words, and highly important words with respect to their deeper meanings, are exclusively defined in terms of this special interest, that is to say, in narrow and restrictive senses. It was originally the intention to entitle this book *Veiled Meanings*, implying thereby that meanings with philosophical bearing had been obscured or hidden in the interests of a dominant cognitive enquiry, as if that alone were worthy of serious pursuit. That what such enquiry as that achieves in the abstract form that it has is minimal as compared with what is achieved by science, which endeavours under handicap of restriction to the phenomenal or the observable world to engage the world of actuality, need not now be stressed. For that is not immediately relevant, except in the sense that, as ideal, abstract or verbal only, analytic philosophy cannot be regarded as having much bearing on life and the problems it really presents. And that is a pity because it is only philosophy which is equipped to consider the nature of value in general. Meanwhile, what is very much more to the point is that philosophy should, in some form or another, give thought to the problem that presents if it is to make a meaningful contribution. The first requirement, then, if that is the form it should take, is that it should examine some of the terms that it uses, largely uncritically it would seem and without sufficient regard to what thought in other fields now brings to its attention, in realistic terms, even should that be alien to its received tradition.

*

There are then a number of terms which demand what might be called analysis, albeit of deeper type, involving investigation into their further meanings as those relate to actualities, to needs as they bear on life. These meanings have been considered in pairs, because, despite claims of making clear distinctions on the part of analysts, some highly important terms have been used in the loosest manner, as synonyms when they in a referential sense are nothing of the sort. Hence, if two terms which have been used as if they were interchangeable, or in loose relation without awareness of what is lost, are shown to have distinctive meanings, their coalescence, which generates confusion and misunderstanding, can be exposed for what it is: an improper use of terms. At times there is a vague awareness that some terms employed synonymously are being used too loosely. But that is seldom made explicit in respect of some words that count, as if the weight of traditional usage were too heavy to permit of serious challenge to it. To consider, for illustration, a term not dealt with in the text, which is freely used without regard to its proper frame of reference, 'truth' might be given attention. A little thought reveals that it has several significances, which are certainly not the same unless to superficial readings. Truth in a moral context, which is contrasted with lying, is surely different from truth in a logical context, the antithesis of which is falsity or error, something other plainly than falsehood or deceit. Truth in religious meaning in which it is bound to the need for a faith, such that it might, as related to differing forms of belief, be thought of as 'acceptance'.[5] is scarcely the same as abstract truth, impersonal in principle, which is little more than verbal and need not in that sense involve acceptance at all, unless in such forms as 'A is A', which scarcely allows disagreement. And if the last acquires prestige by association with the first and the second, as if scepticism of its reach were vicious or heretical,[6] and claims to have a force comparable with or as meaningful socially as the others, that is without question improperly asserted. To glorify truth in rational forms as if it had the weight of truth in other spheres of life, amounts to misrepresentation,[7] a purloining of repute. This correlation, however, scarcely signifies socially, since all sensible persons are aware that lying and error are certainly not the same; and indeed that the last, if genuine, is innocent, simply grounded in ignorance, which is a common failing even in the erudite when they enter other fields than those in which they are experts. Scientists, in contrast to those dealing in absolute truths, have long been content to hold that their findings are merely contingent, and even go so far as to say that "they are approximate only in the nature of the case".[8] This is profoundly different from claims to absolute truth to which scientists make no pretence, preferring rather to speak of 'reliable knowledge', in recognition moreover that there are degrees of reliability, roughly Bradley's "degrees of truth".[9] Yet logic affects to believe that its findings refer to externals, which is surely a dubious claim, inasmuch as reality, as sceptics have held through the ages, is beyond the reach of alethic determination.

Let that pass, however, as sufficiently obvious to all but formal logicians to call for no further attention. There are several other terms which are more significant in that they relate to life as it is actually lived. These are not so easy to deal with, in part because traditional usage in the schools has thus far ruled that what they represent is not recognizable or, if recognized as having real existence, outside rational discourse, and in part because of reluctance freely to admit that there are extra-cognitive interests. To which it might be added, lest another ambiguous usage further confuses issues, that 'rational' as used by logocentric thinkers has itself a limited meaning obscured in its adjectival form, which should rather be 'rationalistic'. For 'rational' means both 'reasonable' and 'ratiocinative', to use another term which is sharper than rationalistic; and these two terms quite certainly have distinctive references, to concrete and abstract discourse or communication respectively. To refer to an aspect of Russell's thought,[10] it might fairly be said that rationalism in the sense of ratiocination is a class of reasoning with special characteristics, which are only by courtesy or dubious extension aligned with those applied by everyone in action against the pressures of reality. This thesis, like any referred to states in actuality, does not lean on logical or rationalistic procedures – a matter to be considered in greater depth in the sequel – although it is fairly held to be reasonably expressed and is submissive in that sense to relevant critique, to disciplined objection as that may be appropriate. Much depends, of course, on the criterion adopted, both when thought is projected and criticism is applied to it. For that need not be logical rigour, which indeed it cannot be, unless in respect of consistency, when the interest that informs it is general evaluation. That adopted here may be described as human need, which is in principle if not in rationalistic practice, the ultimate warrant for all enquiry whatsoever: for even eliciting truth has that as its ultimate justification.

The enhancement of life in some form or another constitutes the end of all genuine enquiry, which is meaningful as that is understood as its warrant. If certain terms in use in the schools delimit or impede a greater depth of understanding referred to this enhancement, then some study of what that implies, of the forms in which this restrictiveness resides, is certainly in order. The exposure of dubious usage or of failure to grasp that certain significant terms have distinctive meanings and should not be aligned with words that refer to different interests, values or functions, is even overdue. For the consequences of misusage have been that serious social issues have been neglected or lost to view, veiled or misrepresented because the terms that refer to such issues have been obscured and even purloined to serve exclusively cognitive ends. To overcome these obstacles to better under-standing, it has to be accepted, even if that is difficult and goes against tradition, that the proper criterion for philosophic enquiry is not cognitive precision dependent on formal logic but human need considered in its fullest and deepest sense. And that can only be understood by recourse to more sensitive means, if only in the use of referential terms, those, so far from rendering discourse 'loose' or 'unphilosophical', are requisite if philosophy is to develop its full potential in the conditions existing today. For if that is a concern with general evaluation, with man's relation to the world in a fundamental sense, it makes a contribution which is distinct from that of science, as it does not if it is cognitive. A movement towards real problems, then, must certainly take start from the proper use of terms as those relate to vital needs. And lest this should be regarded as a dubious form of adventuring, this is suitably said: that concern with the meanings of operative terms is by any token a philosophical role. And if this must involve suggestion as one of its modes of approach, the exploitation of other means than those of formal logic, that is part of the problem that has to be accepted, even though current concern appears to be limited to truth-claims. This is then the purpose of the present

11

book, which makes no pretence to promote any explanatory truth, holding that to be effectively unattainable when the interest is human need, seen, as it certainly should be, in evaluative terms. What then are the terms at issue in evaluative studies? They are clearly those that relate to response on basic or vital levels: reality, sensation, mind, subject and understanding.

Reality: That to which response is made.
Sensation: The form in which it is made at fundamental levels.
Mind, the: The instrument with which it is organized and controlled.
Subject, the: The responsive agent at this level of receptivity.
Understanding: The product of response which is other than strictly cognitive.
Ethics: Interpreted as a concern with the quality of society, of social inter-relations, seen as the primary reason for giving thought to such matters as these, as the interest underlying general evaluation.

Chapter One

Appearance and Reality

A distinction between appearance and reality has long been accepted in philosophy, at least from the time of Plato in the West and even earlier in India, where the doctrine of $m\bar{a}y\bar{a}$ was projected in the Svetāsvatara Upanishad.[1] That this distinction did not always have a similar form is sufficiently evident; but the idea that the world that was received was but a reflection or shadow of reality constituted the common insight of those who attended to this matter. What 'appearance' meant was not in dispute, since it was generally agreed that it referred to the world of phenomenal being to which observation or perception was restricted, as a world beyond which the knowing mind was powerless to pass. And if what is perceived is regarded as reality, as by naïve realists, that is a view that merely confuses ideas on this issue and obscures the point implicit in this distinction. Conversely, with regard to the meaning of 'reality' ideas have always differed profoundly, which is scarcely surprising when it is considered that, given its limited reach, the intellect is powerless to define it in terms which can fairly be held to be conclusive. Hence various ideas with respect to its nature, ranging from Platonic Forms, which effectively render it wholly transcendent of nature, to the materialism implicit in deterministic thinking, have at various times been projected. As answers these continue to exert a certain appeal to those who desire to comprehend reality in terms of their psychological needs, the need for instance to feel that they can be masters of it, and so they yet prevail. But requirement to make a choice between these presented alternatives, and with it some exclusion of what undoubtedly has importance, is scarcely satisfactory from a philosophical standpoint, demanding that there should be but one 'truth', even though it cannot in strict sense be proven.

The main difficulty, however, in discussion of this matter, is that the word 'reality' is itself intrinsically ambiguous, quite apart from what it might mean in any particular theory. For it refers at once, and quite legitimately it seems, both to the whole, to all that there is, including hallucinations, which are real in the sense that they are certainly experienced, *and* to various aspects of responsive existence. In the first sense there is plainly nothing that is not real; in the second what is imagined is denied that attribute because it is not related to concrete actuality. Thus is illusion considered 'unreal', fantastic or unsubstantial, in contrast to what is uncritically taken to be real, that with which we are involved in fully conscious life, the tangible, the concrete, the *apparently* actual. There is a famous passage in Chuang Chou in which he says he dreamt that he was a butterfly and that when he awoke he asked himself this question:[2] Am I a man who dreamt that he was a fluttering creature, flying daintily through the air, or am I a butterfly now dreaming that he is a man? Absurd, one might say, for the answer is quite obvious. But, discounting irony, is it entirely so if it contains a lesson: that things are not entirely as they seem to be. For what he is saying in so many words is that reality, what is given, is present in different guises, and that, if only one is taken as correct, we make a dubious assumption: that what is real to clear consciousness constitutes all that there is, even on the level of human receptivity. To take another comment: it has been said, in this case by a scientist which should raise it above suspicion, that were the rods and cones in our eyes slightly differently structured we would see the world around us as pink or tinged with a rosy hue. Would it then be pink or as we now see it, pictured as having varigated colours over which in these conditions a veil of rosiness would have been drawn? No answer is required, for the notion is but speculative. But that is not all that may be said to make this point convincingly. Dogs, it is believed, to cite a further instance, do not see colours as we do but only shades of grey, relying on smell for the greater part to thread their canine ways through the environment that surrounds them. The dog's reality is patently, then, different from our own; but it can scarcely be denied that it is *a* reality, even though it is one of little concern to ourselves. It is of interest then to note that Bradley used the expression, in this context, "our reality",[3] meaning that to which we are formed to respond with our *human* constitutions.

A more decisive difficulty about the term 'reality' is that it has at least two quite justified meanings: one applying to conscious or perceptual involvement, and the other to what is truly the case, the actual 'state of affairs'. Nor does it require a great effort of thought to realize that ideas such as these are almost certainly different. For though philosophers speak with scorn of naïve realists, of "the vulgar prejudices of simple common sense",[4] they cannot escape that charge themselves if they refuse to acknowledge this difference and suppose that the world to which knowledge applies is the world of external reality, "thinkable but not knowable", in a famous expression.[5] Thus must we grasp at the outset that whereas we can know, or at least have tolerably clear ideas with regard to the nature of "our reality", it is not within our power to 'know' that greater and deeper reality of which that is but a reflection. This undoubtedly makes for philosophical difficulties, since, if this greater world cannot be cognized, then anything said about it cannot be more than speculative. But truth scarcely applies when such a matter as this is discussed, which may render its discussion, as is said, "unphilosophical",[6] as if that stricture were sufficient to dismiss it as unworthy of a serious philosophic attention.

The issue, however, will not disappear, pass away as mis-conceived, as metaphyiscal sophistry, and so for sufficient reason. For what man actually confronts in his state as a vital being obliged in live in conditions which he can never quite comprehend, cannot simply be dismissed as a matter of no moment. It does not cease to be a meaningful concern even though it cannot properly be rationalized. And let it further be considered as this matter is brought to attention, that he who is so involved is without question conditioned by and under the influence of what occurs in this further world. This is indeed implicit in the term 'stimulation', since stimuli themselves are quite certainly brought to being by continual changes in it. And what has now been recognized is that even his thinking is conditioned in this way, not only by interpreted stimuli, on which all perception depends, but no less by influences which are not recorded consciously.

Intuition, which does enter into consciousness, surreptitiously as it were, affords an example of this, in that it seems to involve an exposure of what was latent but had hitherto been hidden. And despite attempts to 'explain' it – as "forgotten inference" for instance[7] – intuition remains a mysterious emanation, which is properly inexplicable. Nor is point immediately served by elaboration on this, since it suffices at once to note that when an inexplicable is recognized as such, good sense demands that that be acknowledged as a 'fact', and so without suggestion that that constitutes loose thinking, as though the sustaining of such an idea were a form of superstititon, or whatever pejorative term rationalists choose to employ. There is much that is inexplicable which has bearing on human life, and it cannot be disregarded because it cannot be explained or discussed in strict rational terms.

It has long been the custom in metaphysical thinking to speak of 'ultimate reality', as something other than and different from 'our reality', as that which gives the latter its ground. This distinguishes one from the other; and however much empiricists may deplore this as a division, in that it projects an empirically unknowable, it is very plainly justified, since without its positing there is no substratum for what is taken to be external and is acknowledged as 'mind-independent'. Furthermore, this conception bears an intimate relation to another ancient but rather neglected distinction, that once held between being and becoming, which is not so much completely overlooked as seen in terms that fail to do full justice to its significance. For if being, like reality, is held to be all-embracing, becoming can be taken as but one of its forms. But that is to misunderstand the essential difference between them as ideas about reality. For being may be said to be a form of 'our reality', something which is knowable, made up of particulars, of Heideggerian 'beings', whereas of its nature becoming cannot be known through induction, since it is, as flowing, indivisible, interrelative, properly speaking without parts. Being for Parmenides, without elaboration, was projected against a Heraclitan becoming,[8] as referred to a world of what *is*, a world that is unchanging. It had for him the character of something comprehensible, as becoming was not, a reading echoed by Plato in a rather different form. Becoming was referred, as it were, to a world that was ever-changing, exemplified by fire; being to a world which was rather static. And although it was not a strict cognitive end that Parmenides had in mind, in principle 'what is' can be known, related to truth as perennial, which was certainly his interest. But, we cannot of course get a similar grip on what has a protean character, as Heraclitus avered. As truth has generally been the aim in later Western thinking, becoming as a doctrine with ontological import has tended to be neglected. But there may be some point in reviving interest in it.

In this there is something a little paradoxical, which divides the present from the thought of classical times, in that it is being in phenomenal form which alone, it is now seen, can correctly be studied by science. Although Parmenides believed that the world as he conceived it could be comprehended by reason, indeed that thought and being or reality were one, as did later thinkers, that is not a view acceptable to realists. In so far, however, as becoming is not, as dynamic, justly to be objectified, this idea of being as unchanging and eternal, an idea implicit in the notion of truth, has won the day as truth is held to be the end of philosophy against attention to an indeterminate becoming. The cult of cognition clearly has roots in this approach, since it could scarcely have been developed as a means of establishing truth on a doctrine of dynamic ever-changing becoming. That in the West has been brushed aside as impervious to proof and so unworthy of attention;[9] and indeed the very term *logos* has so far changed its meaning, or one of its meanings at least, as to refer exclusively to strictly rational discourse, seeking immutable truth. The continuance of the doctrine of *tao*, a doctrine like *logos* in earlier form of dynamic becoming, does something – though by no means all – to explain the Chinese failure to develop a science fully. This thought further allows of an understanding of why the West has had a preference for being, since the world so seen as basically unchanging, uniform or rather regular in action, can also be seen as something which is potentially knowable, something over which reason has some power, gradually in time to bring it under control. Of course, there is in this an intolerable ambiguity, as to what is meant by being in contradistinction to beings. Was it something that could be comprehended cognitively or was it something rather beyond the reach of perception, and so of course of cognition? This issue is still debated today, to constitute a division between the empiricists and the 'rationalists'. But, now that science has shown that there are forces at work behind what is

17

directly perceived, that debate has become outdated, though that calls for further comment. And so let thought be given to the question of why this should be so, why neither of these approaches in their earlier forms dealt with this problem adequately.

*

Lacking the deeper insights which modern science allows, earlier thinkers lacked the power clearly to distinguish *in concrete terms* between phenomenal presentations and a further world. For that further world was for rationalists a world transcendent of nature, one in respect of which concepts could be formed, and not a substantial world, the world of actuality, existing, hidden as it were, below the level of consciousness. This, their thought, had profound effects on the forms of thought that followed, which even now are difficult to reject completely. For traditionally the alternative, rationalism[10] – now using that term in a generic sense – dominating thought in every sphere of enquiry, was a materialistic posture. Hence the sphere to which metaphysics applied was invariably the ideal, not the world below perception, which was scarcely recognized, but a world above and beyond it, the super-sensible sphere, which could not be reached by reason unless that was strictly ideal and without relation to actuality, as with Platonic Forms.[11] That a similar idea or subject for contemplation was never, or hardly ever, entertained in China, where heaven in later times effectively meant nature and where spirit was seen not as transcendent of but immanent *in* nature, is the reason why it has proved so difficult to understand Chinese thought and, paradoxically perhaps, the reason why it is said in some sense to be 'more spiritual'. For, unless it is purely abstract, deductive, a priori, knowledge can only be of what is material, what can be observed, objectified and so given a cognitive form. *Tao*, though a spiritual power in the sense that it was regarded as vital, an animating pulse, was envisaged as wholly natural, as perhaps was the scholastic *natura naturans*, however it was disguised as a divine creative power which produced *natura naturata*.[12] And the Heraclitan *logos* seems to have had a broadly similar meaning despite its apparent relation to *legein* in one meaning, that is to an ideal world. For when the *Fragments* are read without bringing later meanings of *logos* to bear on

18

interpretation, indeed in the thought that it could have meant 'gathering' rather than 'speaking'[13] - one form of gathering only - they seem to house a comparable insight. But the meaning of such early thought is difficult to discern through the veil as it were of later verbal usage, unless in China where such thought persisted as an influence without this form of corruption.

Allowing that received ideas still have meaning in them and were projected in an effort to increase men's understanding of these deeper issues, we might then, with Western thinking in mind, conceive of three modes of reality, conveniently at once distinguished from one another. These may be considered a supra-empiric being, empiric being, which of course is 'our reality', and infra-empiric being, using that expression to refer to 'what is out there', beyond the reach of cognition. If the first is open to sceptical doubt, as to whether it has being in a secular sense at all, the last does not admit of doubt in a similar form, notwithstanding that it is as much beyond the reach of empiric enquiry as is the first of these forms of reality.[14] Nor does its projection as a further view involve an attempt to revive the idea of the mystic in yet another guise, even though it might seem so to dedicated empiricists. The intention in this is simply to show that the empiric is not all, albeit it is all that can in strict sense be known. Though the empiricist may reject the idea of a supernatural world, which he rather scornfully leaves to 'metaphysics', he is, since it gives a grounding for that with which he deals, under obligation to acknowledge this further world. It may be with reluctance that he makes this act of acceptance; but, now that science has shown that such a world indeed exists, without pretence to know or to comprehend it precisely, so that it is yet 'mysterious', that seems to be unavoidable.

Whether he admits the need for it or not, an enquirer cannot really escape the need to adopt an ontology, a view of the world he confronts. Broadly, to secular thinking, two views are available to him: determinism in whatever its several guises, the idea that *all* is causally determined - requisite, it seems, for scientific laws - or a sufficient alternative to it. Under dichotomic rulings, resting for their force on the excluded middle, that can only be *in*determinism, understood as involving powers of moral choice to ground responsibility, though that is rather an axic than an ontic reading. Accordingly, it suffers, when compared with the other, from being but an ideal projection, with little substantive evidence to support it as a contention, apart from this requirement which has only social relevance. Insofar as it constitutes an ontology proper, indeterminism appeals to the factor of chance or *tyche*,[15] as an operative factor related to human involvement – since it does not disallow that the doctrine of causality applies in predictive science – together with the notion of openness to change as a characteristic of nature. But since chance, as random, is not readily confirmed – with a pointed note in passing that absolute confirmation is not always attained in experiment, which, sometimes even fruitfully, leads to unexpected results – it plainly lacks an equivalent, rational, logical standing. Indeterminism is rather then a thesis put forward by moralists to justify the onus of choice than as an ontological doctrine. They can yet, however, defend their position in part by contending that determinism itself is far from completely proven, since it rests on selected instances – initially the movement of celestial bodies and later the discovery of other regularities – which are dubiously generalized to apply to the whole of nature.[16] How the world is structured then remains an open question, since it cannot be studied in itself but only by recourse to intellectual means which do not permit of referral beyond phenomenal presentations. But speculation on this is not simply idle, empty of content or meaning; for it may, when it is supported by oblique or partial evidence, be shown to be highly suggestive when it is referred to conceivable alternatives.

Whatever differences may be, there is one contention at least on which there can scarcely be disagreement: that the world is structured in some way. For, were it not, it simply would not hold together, sustain itself continually in apparent equilibrium. The question at issue, then, is how it is actually structured – atomically, mechanically, or in rather more subtle ways? That it is atomically structured is a very ancient idea which in some sense survives to this day. But the atoms that the early atomists had in mind were different indeed from those distinguished in modern chemistry, which are simply the smallest particles of any discovered elements which cannot be subdivided without destruction of their identity. As all is compounded of chemicals in various combinations, this seems to cover the case, bearing in mind that, though these atoms can now be analysed, their complex interrelations are what really count at this level. For sub-atomic physics now shows that such atoms as these are not the ultimate elements of which the world is compounded, and that such particles are in fact highly complex bodies comprised of charges about a nucleus. So far then from being isolated entities, as if the external world were made up of independent particulars, called 'atomic facts', the charges that appear to comprise the ultimate form of reality are interrelated in ways of quite extraordinary complexity, to constitute a manifold which is effectively indivisible. That the world is atomically ordered, then, is acceptable only in as far as it goes, that is to a certain level. Below that it appears, though this may be crudely put, that quanta or bundles of energy, which interact to sustain the complex in equilibrium, are in state of constant flux and so intricate in their relations that those are far from fully understood.[17] Atomism, accordingly, is at best but a doctrine which proved useful in the past for the study of aspects of nature but which is now superceded by more refined ideas about the nature of reality.

That the world is mechanically ordered is now an outdated notion, developed at a time when mechanics was the most advanced form of science or technology, and the only *modus agens* of nature as matter in motion which was at all understood. It enjoyed a long acceptance because, apart from lack of knowledge of what has now been elicited, it gave ground to rational explanation, not otherwise to be found, and further because it complied with the laws of formal logic, with the principle of causality or causal uniformity. This is the ground on which determinism rests, as a highly selective doctrine confined to the world of phenomena understood in the narrowest sense, to phenomena, that is, observed with the naked eye.[18] With the powers to pass beyond that range developed in modern times, it is seen that interrelations are very much more subtle; and that, though cause-and-effect operates on all levels, the manner in which it does so on levels below direct or natural perception is very far from being a simple one-to-one affair, as it was once supposed to be. This, then, as a feasible theory, can now be disregarded. But, so strong is the bias in favour of such a view as this, which so readily permits of rational explanation that any other idea on this matter of what is confronted has up until quite recently been dismissed as 'mystic', even when developed in such telling forms as emergent evolution or the vitalism of Bergson, as if the idea of *l'élan vital* undermined the principle of natural regularity.[19] Though determinism has generally dominated thinking, because it serves the interests of rationalism so well, yet has there always been uncertainty about it, as failing to account for what might be called 'felt need', admittedly a vague term. That the theme of intentionality was projected at a time when positivism was dominant demonstrates this sufficiently. But mastery through knowledge, based on the idea that "there is nothing in principle that cannot be known to science",[20] then exerted so powerful a sway that any alternative thesis had the appearance of being defensive. And indeed, for as long as the starting point was the 'knowing self', the conscious individual promised power over nature, idea of an ontology that was other than 'objective', meaning rationally determined, simply had no standing.[21] Thus determinists held the trumps, since they could confidently assert that their 'scientific' ontology was rationally respectable, whereas any other was rooted in 'subjective' bias and so could only be seen as answering some psychological need.

Science, meanwhile, without pretence to project a formal ontology, has produced an alternative free from either of these weaknesses, in that it makes no claim that this is 'objective' in strict sense, nor is it 'subjective' in the sense of projecting a view that is personal. This idea of what is confronted when attention is turned to the form of what is truly external is justly called 'holistic', meaning that it is recognized that all is interrelated in a dynamic complex which is effectively indivisible. It is not then compounded of parts, or objects as is implicit in objectification; it is not a world in which the subject as apperceptive plays a conscious part. It is external strictly, in the sense that, though it affects it, it does not enter consciousness as that is an ideal state. Nor is this asserted as a proven finding: it is rather an idea that has to be accepted as the only one that seems to conform with what has thus far been elicited. When holism was first introduced as a descriptive term, by philosophers themselves in the earlier years of this century,[22] it had a meaning related to the current preoccupation with cognitive enquiry, which it very properly sought to deepen and refine. Then, making a sharp distinction between the organic and inorganic, living and non-living action, the contention was that organic wholes functioned differently as wholes than was to be seen from studies confined to the functioning of their parts. How

22

these performed in themselves gave a false or inadequate picture of how they behaved in relation to that of which they were components, so that it was requisite also to consider them in terms of a total functioning – wholes in such a thesis being comprehensible units. Since that time, however, the meaning of this term has undergone some change. It is not now restricted to comprehensible wholes, to be studied in independence, but refers to the whole of all that there is, or of all that can be envisaged. Whether that be the cosmos or the planet Earth, with its circumambient atmosphere, is not immediately pertinent. For how cosmic forces condition the world in which we live is not, to present thinking at least, a philosophical problem, which is rather more modestly that of giving thought to the needs of men as sentient, influenced beings within their effective world. Enough that the Earth itself, within its stratospheric envelope, is seen to be a whole, a dynamic, indivisible, interrelative complex in which all forces, aspects or modes influence all others, directly or indirectly, in an unbroken network of adaptive changes.

*

It is not in this context requisite to make an attempt to describe the findings of modern psychics, nor those, which are no less meaningful, that we owe to biochemistry. Adequate accounts are readily available,[23] written in a way that philosophers unfamiliar with specialist technical terms can absorb sufficiently, which is all that is required to grasp their implications for philosophy itself. Of these two, it would seem that the second is more easily comprehended, since the issues with which that discipline is concerned are sufficiently concrete and free from unresolved theory to render their implications clear to those outsiders willing to make the effort required to understand what is operative. It is then the combinations of various chemical elements, mainly in gaseous form, which have produced and continue to produce and sustain the conditions in which life is possible. These subtle interrelationships, which, almost by chance it seems, brought life initially to being, subsist in a delicate state of fluctuating equipoise. And, so critical is this equipoise that did the composition of the elements that sustain it vary greatly in their make-up, to generate other balances, that might have serious consequences, producing destruction of life. Then, assuming the continuance of this delicate equipoise, what has to be noticed – to emphasize the relationship of everything in the complex – is that the acts of men, however apparently slight when compared with those of nature at large, may exert a decisive influence on the general situation to his own destruction over extended time. What these might be is not as such the real concern of philosophy, unless a little pretentiously it claims to be all-embracing, to enter specialist fields. It is enough at once to accept that man plays part in this process, even without full consciousness, and is not, whilst balance is sustained, independent of it. He could only be so were the balance of forces changed in such a way that he would not then be present, since the conditions for human life would not themselves prevail to allow of his survival. If this contains a suggestion that he does well to take note of how these conditions might change through action on his part, that is not the immediate interest. All that is pertinent at once is to understand that man, although as a thinker he in some sense stands apart from it, is involved in this greater complex, is part or mode of the total structure, or, to put it another way, of the process of becoming.

It is doubtfully possible, then, to make a clear distinction between human and non-human being, so that, if such a distinction is properly to be made, it must be made in other terms than those of relation to nature. For both in nature are aspects or modes of this becoming, to which there has to be persistent adaptation if the individual being, in whatever form, is to maintain his or its continuing existence, balance in conditions. Even rock, without the drive or underlying purpose which characterizes the lives of sentient, mobile beings, must sustain itself in balance, and water, which is fluid, find its proper level. This need to adapt, though less clearly than is the case with individuals, has social or ethical meaning, since societies to persist in any adequate state have continually to adjust to pressures bearing on them. The individual being has, of course, a limit to his or its existence, for he or it must eventually die to give place to new life, which is intrinsic part of the process of becoming, in which the individual has but a transient role to play. This, on a longer time scale may also be so for societies, which can, as history shows, become enfeebled and decay, giving ground, even harshly at times, to more robust successors. But unless in exceptional circumstances, epidemics or massacres, this rather applies to cultures, which yet however often leave a legacy on which those who have overthrown them in their original form can build to bring another to being, a further cultural flowering.

The whole, meanwhile, persists, and indeed persists by changing through continual interaction, adaptation of its components. Elements are replaced, as is the individual, as an aspect of this mutation – just as parts of the living body, the skin and the hair for instance, are renewed in the course of life, until such time as a weakening of the power to effect renewal brings about decay, and at last disintegration, which is commonly called death. All is in process of change, growing or decaying, forming itself or declining, whether in individual or in more general terms: for that is the real law of nature. If then, with stress on the self, the situation is viewed subjectively, it is difficult to slough a deterministic posture, which, although in theory objective and detached, is tied in fact to an entry through the knowing self, and is in that sense subjective. And, with that as the starting point, demanding constant laws referring to all events whatever to secure consistency, the idea of a fluid, ceaselessly changing structure is resisted as unacceptable. Broadly, for as long as idealism is dominant, there cannot be a fully realistic approach. For any ontology then is bound to the need for explanation, which is available only in respect of phenomena, of appearance in other words. Detachment from the external world, implicit to cognition, runs counter very plainly to involvement in it, which is the normal condition of life.[24]

The problem that this presents – and hence resistance to its adoption as a working ontology on the part of rationalists – is essentially methodological: for, if cognition presumes detachment from external actuality, difficult questions arise. It is not of course contended that cognition itself, which has vastly enhanced our lives, strengthened our capacities, is mistakenly pursued, for that would be absurd, even though its limits as engaging observables only must sensibly be recognized. However, a point has now been reached where these limits are not confined to what may fairly be known, which are imposed by powerlessness to pass beyond perception, for they have a further form related to procedure. Knowledge in strict or veridical form is acquired essentially by means of inductive procedures, which are fairly defined as reasoning from particulars to general statements about them, that is, about their relations. These statements cannot be other than intellectual constructs, twice removed from reality, as analytic and notional. For, if they are synthetic, and so establish relationships, those have being only on an intellectual plane. Hence, if what is at last confronted is a holistic manifold, in which there are no objects or parts, since that is dynamc, interrelative, indivisible, it cannot be grasped in its actual form by any such means as induction. All knowledge is not alethic, of course, nor is all science predictive, though claims to this effect are commonly projected. But the making of such claims as if they had universal bearing, though scepticism about them is as commonly projected, affords a clue to the nature of this further limitation, since there can be no certainty except on an ideal plane. A distinction might then be made, a little loosely perhaps, between descriptive or natural and fully explanatory science, which aspires to be apodeictic. For the first does not depend on a rational methodology but on more flexible procedures, on simple observation.[25] When an experiment is successful – as is perhaps best seen in medicine – that is because it accords with some aspect of reality, the truly external world. But when ordered artificially by excluding 'irrelevances' reflection is only partial and to that degree distorted. To reflect reality, then, an experiment should be free from any such modifications as tend to falsify this relation. Nature is encountered in this way directly; and though what is discovered may not in strict sense be 'true', with such an approach there will almost certainly be a greater degree of *vraisemblance* than when conclusiveness is claimed. For this reflection, as direct, is less likely to be erroneous than when absolute truth is claimed to be the character of what is discovered experimentally. The moral in this, now seen from a philosophical standpoint, is that experimentation involves the use of trial-and-error rather than of induction, since what it is referred to is a process of becoming which cannot be objectified or seen as having parts. It engages what is real in the form that it actually has without the introduction of abstraction or analysis. That as a procedure plainly has limitations. But with it science engages reality directly; and, through error or failure to achieve whatever was intended in the theory adopted, is driven to make alternative trials and to explore more thoroughly, which is the way in which it has persistently advanced to its present understanding of natural interrelationships. The methodological problem which emerges with the acceptance of a holistic ontology is only decisive then when science aspires to absolute, alethic explanation, adopts, that is to say, induction as a procedure and relies too greatly on theory. This is not the occasion to consider this point more fully or to propose an alternative. Sufficient that it presumes the need for a measure of rethinking with respect to approaches adopted. In this sense Bacon and others in the early days of science realized that strict deduction had to be augmented by a further system, which came to be called 'induction' and which has proved until this deeper ontology was developed a fertile means of exploring relationships in nature. In other words, the time has come when awareness of nature's complexity demands of those who study it that approaches shall be more sensitive, better attuned to involvement with a volatile actuality.

It is not philosophy's business to tell science how to proceed, as if it sought to force its rationalism on it. For science, which evolved it, scarcely needs to be advised on the matter of an ontology by those who must rather learn from it what its findings reveal. But science has always implicitly tended to be monistic, to accept that nature is an interrelative whole, which is even presumed in the doctrine of 'the laws of nature', now recognized, without doubting that such laws are operative, as very much more complex than was once supposed. And, if logic has demanded that nature shall be atomized, that science should adopt its analytic procedures and the deterministic doctrine to which it tends to cling, that has now lost whatever credit it may have had. That there should be one procedure indeed, as has been urged by certain rationalistic philosophers, under the general heading of 'the unity of science',[26] has never been accepted by scientists themselves, who recognize that many different methods are required to meet the varied problems confronted in their enquiries. Hence science now bids fair to jettison this connection, since formal logic is seen to lack the needed flexibility. So far then from accepting the absolutes of logicians – and these are characteristic of logic for as long as it is formal – science regards its findings as contingent and no more, which amounts to an acknowledgement that reality is more complex than the rationalizing intellect with its finalities can concede. Imagination and insight, intuition informed by persistent thinking on intractable problems, have played a considerable part in the discoveries it has made, which "are sometimes fruitful without being correct". And finally, "There is a feeling", to cite a very distinguished scientist, "that the order behind appearances cannot be fully grasped within any explanatory net".[27] School philosophy, meanwhile, tied to formal logic, cannot easily entertain any such idea. For a changing, mobile, fluid world does not comfortably ride with absolutes that refer to limited forms of language. As will be contended later, when procedures are discussed, the acceptance of this ontology, which can scarcely now be avoided, does not imply the abandonment of logic as an instrument, as a disciplining organon, which is what Aristotle intended that it should be. It merely calls for a deeper and better understanding of the manner in which it disciplines and must continue to do so, which involves the recognition that the search for absolute truth, or its positive application, is not the same as its critical power or its negative application, which, as will be seen, is both firmer and more far-reaching. But that raises very big questions which cannot now be discussed.

The immediate interest is then to ensure that philosophy also adopts this rediscovered ontology[28] and recognizes that it is even obliged to do so if it is to play a significant part in the evolution of thought as it is now developing. Though the methodological problem that science now faces is formidable, it yet accepts without demur the ontology that produces it – that the world is indeed holistic, in process of becoming, dynamic and indivisible – philosophy in its present state, or at least in is dominant forms, does not even see the problem; or, if it does, appears to believe that it is without significance for itself as a discipline. For, if what is in depth confronted is a holistic continuum, that cannot be acknowledged without relinquishing what it holds dear: its received idea of its role as ratiocinative, as the guardian and promoter of truth referred to all enquiry. But, as an end, the promotion of truth, absolute truth that is, simply has no *real* meaning, unless that truth can indeed refer to actualities, which sceptics have always doubted. Formal logic is, strictly speaking, abstract, as its name implies. It promulgates ideal constructs purporting to refer to actual states of affairs; but, as those are only formal, such that symbolic logic alone is beyond question alethic, that reference is a myth. When symbols are replaced by words their meanings are only conventional. That 'grass is green' not 'grue' is as a statement true because linguistic usage has given certain sounds certain meanings or references rather than because it defines some aspect of actuality: waves perhaps of certain lengths impinging on the eye. And however complex the form that a proposition is given, it remains the case that its reference is, as it claims to be rigorous, confined to the ideal world, to what can be defined with absolute precision in immutable terms. Since assertoric logic cannot truly refer externally, but only to conventional acceptance in some language, it cannot, as a formal and strictly linguistic discipline, even begin to engage the dynamic of becoming. If then philosophy is to deal with relations in actuality, that is to say, to contribute to an understanding of them, of how they bear on life, it must take another form. That is not to abandon discipline, which would be disastrous, but to change its mode of approach, which means its presuppositions with respect to real confrontations. To pass from a rather empty pursuit, empty because natural logic – implicit in good English or any other language – is infinitely more flexible. It can reach to understanding in a way that formal logic with its rigour cannot, to one which is vitally meaningful, though that may not be an easy task. None the less, it has to be done lest philosophy, lost in verbal abstractions, ceases to be an influence.

Reality, now regarded as a process of becoming is not to be defined in rigorous terms at all, so that ideas developed about it must have another character. This is not to say that suggestion, disciplined by negation, is the only means to hand; but it is certainly a means that could be made available were restrictions on it rather less oppressive. But indeed, it is often employed as a means of bringing ideas forward despite official stances. Thus, when it is said that all, meaning nature at large, is in dynamic equipoise, undergoing persistent change through continual movement off centre,[29] that should not be taken as a formal definition, as if it were fully proven. It is, to use a term adopted by Leibniz, simply a 'proposal',[30] which could conceivably be shown to be fallacious. Though valuable as permitting a better understanding of the nature of involvement, it cannot be asserted as true, as 'A equals A' may be. It is not the phenomenal world to which attention should be directed, as it has been almost exclusively in philosophical discourse when that is turned to other than ideas about the

29

transcendent. It is the world in which man acts, in which he has his being, the dynamic world of becoming, that has to be engaged if his relation to it is to be studied more sensitively. Some astute philosophers have recognized that as the problem: that it was the external world, in itself unknowable, that had first to be considered as that in which all else is grounded. But their weakness generally lay in this: that they believed that that world could be defined in rational terms, when those in fact were little more than verbal formulations, such as 'Being in itself', 'existence in its essence', 'esse ipsum subsistens', and even as 'the timeless, perfect, organic whole of self-thinking thought', whatever that might mean.[31] Reality was idealized, which might of course be said of any verbal statement about it, but only so essentially as it claims to be veridical. The most remarkable form of such rationalized projection is that 'Being is static, the unconditioned ground', when 'unconditioned' appears to mean 'absolute' or 'unchanging'. All this is now outdated, since there is no alternative than to accept that such statements as these are conceptualizations only, which may satisfy metaphysicians, but do not by any token relate to living actualities, the reality in which man is enmeshed as a living being. The world is undoubtedly one and doubtless the ground of everything that bears on human existence; but that is surely evident without the need to state it, as though it were a profound and illuminating discovery. And continually to harp on it, as if that were required of philosophy, to evoke the term 'perennial' as characterizing its problems, is to give it a false dignity, as also to lose touch with what has fuller bearing on life. The idea that man can view the world as something apart from himself, can dichotomize mind and matter, when he as a sentient being is a mode of it himself, is to misunderstand the nature of his involvement.[32] A duality, if there is one when thinking is realistic, is rather a restriction on thought than a licence to develop idealistic pictures of the nature of reality. Only by accepting involvement with reality as the problem he confronts is the philosopher concerned with a primary issue, not verbal merely but concrete. If philosophy is to contribute to the unfolding of modern thought, its 'becoming' so to say, and to grapple with the issues it forces on attention, revealing in the process the limits of past thinking and the damage it has caused by promoting with idealism at least one dubious doctrine,[33] it has then to review its idea of its role and to modify it accordingly. With reservations, then, about the presuppositional set which once seemed to give it its warrant but actually delimited it, there is no reason to cling to it but every reason rather to adopt another. For only as it does so can it play a significant part in enhancing understanding in that sphere of interest with which it alone can properly deal: namely, general evaluation.

*

Everybody knows what 'appearance' means, even though the simple should mistake it for reality. What 'reality' means, however, is very much less clear, since, as has been said above, it has several meanings, all of which are justified in as far as they go. It is not then that that term is in its various meanings improperly used by thinkers: it is rather that its meanings are not always clearly distinguished, such that assumptions are made or allowed which obscure the essential issue: man's relation to the world which continually plays upon him. Reverting to what has already been said, there are three legitimate meanings attached to the term 'reality'. The first, to be taken as primary, is that it signifies all that there is, the sum total of all that exists, in respect of which little can be said, since it is too vast a notion to be properly comprehensible. Then there is 'our reality', which is all of which we are conscious, a world which is not confined to phenomenal presentations, since it embraces dim thought in respect of what cannot be clearly located, nebulous musings, for instance, about a greater world, vague fears and premonitions, hopes and distant goals, in sum, the innumerable psychical states which impinge on consciousness. For the tendency to confine it to what we observe in full consciousness, to sustain an empiricist stance, is evidently to limit the part it plays in our lives; indeed, in our experience, which quite certainly covers more than "actual observation" (to cite a dictionary definition), to include the whole complex of affect and the influence that it has. The third of these meanings is that which relates to what is surely external, something other than ourselves against which we react, something standing over against this internal reality. That is sometimes taken to be the phenomenal world, which, though it may relate to or reflect what is truly external, is properly internal, inasmuch as the world of objects is one that we ourselves create with our particularizing intellects or, more deeply, through mental action, which allows us to separate out from the whole that which at once concerns us. But that is another story. Very properly, philosophers have referred to that world as "out there" or as "mind-independent" – though the last of these expressions may be open to question, in that the mind, at once contrasted with the intellect, certainly has to contend with certain aspects of it, commonly called 'stimuli', with the pressures of stimulation produced by changes in it. So seen, it is the world to which we respond *directly* without any process of filtering, which invariably accompanies all conscious objective responses. But that cannot be justly considered in a statement as brief as this, and the nature of response must be the subject of further discussion. Enough at once that there is a truly external world lying beneath or beyond the world of which we are aware, which influences that awareness in ways of which we are not fully conscious.

As consciousness is brought into play, we are plainly conscious of something the ultimate source of which is not phenomenal simply, but that which grounds phenomena, *le mystère onto-logique*. And as that is an expression used by a philosopher,[34] it gives an indication that this something has been recognized, not only in religion but in philosophical thinking, if not also in the thought of many ordinary people. It is indeed mysterious or, otherwise said, unknowable; and to disregard or to dismiss it for that reason is to refuse to face reality, which is a grave fault in a thinker. Even more to the point, it is that which should be the concern of philosophy in contradistinction to science, which can only deal, as it claims to describe, with what is observable, directly or now indirectly with the aid of elaborate instruments. And if in that form this concern refers to what rationalists regard as illicit preoccupations, as "fishing in muddy waters", scarcely to be distinguished from clairvoyance or parapsychology, the prejudice exhibited may very well be theirs. For, in dismissing thought addressed to deeper human involvement, they effectively renounce any responsible role, any concern with the problem which uniquely confronts philosophy.[35] Man's relation to the world in its most basic meaning constitutes a problem with which science is powerless to deal, albeit that some of its findings may illuminate understanding. So, if the requirement to study it presupposes some form of extracognitive thinking, that must be accepted; and if such thinking as this is designated 'mystic', that is of little moment, since it is mystic only in a special sense of that term in which it is merely contrasted with 'rational'. What is unknowable in strict sense is not for that reason wholly incomprehensible. It is, as Kant said, "thinkable", which clearly implies that ideas *can* be formed about it, and so in a disciplined manner with the devising of fitting procedures.

The adjective correctly applied to such deeper thinking as this is properly 'realistic', which means that it refers to influential forces which emanate externally, the study of which demands an attempt to pass beyond the subjective, the realm of the knowing self, into a deeper world. And that that is not impossible will be shown in a later chapter, after other terms, which must first be considered more closely, have prepared the ground for a deeper discussion of what it involves.[36] This is, of course, the antithesis of traditional rationalist thinking, which is so idealistic that it is without power to pass beyond what concerns the conscious self, as if externals had no influence or no character in themselves, as comprising mere 'matter in motion'. Hence, though it is well aware, whenever it gives attention to moral or ethical problems – if it makes a distinction between them, not easily done when the only approach conceived of is idealistic – that determinism undermines the idea of responsibility, it is impotent to provide a firm alternative to it. It flounders, so to say, in an ontological swamp, inasmuch as it is trapped or sunk in subjectivity and cannot grant that reality, in its essential meaning, is the ground of everything, thinking not excluded, and constitutes an influence that cannot be disregarded. Vague talk about 'world-order', 'world-ground', 'world-soul', and so on, is ideal when it is little more than conceptualization and lacks a concrete reference. 'Mystic' thought may well be when it is other than rationalistic. The real question, however, is this: which of these forms of thinking is more restrictive and limiting, which penetrates more deeply, suggestively perhaps, into actuality as it bears on human life?

If, in this essay then, thought is referred to reality in its external meaning, without pretence to define the nature of all that there is – as if that were possible in any adequate form – the reason for that is that it permits an escape from subjectivity, which confines us to clear consciousness, or rather to an involvement with the self as opposed to externals. To suppose that all response is necessarily conscious is to misunderstand the nature of man's involvement, the more especially as he is seen as a vital agent as opposed to an intellectual, seeing his situation in intellectual terms and blind in that sense to any idea that there are certainly others. Love, affection, sympathy, action itself indeed, are *not* involvements of the intellect, which intervenes obtusely since its acts are not spontaneous, reflective of life as such.[37] And that these are unimportant in comparison with knowledge, which is at best a means of furthering one of these ends, action which is deliberate, is a ridiculous notion: for they are the substance of life. What man confronts in reality as distinguished from what he confronts in cognitive enquiry, the environment in which he lives as pressures bear upon him, both in natural and social forms, is not something he cognizes in clear or scientific sense; it is something rather of which he is largely unaware. It is not the philosopher's business to wake him to full awareness, if that is really possible when philosophers share his fate, of having to act spontaneously in the normal course of life and can only themselves acquire that attitude at all by adopting a form of detachment, which is at best but partial. But is is his business, his *raison d'être*, to develop better ideas about what these conditions are, since they are the foundations on which, if nothing more, prescriptions must be laid: though his burden rests essentially in deepening understanding, to the end that men may live a little more sanely. And that does not mean aspiring to the domination of nature but rather learning to live with it, in attunement to its pulse. Thus should we, as thinkers with this responsibility, accept that idea of reality which is better related to the real conditions of life, adaptation, that is to say, to the ceaselessly changing pressures which, though not in the main apparent, are continually bearing on us. Reality is, then, in the present context, that with which man must come to terms if he is to live more sanely and to establish better relations through that, the complex in which he *acts*, with his fellow men who have to adapt to similar pressures.

Chapter Two

Sensation and Perception

We are therefore called upon to review the information
with which the neurologist provides us not simply as
yet another specialization but as a matter at the very
heart and quality of our cultural being.   Barlow

Whereas the only ambiguity that is likely to breed confusion
between the two terms already discussed is that the first,
appearance, is interpreted as the second, reality, which is in that
way misrepresented, the distinction between sensation and
perception, when not properly made, leads to ambiguities which
are less easy to summarize and so are more insidious. For their
meanings are confused in a more subtle way, which obscures the
point that the difference between them is even decisive. Sensation is
not perception, not to be muddled with it, but something very
different, both in nature and in function. As both of these
expressions have a Latin origin, and may have been introduced
more or less simultaneously, they presumably at that time had
distinctive meanings. For, if they did not, why were two terms
brought into use when what they referred to was effectively the
same, a similar form of response. Later usage, then, seems to have
brought them together, though not entirely so. For there are still
two words with slightly different meanings, which, with careful
employment, they retain to this day. That their earliest users,

without benefit of the findings of modern neuroscience, fully grasped the difference between nervous and conscious response is not to be supposed. But a glimmering of that, grounded in common sense, must have been present to justify the coining of two terms. This common sense distinction between them still survives, although it is vague and wanting in clarity, not only with simple people, little given to making nice distinctions in verbal usage, but also in the discourse of sophisticated thinkers, some of whom fail all too often to make a clear distinction between these two forms of responsive action.

In later classical times the term 'sensation' or its equivalent, *sensus* – for the English word 'sensation' is a later formation on the low Latin *sensatio*[1] – came to have the meaning of 'feeling' or 'emotion', at once somatic and psychical, to which we are heirs, at least in popular usage. And with a growing tendency to cultivate self-consciousness in place of a more basic, generalized sensitivity, that meaning should change to that which is apparent to consciousness is not a surprising outcome. Emotion is usually viewed as impinging on consciousness, though feeling need not have the same degree of awareness, in which case it may relate to the earlier meaning of the term in question. Naïve realism, which takes appearance to be reality, is, paradoxically perhaps, a latter-day development, emerging with increasing interest in cognition, which implicitly subscribes to it – as in the use of such terms as 'fact' with reference to phenomena as opposed to actualities.[2] Thus do modern dictionaries define 'sensation' as "consciousness of perceiving or seeming to perceive some state or affection of one's body, of one's mind or its emotions; contents of such consciousness". But, if some state is perceived, it surely involves perception, however dim that may be. Yet there is undoubtedly some difference between sensation, which is direct response, and perception, which is now seen to be indirect; and that differentiation has not, despite this stress on consciousness, been entirely obscured or forgotten. There is something which is intangible, more basic and elemental than that which is received in and recorded by clear consciousness. And that that something has this elusive character is the reason why there is yet a degree of obscurity, a measure of muddled thinking about the import of sensation.

Clarification is aided if closer consideration is given to the etymon, or better the derivation, of the second term 'perception'. It was formed from a prefix attached to a verb, to give the combination or the compound *per-cipere*, when the verb itself was a variant of the older form *capere*, meaning 'to seize', 'to hold to oneself', 'to take possession of', of which an English derivative is 'capture', giving 'captive'. 'To seize' is a deliberate act scarcely done with 'feeling', which, even when recorded subsequently in consciousness, comes upon one so to say, one knows not whence precisely – the stomach, the heart, the liver, all have been suggested – to show, as modern science confirms, that feeling or emotion has a bodily seat.[3] This marks it off, in a sense at least, from conscious intellection, which is held to be disembodied. 'To take possession of', or better 'to take to oneself', has other, then, than a physical meaning, since it is plainly a conscious act undertaken in full awareness, as reflex response, a mere reaction, is evidently not, since it is involuntary. And that is noted to ensure that there is no confusion between an act which is done deliberately and one that is spontaneous. What is taken in in thought is a presentation, later called an 'object', which is held in order that it may in itself be analysed by the conscious mind, correctly by the intellect, in a manner to be discussed more fully in the sequel. What is received *directly* in response to stimulation cannot be so dealt with, since it is not detectable. And if that is not at once evident when cognition is the interest, almost to exclusion, its meaning in this context may be seen as discussion develops. Sufficient now that there is a distinction to be drawn between that of which we are aware, because it is perceived, and that of which we are not because it does not enter consciousness.

It is not invariably the case that the term 'sensation' is employed improperly, specifically by philosophers, but rather that it is vaguely distinguished from perception, though that is seen as its base, which it undoubtedly is. But at times misuse of the term occurs and is too seldom checked on account of this vagueness, with roots in a cognitive bias, which tends to inhibit clear thinking on such a matter as this which refers to what is beyond its reach. The classical instance of such misuse is to be found in Wundt's still accepted expression "the threshold of sensation". For, since there is no detectable threshold of sensation when that term is properly used – to refer to response effected on subconscious levels – his wording should surely have been "the threshold of perception".[4] This is echoed again and again when philosophers

37

speak of pain, or rather more precisely of conscious awareness of it, which, as consciously recorded, is perceptually received. Awareness of pain is a rather unusual form of perception, in that consciousness of it is *apparently* immediate. But 'apparently' is perhaps the pertinent word in this context, since a disturbance in the system, of which clear warning is given with pain as an index of it, has plainly some history behind it, which, as prior to perception, cannot be detected. It is doubtless convenient to have such a seeming convergence at philosophic disposal, as evidence that perception is immediate and direct, in order to show that cognition relates to actuality. But this would seem to give a rather deceptive picture, as if to suggest that what is in this way drawn to attention were the same as that which lies below the surface. For that identification, which amounts to improper conflation, conduces to a blindness with respect to the distinctive meaning and function of sensation, which is delimiting philosophically.

Apart from a Latin etymon, then, a German word is instructive. For *gewahr*, giving *gewahren*, meaning 'to perceive', whence such English words as 'awareness' and 'beware', suggests that perception is a power given to sentient beings to render them alert to potential danger, the greater inasmuch as they are free-acting agents. Those who do not possess this power, as is the case with plants and lower forms of animal life – though they certainly have sensations, in respect of light, for instance, as when they turn to the sun – do not in this sense perceive and do not have the organs in any case to do so.[5] Perception is therefore something which has been developed in certain higher species in the course of evolution, in effect to permit the taking of more decisive action on the part of mobile beings, either searching for pasture or prey or avoiding the fate of becoming the prey of others themselves. With the human advance into relative safety, this meaning of perception has largely been forgotten. But, despite the idea that it was primarily given to men as a grounding for conception, this more basic meaning survives and is evident to those whose lives involve the taking of risks. The dangers men face in urban life are doubtless very different from those they once faced in the jungle; but still such acts as crossing the road or driving a car along it demand this animal alertness, as do many other occasions in the normal course of life. It is those for which perceptual power is essentially given, although its function in that sense seldom seems to be noticed by philosophers of mind, for whom the later meaning is the only one that counts. Vital needs are primary; and, in comparison with them, cognitive interests cannot be regarded as more than secondary, unless knowledge is a means of strengthening powers of alertness. To overstress the second at expense of the first is then to misinterpret the real nature of response in relation to vital action. But this, the aim of which is to direct attention to what is basic in human life, is no more than introductory. The time has come to give it more convincing support.

*

Empiricist psychologists may contend that gestalt psychology is either outdated or flawed as a doctrine, for reasons which to them appear to be sufficient.[6] Philosophers, unless they are empiricists themselves, would be ill-advised to adopt such a stance as that without a closer study of what that doctrine implies in terms of their specific concern. For though it may have weaknesses in the eyes of those pursuing cognitive ends, it has a pregnant meaning for those concerned with what is *not* phenomenally presented but has a deeper reference. Gestalt psychology, then, has in effect two aspects, explicit and implicit, the last of which has been curiously neglected, notwithstanding its immense significance for philosophy. Several terms could be used to distinguish these two aspects, of which those considered most suitable in the present context are its pre-gestalten and its post-gestalten dimensions. It is the first of these that now demands attention, because of its special bearing on how we should view or understand the nature of response to real external pressures, to stimulation, that is to say, taken to be direct. That level of response is not of itself observable, even if aspects of it may on occasion be so, simply because it is 'sensuous' as contrasted with 'mechanical', which it is when we have some knowledge of the nervous system in action. For the nature of direct response, which constitutes a relation between two different forms of activity, external and internal, physical stimulation and psychosomatic reaction to that stimulation, is, since it is indeed direct, hidden from inspection. Between innervation itself and the effects that it produces in the form of responsive reaction, there is a gulf which has never been bridged, and doubtfully ever will be, simply because it is sensuous and involves *immediate* contact. It is possible to arrange an experiment in which one sharply pointed instrument touches one point in one thing to secure a one-to-one relationship. But that is both exceptional and rather artificial. For normally, in the act of gripping for example, many nerves and muscles have to be brought into play and pressures bear on whatever is gripped not in one but in several ways, the more so as that is spongy. Thus what is being referred to is a largely hidden sphere, which, in so far as is known, is intricate in the extreme, a complex of involvement. Comment on this relation, then, may well be 'metaphysical', in that it deals with what is not phenomenally observable, but rests for the greater part on unsupported inference, so that it is conjectural rather than demonstrative. If it is thought of, however, in such terms as these, it is possible to conceive of a thesis that is reasonable, which stands, if not as proven, as alethic, established truth, as a doctrine which cannot simply be rejected on the score that it lacks substance.

Let us then begin with what is scarcely to be doubted, though again it cannot be given conclusive demonstration. That is that we, in common with other sentient beings, are persistently saluted by literally showers of stimuli, which bear upon us unceasingly throughout our waking lives and even, it seems, in sleep, which may at any time be disturbed by something which threatens the system, a noise, a smell, or even a cutaneous irritation. 'Showers of stimuli' is an expression that merits further attention, since it has in the present context more than a metaphorical meaning. For, were we aware of *all* the pressures bearing on us, of every slightest change in the environment about us, we should be so distracted, disconcerted, befuddled that we should be quite unable to live our normal lives, indeed to act or think with any semblance of precision. Nature, then, protects us against such a calamitous outcome, by developing a process whereby this disabling consequence is avoided or overcome. And the way in which it does so is by subconscious mental action. Acting on this level the mind performs as an ordering instrument, under guidance of intention and with the aid of memory, both active on this plane,[7] selecting from among this multitude of stimuli playing upon the receptors those that are of immediate significance for well-being. If we care to put it this way, mind governs the nervous system,[8] orders innervation in the organism's interest: though this must be said with caution, since all that is observable, with the aid of elaborate instruments, is the action of the nerves threading complex paths through the neural network to the cerebral cortex and other parts of the brain which act as mediating centres. In other words, it generates a synthesizing process, with extraordinary rapidity, in order to produce a whole – which is other, of course, than the whole of current stimulation – which we, now in awareness, can comfortably accept. That whole is called a *Gestalt*, which is a German word for a form or a figure, something, that is, that has definite shape, a demarcated outline, and something as a consequence that can readily be grasped. It is only then, when a gestalt is formed, that we become aware, conscious, clearly or dimly, of something that affects us, reflecting some significant change in our external environment. And, with this in mind we may fairly speak of two quite distinctive processes: that which leads up to or orders the formation of gestalt syntheses, which form a sort of watershed, and that which follows from their making, analysis and other intellectual acts.

This is all too simply put, for such processes as the first are extremely complex, for various parts of the brain are involved in bringing gestalten to being. And, as the movements in play cannot be observed, except in isolation, what actually takes place can only be inferred.[9] It is sufficient, however, firmly to mark the point at which sensation, subconscious response, passes into perception, which is broadly a conscious involvement. And though philosophers may be vague when they use the term 'sensation', scientists, neurophysiologists and those concerned with action on this preperceptual plane, use it in a proper sense, relating it to terms, 'sensorial' for example, which have strict neural meaning, free from the ambiguity that attaches to 'sense data' and kindred terms which philosophers use to refer to something observable. It was one of themselves, however, familiar with this field, who made the rather scathing remark, paraphrased for simplicity: "The word 'sensation' has two meanings, one of which is philosophical or popular whilst the other is scientific, meaning simply 'caused sensory reaction'".[10] But that, if it implies that sensation is simply physical, which the use of the qualification 'caused' might at first sight suggest, is perhaps a little insensitive. In one sense, of course, such response is physical, nervous or corporeal. That will only stand as an interpretation, however, with uncritical acceptance of the all too common dichotomy, that between spirit and body, or

41

more commonly mind and matter. These are supposed to be wholly distinct, since the former is exalted as transcendent over nature whilst the latter is regarded as material or natural, as though those terms were synonymous. But if spirit is regarded as immanent in vitality, as natural in itself, a different picture emerges. Without at once discussing this idea at length, despite its great significance, it suffices at once to remark, with Brentano as a witness, that memory and intention play part in subconscious response. In other words, there is in sensation a psychical factor, a notion presenting no difficulty once we can abandon this crude mind-matter dichotomy, which assumes that the psychical, the spiritual for that matter, must always have a conscious, intellectual seat. This delimits ideas about it, since its sphere is certainly wider.

It might be supposed from a study of the writings of those who believe that meaningful response begins only with the conscious reception of sense data, that all below that level is involuntary, conditioned, automatic, mechanical, as befits the movement of matter. But this idea, it need scarcely be said, is altogether too simple. For. as the great majority of all responses made – some 90% or more, it is held[11] – are made and mediated below the level of consciousness, they may, if only by reason of their very preponderance, be presumed to serve a meaningful, vital function. Those pressures which are not clearly recorded in consciousness do not simply fade away as if they were redundant, had no part to play, they also have to be countered. And since consciousness does not intervene on this lowly plane, they must be mediated subconsciously. In fact, the function of the mind on such subconscious levels is in part the maintaining of balance in the body, the organic whole in its widest meaning – including deeper psychical needs, acknowledged with the use of the expression 'psychosomatic' – to permit of its sustaining its being in active life. For the system must adapt to the pressures bearing on it, as must every living system: and this adaptation plainly calls for more than reflex reaction, occurring only as pressures are placed on certain specific muscles. And it is well that it does so act; for, if pressures can be met without need to call on consciousness, so is consciousness relieved of the onus to deal with them, and thus acquires the power to act with a greater freedom. Consciousness is only evoked in natural or normal conditions when there is occasion for it, when action against pressures had to be more decisive. Hence, it has to be understood that what takes place subconsciously involves and must involve highly meaningful processes in that they are vital, if only in the sense of maintaining homeostasis, which may in itself have rather more than mere physical connotations.[12] But in fact the role of subconscious response is infinitely greater, inasmuch as it is direct, a meeting of reality, the world as it actually is in all its richness and complexity. And the better to grasp the meaning of this, its further implications must be given consideration.

*

An almost exclusive devotion to rationalistic interests has blinded the West to the idea that there are certainly others which are *not* by contrast transcendent, seen as the only alternative to what can be cognized. The effect of this has been, to say the least, unfortunate, since it has conduced to grave misunderstanding of the nature of life as it is lived by normal, ordinary people; and, what is no less significant, of their natural spontaneous culture. For the latter was in the main developed on this level, as the product of spontaneous natural sensitivity, which, if it has weakened or taken degraded forms, may possibly be a consequence of placing too much stress on intellectuality. The very word 'sensitivity' indeed suggests a relation with the word 'sensation', as if that were its base. For many social acts of delicate, elegant form are 'sensuous' through and through. To take a simple example, the dancer who deliberates on the steps that he is taking will be a poor performer. And it is common knowledge that the trained executant, the ballet dancer for instance, does not think about technique, which has been 'internalized', but throws herself without thinking about such rationalizable matters into the rhythmic sequence, the sensuous unfolding. So the musician, who certainly does not give conscious thought, for which in any case time is scarcely available to him, to the chords that he is striking. He acts with a kind of subconscious flair,[13] paying overt attention only to effects, noting, for example, some failure to develop the right degree of 'colour'. So the sportsman, so the craftsman, acts with a certain finesse, critically conscious essentially of the results that he obtains, of failure to achieve what he set out to do, aware that he had not attained to an indefinable standard to total satisfaction.

Let us, to illustrate this, consider the artist at work, the painter or the sculptor. He starts with a broad idea, a rather vague mental image of what he intends to do. He then proceeds with a series of thrusts, 'stabs' as is sometimes said, inspired by powers that seem to come upon him as it were, though fed in part no doubt by what he has already done; and is only conscious of effects as he stands back from his work, critically to review it. The creative process is very obscure, but it seems to have the tentative form of trial-and-error, which is requisite to secure the needed spontaneity: as if a fully conscious, algorithmic approach would issue in something lifeless, devoid of the vivid quality of that which emerges immediately. Thinkers may, perhaps, proceed more systematically, though less so than they like to believe in conformity with their image of themselves as rigidly rational. For sequences of ideas spring out of one another, such that what is written or said conditions what will follow, to the point indeed that one inadequate word or sentence may alter the tone, the meaning as well, of all that is written thereafter. And hence the need for several drafts to ensure that the expression of ideas is as it should be, a kind of polishing based again on a form of trial-and-error. Ideas themselves have elusive and scarcely detectable origins: they emerge quite unexpectedly in very varied conditions, when walking, when waking from sleep, when the mind is otherwise occupied, and form themselves, at large over time, as though through slow maturation.[14] Indeed, that they are the products of contemplative calculation – in the manner of Rodin's Thinker – is a misrepresentation, confusing a later process, critical in character, with original inspiration.

Without enlarging on this at once, interest will now be directed towards rather less exalted and rarefied forms of action. Not all men have creative gifts, but all have responsive powers, though, with the romantic movement and its emphasis on genius, those tend to be overlooked, even in some sense inhibited. Hence, if thought is concerned with value, value in general terms, it is well to understand that it accrues less significantly to the creative artist or thinker, whose delight in his work is personal, than to people at large to whom he properly addresses it. With idealism indeed, the cult of the self that is, there is a tendency to forget this; a

44

consequence of which is that individualistic grotesques are foisted on the public, admonished to admire them, not for intrinsic quality, a universal value, but as "expressing the artist", as if his emotions or options had some special virtue. And thus is taste debased in the service of personal vanity or the current trend. These deeper responsive needs are, of course, difficult to define, inasmuch as they are sensuous rather than conscious or personal, and so are lost to view when subjective pretension carries all before it. As value, then, can only be seen in such personal terms, as all is intellectualized to conform with passing fashion, normal sensitivity is pushed into the background, even viewed as commonplace, insipid, uninspired. Let it then be understood that when the term 'general' is used in such a context as this, it refers to what is common to men as sentient, sensuous beings with power to respond directly to rhythmic presentations. In as far as consciousness tends to be subjective and so varies with the person, with age, with sex, with background, it is only universal in a restricted sense – as with logical universals – so that it is not related to life as it is normally lived, still less to nervous responsiveness, without which, a point of importance, there can be no general culture. Consciousness, of course, plays a highly significant part in the lives of human beings. But stressing it unduly, as uniquely human – which it is certainly not – to the point of disregarding any other state, is to misconstrue the full nature of human capacity, the situation of man as a being involved with reality.[15]

It is then incumbent to understand that what is common to men on this more basic plane has rather a relation to forms of nervous responsiveness than to intellectuality, seen as something different from the exercise of reason in the life of action. And this is of significance when applied prescriptions, which must of course be general in their application, have to be considered. For they must relate to what is common as a capacity in terms of social requirement rather than to such interests as appertain to a class, of which liberal ideologies might afford an example, in that they are divisive and so may meet with resistance. In fine, the claim so freely made by the 'knowing' classes that these social needs, which are general, must be intellectualized – by such means, for instance, as statistical enquiry, which tends to be superficial – must mean that their nature is misunderstood, as when it is assumed, since those alone are measurable, that needs are simply material. And though

45

they might in that sense be regarded as 'sensual', in the classical meaning of *le moyen homme sensuel*, they are certainly not 'sensuous', if a proper distinction is made between these two expressions. For the first is *consciously* appetitive, whereas the second, though nervous and in that sense bodily, also comprehends deep psychological needs, many of which are impalpable and do not rise into consciousness. Somewhere within the subconscious sphere a development takes place in which the physical and the psychical blend or come together in a convergence which, though evidently functional, cannot be known as it is. So that, although related to intentionality, which is to say to need, in the second of these forms, it is not in itself a realm that can be cognized, as can overt material needs or conscious psychical goals. That it has been neglected is not then surprising – though that thinkers have endeavoured to align these inner movements with what is exposed to consciousness, and so is rationalizable, shows grave insensitivity, as if this deeper realm were without meaningful existence and exercised no influence on their rationalistic thinking. But then, with the ancient dichotomy, which, with the excluded middle, allows of only two spheres, a bodily, which is accessible to empirical enquiry, and a psychical which, as conscious, is open to inspection, if only introspectively, a blindness to what is excluded is naturally a consequence. Since what is then unheeded is beyond the reach of perception, it defies the examination which can only be applied to neurological aspects, regarded all too readily as completely covering the form of subconscious response.

Hidden in the sphere of the extra-perceptual, there is then an unexplored area of response to stimulation, which has the significant feature of meeting, and mediating in part, psychosomatic needs, and thus of bringing together the physical and the psychical. The point is then that little is known about this correlation. For plainly psychical factors at this level are undetectable, whilst those of a physical nature can only be known in a limited sense. It is possible to follow a single charge or pulse as it passes from a receptor to some mediating centre through synaptic links and by means of action on the effectors. But the complexity of that passage when innervation is thought of as operating pervasively with multiple interconnections can only be inferred, inasmuch as this process cannot be comprehended except in relative isolation. The psychical factors, meanwhile, can only be observed through their later effects, that is, as they enter consciousness. Accordingly, the play between the physical and the psychical at this level of reception is beyond an empiricist grasp. The idea of its presence as a stage of response can then never be more than speculative, tenuous at best; but it cannot for that reason simply be discounted. And indeed, if the real concern in studying response in its basic nature or its form at vital levels, regard must be had to this. Some highly complex process – more complicated even than physiological action – seems, no more can be said, to occur on subconscious levels. And that is what is meant in this text by 'sensuous response', which quite certainly plays a significant part in life, even if the manner in which it does so is obscure. Sensation considered in depth is not, then, a mere prelude to perception, nor is it merely the 'animal', or better said the 'sensorial', aspect of response.[16] It is something that has to be seen in its own, its specific character, as vital or direct response to the pulsing rhythm of nature, the dynamic of becoming, with which all sentient beings, man included, are involved.

*

Failure to see things in this way constitutes a failure to understand the springs of basic human culture. Had there been no more than what the intellect develops, the outcome would have been limited, fragile, thin, lacking in body and substance. And those developments themselves could scarcely have come to flower unless in a deeper soil; and indeed, they had their origin in something which was other than deliberative thought. For they were brought into being to refine on intuitions, vague thoughts about the nature of an indifferent and so mysterious world, not wholly comprehensible to the awakening intellect. What was man's place within it, what was its purpose or meaning seen in human terms?[17] And even in comprehensible aspects of human life, there were interests and even vital needs which were not clearly definable. The essence of law is surely the securing of justice, which is a form of balance between or a reconciling of interests. Justice does not of itself allow of strict definition, since it is for the most part attained in relation to circumstances; and is seldom, unless in principle – involving established rules to ensure a measure of consistency – absolute or unchanging. It has to be more or less flexible in order to meet contingences, conditions as they evolve. The idea, then, that grounds it is rooted in a 'sense', innate in the human make-up, of what is just in conditions. This is apparent when it is said, and with considerable insight, that "Justice must not only be done, it must also be seen to be done", implying that the power to 'see' is given to men at large. In humbler form justice is called 'fair play', which, though often related to rules, devised in order to secure it, is rather 'understood', as is shown when actions are condemned as 'underhand' or 'dirty', as going against the grain of what is 'felt' to be right and proper. And if this is a rather far cry from great metaphysical questions, still further from cognitive issues, it seems that the earliest thinking turned rather on ethical problems,[18] seen as more fundamental, to the point that the frame in which life was lived, the encompassing natural order, was only considered later as social order allowed of it and afforded sufficient leisure. The point, however, is still that these interests are related, since both refer to man's relation to man through nature, of which he is a mode, for his 'nature' is what nature gives. Hence, what aroused the interest of the enquiring mind – since neither could be met by simple, straightforward answers, when both nature and society were interrelative structures, to which man responded sensuously and not in strict rational terms – were the difficulties presented. It was only later, specifically in the West, that absolute solutions were taken to be the aim, with the consequence that a sense of the tenuousness of all answers bearing on relationships was lost or sublimated into a quest for irrefragable truth. Since nothing in nature is true in any axiomatic sense, that preoccupation has had the effect of inhibiting a deeper understanding of actual involvement, indeed of the nature of man in his actual situation.

Man is a sensitive being, and if also a 'rational animal', that is a part of his nature which has been overrated when stressed at expense of the first, unless 'rational' means no more than having the power to think, when it is rather more characteristic.[19] For then a general potential, implicit in this 'sensing', which, though it may be reasonable, has little rational standing, tends to be overlooked, and with that its *social* significance. Justice affords an obvious form of this sense of what is appropriate. But an even deeper form of it is to be found in courtesy, a characteristic evidenced even in primitive peoples, who do not have to develop a theme of "the sacredness of the person" – which exonerates even reprobates – to grasp that social relations are linked to human dignity: and that that is lost, with self-respect, if others are not respected as their behaviour demands that they should be. If his approach is not aggressive, to constitute a threat, a stranger is received with grace and hospitality, as many travellers' tales evince throughout the course of history.[20] Diplomats have traditionally enjoyed a certain status, as representing peoples with potentially common interests. And if they were regarded as vice-regents of authority, that does not imply that their reception was exceptional. For hierarchic relations, linked to age if no more, are part of the structure of courtesy, a means of maintaining dignity beyond those with responsibility endowed with greater power and, in principle, fuller experience and those for whom they act. None of this is explicit, as if it were the product of conscious deliberation on the need to sustain a balance. It is innate, it seems, in the human make-up, rooted in a deeply felt need for decency in relations. For it is likewise realized – 'sensed', to use the expression that better fits these conditions – that aggressive acts, which are personal and not formalized and disciplined by legalized authority,[21] are socially disturbing and have repercussive effects, such as a loss of confidence, on the part of the weaker especially.

Courtesy is linked to a sense of what is appropriate, not only in social relations but also in public acts. There is thus a call for propriety in the making of decisions, which ought to be observed in everything that is done, inasmuch as those bear on others, who, in great affairs, comprise the great majority affected by what is decided. Thus, most of the cultures of the past aspired to a sense of propriety even in great works, since its absence would have meant a lowering of trust, a division between authority and those on whom it bore – recognizing that interests such as self-aggrandizement instead of responsibility had become the motive for action.[22] And authority here means any form of exerted influence which has effects on others. Indeed, without this social sense, the sense which the artist reflects in his own sensitivity to the basic nervous needs, for rhythm, scale and proportion, of the normal man – now unhappily blunted by the romantics' disregard of them – there would be no general culture, only transient excitation for a 'cultivated' few. For a universal culture develops through the involvement of everyone in society, not playing a creative part, though that is the role of all craftsmen, but by responding naturally to well-formed and shapely artifacts – or to appropriate action. That there is a like response to statesmanlike decisions, to wise and needed policies, might also then be mentioned were it not that the notion of that is clouded by partisan passions, which turn on desire for power, so that what was statesmanlike can only be seen in retrospect, when those have ceased to be operative. But thought is wisely confined at once to what is non-controversial, the nature of sensitivity on strictly *social* levels, in manners, in the arts, in the gracing of the environment, to which everyone may contribute, in however modest a way, thereby to sustain a quality both in relation to others and to nature itself, the determinant of all value.[23]

In fine, it is not too much to say, with courtesy as the key, since that is a universal capacity, shown even in those societies which are not greatly creative, that all refinement has its roots in human sensitivity, in spontaneous responsiveness to what is naturally elegant. And if that had finer forms in the higher classes, where freedom from grosser pressures allowed of its fuller flowering, it seeped down, as those were seen to have a greater quality, into society generally, enriched by growing maturity.[24] The decay or weakening of this natural endowment, contempt indeed for what is implicit in it, is a sufficiently serious matter, if only because that makes for conflict and discontent. For it is a *general* refinement, with some schooling of self-interest, which permits of those relations, graced by ease of manner, that fosters forms of fulfilment in life free from upsetting consequences. Or, if this is too idealistic, it affords at least a prospect, in as far as men, with their human weaknesses, are capable of developing it. Humans are passionate creatures; and it would be absurd to suppose that that aspect of their nature could or should be retrenched, the effect of which could only be a listless, languid society void of fire and spirit. But only dichotomic thinking, referred to absolutes or extremes, allows of the idea that passion and refinement are irreconcilable, when the latter gives a sharper edge to creative thrust and raises desire from lust or greed into something more fulfilling. A sensible aim is then no more than an inducing of attitudes which are less destructive than those which glorify self-assertion, which, despite the veneration in which that cult is held, is the product of individualism. And that aim is one that philosophy might reasonably pursue were its attention turned to dealing with other problems than those, which, if they impinge on social modes at all, do little to change or modify these aggressive postures, bred in part of stress on the 'knowing self', never far removed from an affiliation with acquisitive self-advancement.[25] The stressing of autonomy, to put this another way, stands in the way of the growth of a universal culture, of greater general refinement.

The point is then that the seat of this natural human endowment is sensuous responsiveness, inhibited or submerged as intellectuality is given undue importance, apotheosized indeed, seen as an end in itself rather than as a means to a deeper, more general end, the enrichment of sensuous life in its various aspects and guises. The cult of the individual, though theoretically all-embracing as an intensification of selfhood, in fact has the effect of creating a division between those endowed or gifted with intellectual powers and those whose lives are lived on less exalted levels. And however great its achievements, however enriching the freedom which it makes available, when refinement is wanting it all too often degenerates into forms of belligerency, as the only form in which its potency is exploitable.[26] Let it then be stressed that if culture is to be general, if the potential tone of society is to be raised, there must be some understanding of the qualities common to men, until now supposed to be rational whereas they are rather sensuous, which might well incorporate 'reasonable'. For, with almost total failure to pay attention to anything which is not intellectual or intellectualizable, even one of the meanings of 'reasonable' only survives because ordinary men have need of that term to refer to what is appropriate.[27] When then it is equated with a logocentric 'rational' to the point where its deployment is assumed to be the prerogative of an *élite*, it is not surprising that the notion of sensitivity has itself been intellectualized.

It is not easy to make the point that sensuous receptivity has value in itself, since every term employed in attempt to distinguish its characteristics has in this way been purloined. So strong has been the bias in favour of cognition, of intellectuality, that anything which is not to be brought within its range is, albeit implicitly, taken to be inferior. The sensuous and the sensual are regarded as broadly identical, and sensitivity scarcely escapes coalescence with sentimentality – intensified as a counter perhaps to rationalistic pressures – with the consequence that the whole of life that relates to direct responsiveness, as in artistry for instance, is misunderstood and corroded. The idea of a general culture which has any other form than that of the universalization of intellectuality is simply inconceivable, as if to advocate it invited decay into debauchery. The paradox is then that that is roughly what has happened with the failure to understand a natural human capacity and the real springs of refinement. A contempt for the 'contingent',[28] that is, for normal responsiveness, held to be gross because it does not have an intellectual character or aspire to rise above nature, is precisely the error that has to be corrected lest a greater coarseness and resentment be unleashed. The natural man is not a boor; he is made so by divisiveness, by contempt for, disregard at least, of his natural powers, by failure to take account of what is innate in his make-up, by warping it indeed in an attempt to mould it into conformity with a rationalist ideology, a strictly ideal conception of the characteristic of value. Sensation is not something of interest only to scientists, and is certainly not touched by sense data theory.[29] It is something that relates to spontaneous, vital response or, in more intimate terms, to man's direct relation to the world about him, without some understanding of which all is misunderstood as it relates to man in his state as a sentient being. Nor is this understanding that which is the outcome, the terminus so to say, of cognitive enquiry, which has quite a different form. For, in the attempt to effect a form of detachment, such that all approaches are idealistic only, ideas themselves are distorted; and, in so far as they refer to involvement with actuality, are false of their very nature, since they idealize the real. Sensation is not to be seen simply as a preliminary to intellectual action, but as the very basis of life, as that indeed which gives it its richness and its meaning. And if this contention does no more than bring that point to attention, it will not have been stated in vain.

*

With acceptance that sensation must be distinguished from perception, not vaguely but sharply as serving a distinctive vital function, in the fullest meaning of that very basic expression, the form of perception itself must be examined more closely. For, with the cult of cognition, analysis and detachment, even the form of that response, a conscious reaction to pressures, is largely misunderstood. What takes place when gestalten are formed is not quite so simple, so readily comprehensible as empiricists seem to believe. Starting, then, from their approach, the post-gestalten process is taken to have this form. That the whole that is then presented is taken to be an 'object', something standing out from, detached from all about it, to be gathered in isolation; for relation to other objects or particulars is effected in the intellect, by intellectual means. And it must be so for cognition, dependent on observation, which requires that what is so seen is seen in just that manner in order to permit of close examination. The object thus distinguished is then subjected to analysis, which might either refer to the act of tearing it from its context or to the act of dissecting it in order to study its properties, colour, shape, texture and so on. Its features are then related to ideas stored in the memory, now consciously evoked, so that various intellectual acts, comparison, correlation, generalization and so on, may be undertaken. Thus a clear picture is formed of an aggregate of particulars, sometimes called 'individuals', bound together into a whole which is other than that of the gestalt, and which, to indulge a not wholly improper analogy, is like a finished jigsaw puzzle, giving a composite picture of what is believed to reflect reality. But this picture is not of reality, it is an *ad hoc* construct, the product of intellectual acts of great sophistication, which, based on adequate theory and confirmed experimentally, reflects external becoming only in as far as it *seems* to fit.

In this way knowledge is acquired with greater or lesser *vraisemblance*,[30] of which the lesser only affords a conclusive answer, because by reason of a detectable flaw in finding or reporting, it is shown to be 'non-fitting', patently erroneous. If knowledge is the aim, and a worthy aim it is, a filtering process must take place between gestalt reception and formation into knowledge: first of objectification, then of analysis of the object, and finally of the relating of what has been elicited to what is already known, to allow of generalization, and possibly of prediction. These are meaningful ends, which have proved so beneficial that it would be invidious seriously to question them. But there must also be recognition of the limitations present in the procedures required to attain to such ends as these. And the greatest, without doubt, is divorce or separation from the living actuality, which is particularly unfortunate when what is under review is not the material simply but response in its complexity, its psychical dimension, to external stimulation. Hence, when seen as an end in itself, cognition has clear limits. And those refer not only to the procedures it must adopt, but also to the fact that there is something it cannot engage by reason of these procedures, which do not permit a grasping of relations in the complex of dynamic becoming where they have real existence and effects on those who respond to them. For nature with such procedures is viewed as compounded of objects, which, as intellectual constructs with a phenomenal base, have no real existence in the external world and do not even reflect the way in which gestalten are received in normal responsive action. Knowledge is of value, then, is as far as its reach extends. But if it is regarded, potentially at least, as embracing everything that influences life, much is left out of account, or rather disregarded, which is beyond question meaningful. And that includes the whole of what is not in strict sense cognizable, and in some forms never can be, albeit that in aspects that enters into consciousness, though so in such a way as is yet beyond a cognitive grasp. And if this as a statement seems odd, the reasons that warrant its making are suitably considered, suitably because they play a significant part in the proper understanding of the nature of response as it in fact takes place on one of its several levels.

In an earlier paper a distinction was made between clear and dim perception, which could not of course be sharp as they flow into each other, but which was very properly made in terms of the functions they serve.[31] The function of the first is the acquirement of firm knowledge, supposing the isolation of part of the presentation and its immobilizing for the purpose of inspection, which means in effect its detachment from all that is about it. The function of the second is by contrast vital, not to know in any strict sense, precisely or scientifically, but to live, to adapt to the pressures immediately in action, which may involve some knowledge or its application, but has a purpose other than cognition as its end. In living we confront the dynamic flow of events, from which we cannot normally detach ourselves with ease, as if that cavalcade of occurrences took place apart from ourselves. Normal living in fact involves continual adjustment, attunement might be better, to changes which affect us, not all of which can readily be mediated subconsciously. How then do we react when such pressures impinge on awareness? To empiricism, it seems, we always respond in clear consciousness, cognitively that is; but cognitive response in that empiricist sense calls for certain procedures which not only take up time, which is not normally given, but separate us from the flux in which we are enmeshed. Neither of these can we really afford, unless on rare occasions we have leisure to indulge them, to hesitate, to contemplate, to stand back and observe.[32] Living, that is, adapting to the pressures continually active, presumes an unbroken relation with all that happens around us. The manner in which we then respond is fundamentally different from the manner in which we respond with cognitive intention. For then, now on a perceptual plane, we generate gestalten, that is, acceptable wholes, in extremely rapid succession, one following on another, in effect without respite as changing conditions demand the making of new formations. In place of holding on to a selected presentation, we substitute another, indeed a continuing series, only retaining one gestalt for as long as it serves some purpose. In fine, we respond to the pulse of events, the sequence that is unfolding, much as we respond to the rhythm when we dance, instead of holding ourselves apart, as if we were not involved in the stream of unceasing stimulation. Perception, to reiterate, was primarily evolved as a power permitting us to react with greater acuity, alertness and precision, notably as anything constituted a threat, either to homeostasis or to psychical balance, in this way to secure a keener relation with nature, through which all needs are met. And that is the *normal* relation we have to the world around us, which is more closely linked to sensation, as response to dynamic becoming, then to a cognitively oriented desire to accumulate further knowledge.

If memory and intention, or better intentionality, play a part in subconscious response, that they are active on this plane is scarcely to be doubted. Indeed, all acts are intentional, with very rare exceptions, if those in fact exist as other than reflex reactions: a decision to do nothing is an intention to relax. But to hold that intention *must* have the form of fully conscious resolve, the product, normally over time, of careful deliberation, is a restrictive contention. It may perhaps be an aspect of a broader aim, as when the artist makes a 'stab', not in terms of itself as a self-sufficient action, but in those of a compositional whole in process of formation.[33] Perhaps, when something presents itself as an impending threat, intention involves a decision, to step back on the pavement as a car approaches too closely, to restrain a child as it moves too near the fire or the water's edge. And both of these, of course, presume a recourse to memory, commonly called 'experience', of past events of like character known to have certain consequences. To suppose that such mnemonic acts are similar entirely to the scholar's effort to recollect some passage bearing on the matter on which he is thinking or writing is to carry analogy to the point of misrepresentation. For one is a spontaneous act, the other is deliberative, and that, from the standpoint of function, is a very significant difference. In sum, if we are to understand the nature of perception in deeper terms than those which concern epistemologists, we must not omit to see it in this more basic and vital form, when its character is infinitely more fluid and more subtle, its meaning more closely related to the actual process of living. And need it be added that that is the real concern of philosophy.

*

The meanings here considered, which have reference to responsiveness, show – reflex reaction discounted – that three broad forms of response are more or less distinctive: sensation, dim perception and clear or fully conscious reception. Whether then it is requisite to use a further term for what is here called 'dim perception' is an open question.[34] For it seems that the traditional employment of three terms, sensation, perception, conception – which last refers to strictly rational acts and not to objectification, which is preliminary to them – is a little too limited, in that it excludes or conceals an aspect of response which is far from insignificant. It goes against the grain to call for a change in accepted usage. But, if there is a difference between two forms of perceiving, a better distinction than 'dim' and 'clear' seems to be required. And that is perhaps the more needed in that both the more basic terms, sensation and dim perception, refer to vital response, which should surely be distinguished from that which is simply cognitive and which, if vital at all, is so only indirectly. On the nature of clear perception a quite extensive literature has in recent times been produced, under the general title of 'epistemo-logical studies'. Conversely, little serious thought has been given to what lies outside them, though curiously in early Greek *epistēmē* meant that to which attention has been brought in the present context, subtler forms of response.[35] Balancing on a bicycle or riding a horse successfully, that is, with some feel for the animal, are acts of sensuous character, corrected by dim perception, as when balance is restored by immediate counteraction instantly undertaken. That matters such as these should fall to another discipline, empiricist psychology, is a mistaken idea. For, as such a study aspires to strictly cognitive ends, that is, to be a 'science', it is powerless to comprehend them in the forms that they actually have; and, from a vital standpoint, those forms are what really signify. Philosophy must then give the lead, since it at least establishes that such forms of response exist, with the rider that they quite certainly bear on life as it is lived.

If they are then to be given thought, that must be related to response in more subtle forms. That is not in personal terms in which faults are corrected spontaneously, nor, it need scarcely be added, in terms of conscious action, which lends itself of course to rational explanation, but in those of more complex social forms, which are not in strict sense explicable. For action in those forms relates to interrelative networks, to man's relation *through* the world to his fellow-men – the ethical problem precisely – so that means of comprehending it cannot be simply empirical. It is true that moral problems have traditionally been considered the province of rational thought. But, seen as moral problems, turning on choice and motivation, they are not, as will later be shown, in any strict sense ethical. If ethical issues, then, are traditionally philosophical, what they entail may be other than Western tradition supposes, when it places the emphasis on deliberative, rational action, which turns on the knowing or, by extension, the moral self. The upshot is that philosophy, if ethics is still its interest – and that has no other home – must accept what its study entails. Thus, as social problems, problems of value in general, of priorities of importance, are not to be answered by science, which can deal with observables only, they presume a study which has rather different form. This is not the occasion to press the distinction between ethics and morality, which must wait for fuller development. But it is the occasion once more to mark a needed distinction between conception or cognition and other forms of response. For once consciousness is introduced and linked to rationality, there results a passage into subjectivity, and ethics in effect turns into moral philosophy, which may or may not exert an influence on society, little given to seeking guidance from learned discussions on virtue, but relying even yet on a 'sense' of propriety. And that is so valuable socially that a deeper understanding of that on which it rests, which is something other than consciousness, is surely a worthwhile pursuit, which, though it may take time to have a real effect, might none the less exert an influence on attitudes. But that cannot be undertaken unless thinkers are prepared to give thought to what is involved in this interest, and to the manner in which this sense develops in responsiveness, that is, from a base which is innate in the human make-up and awaits, as it were, release, which right thinking alone can secure.[36]

With idealism dominant in every branch of philosophy, where cognitive interests only are seen as worthy of attention, sub-jectivized morality leads to a general neglect of the problem presented by ethics, not to mention other forms of relation to actualities. And when moral philosophy is itself disregarded in favour of logocentric involvement, ethics as an issue, or rather as a sphere involving sensitivity, ceases to be recognized, and with it all relation to the complex of becoming. Drawing attention, then, to the nature of vital response and to a human potentiality which is deeply embedded in it, finds its ultimate justification in its social or ethical bearing, since it is only in thought of the 'general in actuality', of what is truly common to men, that the problem presented in this form can properly be considered. To which it is fairly added that, if philosophy has traditionally been concerned with further problems, of the nature of reality, of essence, of causality, of what can truly be known, of the meaning of life, and so on, the question of how man meets the world external to himself is surely related to these. For, if the fact that 90% of his response to externals takes place below the level of consciousness is taken as affirmed, then concentration on conscious response, specifically on a form of it, on a clear cognition that is, is to restrict ideas in a most unfortunate manner. If the notion of reality has a strictly conceptual form, supposed to be true for all time, we have but a narrow idea of it. If the idea of causality is confined to knowable instances, only properly recognized in one-to-one relationships generalized in the intellect, interrelativity is not properly understood. And if sensation is only a prelude to what has 'meaning', perception, many aspects of meaning, interpreted as that which exercises an influence, are effectively lost to view. Addressing attention, then, to the nature of vital response, though that can only be grasped through speculative inference, touches all that has been of interest to philosophy in the past, logic perhaps excepted since that has in the Western tradition been confined to an ideal plane.

The full implications, however, of what that attention might mean cannot be properly seen until a better vocabulary, beginning with what terms should mean when applied to direct response, can be framed to refer to what is not in strict sense cognizable, since it is not phenomenal, even in its effects. What renders words deficient in extended discourse is a demand for logical rigour, which delimits by definition. If then what they refer to is not to be defined in a rigorous positive manner, perhaps the meanings to be conveyed can be sharpened by recourse to negating limitations, which, by criticizing improper use clear away false ideas – as when sensation is linked to cognizable sense data or as when perception is supposed always to be clear. But enough that, if the problem is seen in realistic terms, that is to say, as referring to what man in depth confronts, and the means in which he does so as a sentient being, the reference of terms must be other than idealistic. And much depends on this if it is accepted that philosophy should be concerned, whatever its other interests, with what is truly general in a realistic sense. For that, in terms of response, has universal bearing, and is plainly related to action as that takes place in the actual world, as it does even when ordered by thought. Both sensation and perception constitute words which are, if greater depth is the aim, in need of better definition – though that should be but negative – in order that the meanings that they most fruitfully have, as also the implications that such meanings carry with them, may be given the attention that should be accorded to them, which can never be given whilst the interest is merely cognitive.

Chapter Three

Mind and Intellect

That there is some difference between sensation and perception is generally recognized, notwithstanding that it is somewhat vaguely conceived. That there is any between intellect and mind is scarcely recognized at all even by those who devote themselves to that branch of philosophy which goes under the generic name the 'philosophy of mind'. The idea of a difference between them is almost inconceivable, since the only difference to rationalistic thinking is that between the mental and the cerebral or the bodily, when 'mental' is taken to mean ideal or fully conscious thought poised against what is 'cerebral', held to be material – though the first of these terms, when so defined, is used a little loosely. At once discounting that dualism in this too simple form is now subjected to question in several different ways – and not only by determinists – it may be observed that a proper distinction between intellect and mind might do much, without dependence on duality, to clarify ideas on the relation subsisting between thought and its physical base. But let that pass immediately whilst note is made of readings which are less obtuse than simple interchangeability, conflating these two terms against what is without question non-mental. Allowing for a failure to make this distinction sharply – and hence the common use of a single leading term – the scholastics, with some awareness of a difference in responsive modes and functions, even on a conscious plane, distinguished between the active or involved, reactive intellect (*intellectus agens*) and the passive or possible intellect (*intellectus possibilis*) in what were effectively directed or functional terms.[1] And since function is the key to differentiation, this amounts to an insight worthy of attention, such that its refinement on what is known today so far from discrediting it as an outdated projection shows it to have been a step towards a better understanding – though the lesson that it teaches seems to have been disregarded. It suggests, for an example, that the argument intended to place a distinction between the mental and the physical quite beyond dispute – that the mental had no locus in space whereas the physical was 'extended' – was at best but limited. For if thought is not embodied, as Descartes' earliest critics saw to be the case,[2] it must yet have some relation to external pressures, since, if nothing more, it both reacts against them and further acts upon them and must surely relate to them in some way if it aspires to refer.

Thought is very surely a mysterious emanation, if only for the reason that its features cannot be defined in scientific terms, or so without accepting its dependence on the brain, since it is plainly not phenomenal, subject to observation, unless by means of introspection. And if part of the cerebral cortex appears to be its seat, that, apart uncertainty as to its location, is at best but a limited finding. For it seems that all parts of the cortex, not to mention parts of what is called the lower brain, act together and interrelatively in extremely complex ways – of which the EEG's afford sufficient instance – to bring thought, and consciousness, to being. That thought is in some sense ethereal, may even warrant the making of a distinction between it, as having this characteristic, and what is physical, tangible, substantial and amenable to measurement. But that certainly does not justify the simple lumping together of every form of responsive reaction to externals, as if all in effect were to be equated with one far from typical aspect of mentation or mental power, that of special interest to those whose ends are cognitive and no more. It is easy to single out fully conscious thought, but that is even illicit and it certainly presumes a measure of falsification, some misunderstanding of the character of involvement. And in terms of modern thought it is too simplistic, whatever it may have been in the past when recognition of a power uniquely given to men gave those who most fully developed it a sense of exhilaration and justified claims to authority.[3] We must now be a little more cautious, since it seems that this extraordinary power had roots in natural conditions, that it was not the product of some form of autogenesis and did not spring up in a day as did Eve from Adam's rib.

This capacity doubtless developed through process of evolution, which itself was always functional, related to needs that had to be met in the interests of preservation. Thus sensation, the power at all to respond, presumably came into being with the emergence of animate life, and perception, as a development on this basic capacity, with a curious feature, consciousness, the genesis of which is wholly inexplicable, plainly had that as its base. It is likely, then, that self-consciousness, which permitted degrees of detachment and with it introspection, was a relatively late development, which, since it allowed a measure of self-knowledge, could be more or less understood, if not with respect to its emergence as a power then in terms at least of its character. That, even so, when seen by itself, in isolation, may and does indeed generate false pictures with respect to a being's involvement, as if he had power to stand alone, uninfluenced, unconditioned by external forces continually playing upon him. But the question is rather how consciousness arose, to be present as a power in all higher species. For, as had already been said, it undoubtedly came into being, as a development on perception, with the need for alertness to danger as animate beings became locomotive and thence subject to greater risks. In fine, the power of conscious thought grew with the conditions that called it into being, to suggest that *intellectus agens* long preceded, as more basic, *intellectus possibilis*, the faculty, that is, for developing abstract thought.

It has then to be understood that there are at least two powers appertaining to response on a conscious level, so that to deny, to forget or to ignore this with the idea that there is but one is to harbour an illusion. Failure, however, to make such a distinction as this would not of itself be especially harmful were it not that the mind with this conflation of terms is identified complet;ely with the rationalizing intellect – with the upshot that much confusion ensues when thought is directed towards response to external pressures. The mental, now considered as the capacity to reason – thinking of it immediately in but one of its aspects – is a power that all men enjoy simply by being human, since it is a trait of their *hsing*, a species characteristic.[4] Intellection, then, is but an aspect of this capacity, an emanation out of mind, itself *directly* responsive, with a clearly limited function. So that a coalescence of these two responsive terms, as if all mental action had to be intellectual, imposes limits on mentation and deprives it, in as far as that is at all achievable, of its greater range and its invaluable flexibility. Under the rule of rationalism, or ratiocination, intellection is supposed to have universal reach, as if all communication had, in order to be adequate, to have a precise, demonstrative or categorical form. It does not; and the demand that it should is too freely projected and, taking advantage of apparent similarities, asserted, exploited in this case is not too strong a term, as the sole criterion for all communication, to render rationalism superior to any other approach. Men *ought*, that is the implication present in this claim, to speak in propositional terms, lest otherwise what is said is loose and lacks sufficient discipline. Such talk is also labelled subjective, as if that were the only alternative to rational objectivity. But it is not, or need not be, anything of the sort; and, if its aim is precision, that is precision referred to action, in respect of which language is but a means. When used, indeed, it often has to be suggestive, since if what is called for is appropriate action in the external world, circumstances may well be such that that alone is appropriate, so complex is the involvement that rigorous expression may not be expedient and may even, if applied, falsify the issue.

If logic is regarded as essentially an organon, a disciplinary instrument, developed to secure the appropriate use of reason, it may fairly be said to have two forms or characters, here to be distinguished as natural and formal logic. Then, whereas the first is employed by everyone, since it is a given endowment, given to permit the adequate application of thought to the conduct of normal life, the second is only applicable, properly and usefully, in a rather narrower field, which is different from that confronted in the sphere of concrete action. Hence the case is that, morons perhaps excepted, everyone in ordinary life makes use of natural logic. For without it, which is rather absorbed than acquired through special study, there could be no communal life, no communication between persons in society which was mutually understood. All language is based upon it and develops the various forms that it has precisely in the service of such demands as these: a measure of consistency, broad agreement on terms and on their meanings in context, as also on their use in various combinations.

It is known that every language, as it seems without exception, for none is really primitive, has a quite extraordinary subtlety, such that there is nothing which pertains to normal life that cannot be expressed in it in some form or another.[5] Simple affirmations and denials are apposite only in certain specific conditions, to which of its very nature formal logic is confined. But formal logic itself is no more at last than a stiffening, an induration of a more flexible natural logic, without the power, because of its self-imposed restrictions, to compete with natural logic in the actual world, which it rather awkwardly endeavours to engage[6] – a point to be considered more fully in the sequel. This, then, is said at once simply to show that reasoning finds its base in what has here been distinguished as natural logic, wherein it differs greatly from rationalistic thinking as that is tied to formal logic, and remains, because it is so bound, a marginal activity.

That natural logic lacks the precision of the other must, of course, be acknowledged. But so, none the less, with the rider that the precision that it lacks is not that required in ordinary life and discourse, in dealing with things or events, properly with pressures, which its forms are specifically adapted to encounter. To sustain its rigour, formal logic cannot so adapt to conditions, and can only as a consequence deal with a limited form of language. In science it is not such a form as that which really counts, since its ultimate interest lies in relation to reality, established, contingently as is said, through successful experimentation, which, against reality, affords the only real test. And that is broadly the test that applies in normal life, where action has to be taken in terms of real conditions, even, for example, when a speaker endeavours to influence his audience by means of the words, the tone, the stress and the gestures that he uses to ensure that what he says shall be fully understood. Between reasoning so considered, as flexible and persuasive, and rationalism proper, which is in principle rather compulsive, there is an undoubted difference, which is not unrelated to the distinction subsisting between mental and intellectual modes of deploying thought. Hence, if both are regarded as active on conscious levels, it is requisite to take account of this divergence of character and to show that it is related to function, purpose or need. But merely to note this does something to show wherein that difference lies, and thus to clarify ideas on the nature of response on higher or conscious levels.

However, in exposing the limits of formal logic and the restrictiveness of a narrow logocentric rationality, it is not to be supposed that all intellectual action shares these limitations – though it will be seen to have others. For though it may not be a power that everyone deploys in its higher forms, it is one in the hands of those who cultivate it sensitively that has so enriched the lives of men that to misrepresent it is even to impoverish or circumscribe what it has given and has to give to a continuing culture linked to the sensitive use of language. But the present point is simply to show that reasoning as a capacity is narrowed when eristic debate is considered its only authentic mode of procedure, its standards the only standards by which statements are to be judged, to the point that they cannot be challenged without an undermining of discipline.[7] For the confusion engendered by such restrictive notions tends not only to falsify ideas about rational powers, which must be deployed in any serious discourse, but all ideas in respect of the nature of response, even on conscious levels. Accordingly, there was need to make this critical comment as a prelude to proceeding to further thought about the nature of deeper forms of response viewed in terms of function, notably with regard to their bearing on life as it is, with language, normally lived. For that is misunderstood if function can only by seen in a way that excludes its vital meaning, its meaning for action in life. So, let further thought be given to intellection as a power with wider reference than its identification with rationalism allows. But, before that can be done with any show of adequacy, it is well that both intellection and a more far-reaching and extensive mental action be defined with greater acumen than is given to them when they are taken to be synonymous.

*

Resisting the temptation fully to equate *intellectus agens* with mind, which would be too crude, it is fitting to observe that, considered in itself, *intellectus* is not immediately or directly active against externals. Those, when suitably treated, simply afford it something on which it is able to act, operating, after this treatment has been applied, in its own terms and with attempted detachment from them. Its act when it does this may be called 'the act of objectification', though that is but an initial move whereby what is

65

received in perception is rendered a distinct, that is, a definable object, symbolized by attaching a suitable designate to it, so that it can have the form of a clear idea. For an object as such, a thing apart from whatever is about it, need not be named if action alone is exerted on it, as in the act, for instance, of picking up a cup, and may itself have a transient life, as in dim perception, which is mental not intellectual. Hence objectification, which has wider application, is not intellectually meaningful until a term has been placed upon whatever is selected for closer examination, when the object is taken as something subsisting in itself, a particular set apart from the dynamic of becoming and related only to ideas that may be formed about it, by comparison, quantification or other rational transactions. And thus is impression, which is vague, fluid and pervasive, changed into ideas which can be sustained. For, whilst the intellect acts with ease in the world of clear ideas, it tends to be uncomfortable when it essays to pass beyond them into realms that cannot be given clear ideational forms. And its etymon seems to conform this, since it shows that a term with this import was a later formation, which could not have been produced until conceptual powers had been sufficiently developed to call for a word that referred to this specific activity. The knowing self is then a conscious intellectual in a sense that the active agent is not, or rather need not be when he responds to the world spontaneously. For he stands apart from what is known, regarding that – though this brings up a host of questions – as something outside himself with which he is not involved directly, as that on which clear thinking is developed internally.

Intellect in English has its roots in two Latin words, *lectus*, the past participle of the verb *legere*, prefixed or combined with the preposition *inter*, to form the composite *intellectus*, which is the nounal form of *intellegere*. The meaning of *legere*, the key word in this compound, is best understood by reference to the first person singular in the present tense, as *lego* that is to say, when it may be translated as 'I gather', 'I collect', 'I select' or 'I pick out', with *inter* in this connection meaning 'from among'. Hence *intellego* itself may be rendered 'I read into or from among – what is placed before me' or, in a yet more specialized sense, 'I read between the lines', which is an intellectual act of great sophistication. Note, then, that *mens* has no verbal form, which brings out the subjective character of the term *intellectus*, which cannot in the same sense be attributed to mind. What then emerges is that intellect, *intellectus*, refers to fully conscious response. And though not to be aligned exactly with apperception – in which attention is addressed to one's own inner states, with little or no relation to referred perception – it must be considered as a form presuming detachment from what appertains to normal forms of involvement.

In the last analysis there is no such thing as absolute detachment, just as there is no unqualified *a priori* except on narrow abstract planes.[8] For, even involvement with one's own states presumes, and cannot but presume, some influence from outside; for without that, as it affects the self, there would be nothing to contemplate, to stir one to thought about what has affected one's condition. Even mystics must think about something, if no more than the ultimate void, until they attain that extraordinary state of relinquishing all forms of thought, a state which, since it is scarcely an involvement of the intellect, may be disregarded here. Turning, then, to what is operative in context, let thought be given to what intellectual action is often supposed, uniquely and exclusively, to comprise. In science and philosophy, its specific realms, it is commonly taken to embrace cognition, or that culmination of it, final explanation. This is seen in expressions such as 'intellectual knowledge', a qualification applied clearly to distinguish it from other forms of knowledge, 'tacit knowledge', for instance. To those it is supposed to be unquestionably superior, 'scientific' in a sense that the others plainly are not. The intellect, again, is commonly defined as 'the faculty of knowledge' or 'the cognitive capacity'. Nor is it without bearing here that logic, formal logic, claims to be a science, that is to project or to establish knowledge, though that knowledge can never be more at last than the revelation of abstract or formal relations.[9] Hence, to attain or attest to knowledge is held to be the essential function of the intellect, since it alone can collect, collate or evaluate knowledge strictly, in a form that is properly judged to be scientific, in one, that is to say, which presumes systematic acquirement and the subjection of what is discovered to methodical testing.

The process, then, whereby this is done, by employment of such means as analysis and induction, is fittingly described and distinguished as intellectual and defines its peculiar character as uniquely a human capacity. But it cannot, if that indeed is the only form that it has, do other than observe its evident limitations: that it is either confined to the phenomenal world or to the world of abstract discourse. It deals, and can only deal, with preselected 'objects', which have no existence in the world of actuality, in which nothing stands in objective isolation and where everything has being in an interrelative complex, exists as a 'mode' in the manifold, the dynamic of becoming. Hence, the knowledge so attained is always filtered knowledge, acquired through a process requiring the arrest or objectification of gestalt presentations and the analysis of the particulars distinguished in this manner. This is not, of course, to deprecate the achievements of the enquiring intellect, which have proved beyond question fruitful. It is simply to state what is in fact the case: that "even the most complete understanding of all the natural phenomena present to the mind (correctly the intellect) could not overcome the built-in dilemma inherent in man's thinking: the fact that he perceives the world with the help of a mental apparatus which imposes its own forms (the categories) upon the raw material of existence... a world independent of mind".[10] The constant struggle of rationalists to overcome these restraints is surely to be regarded as a highly commendable effort, even should it end, as it must, in comparative failure. But the price of acquiring the power of relative detachment, for that can never be complete, is precisely this limitation.

How far the intellect is or apparently should be confined to cognitive enquiry is a question of some moment, since this rationalistic reading of what it is potent to do gives but a restricted idea of its latent capacity. Thus, it is fairly, properly asked: to what extent are creative and imaginative activities to be ranked as intellectual? That they are in a certain sense granted such a status, though not in rationalistic philosophy, unless in a dubious form in which they are regarded as subject to rational treatment, cannot be denied. But care is required in discussing this point, since it is open to question whether this subsumption is wholly to be welcomed, since with stress on cognition as the essential characteristic of intellectuality what artistry really involves is widely misunderstood, with unfortunate consequences for cultural growth and refinement, its diffusion into the complex of social life at large. For this bias has had the effect of obscuring its basic, sensuous, universal meaning, of replacing the value of spontaneous response to form in artistic meaning, of plasticity, musicality seen as natural endowments, with a wholly alien, adventitious interest, in 'what does it mean', 'its provenance', 'its self-expressive power', and other attitudes introduced with the romantic movement.[11] Classical universality has been sacrificed to serve specialized cognitive interests. The inspiration, then, that lies behind the creative thrust does not have *in this sense* an intellectual character, since with it there is no standing back, no detachment from involvement with the pulse of reality, and no suggestion even that it was prepense or preconditioned. It seems to surge up uninvited, to spring, so to say, from the blue. But inspiration is no more at last than stimulation, stimulation with an apparent external source – though it is sometimes brought to birth by suggestibility, urging its recipient to effective action. It is said that some poets have received whole poems in this way, which they had simply to transcribe. Usually, he who is so inspired – and this gifted he includes not only artists but thinkers, statesmen, men of action, even entrepreneurs – sets to work to develop the 'idea' that he has received. And this working may comprise a long and arduous process, involving continued refinement and repeated review, the careful application of the critical faculty.[12]

To mention the last is, of course, to cite intellectual powers, though those in such forms are scarcely ratiocinative or tied to formal logic. Then, that something other than blind or strictly subjective involvement informs the creative act cannot but be acknowledged. Indeed, man cannot escape the powers that are given to him through the evolutionary growth of a critical capacity with its neurophysical base; he cannot return to a state in which he is without it. But he should surely use it to see himself as he is: an animal with certain psychical characteristics. It would be a mistake, however, to regard these rational powers, because, in as far as is known, they are unique to humanity, as those alone which merit serious attention. For man is also, and in another sense uniquely – meaning that it has special forms as a human endowment – gifted with sensitivity, which is certainly not to be aligned with intellectuality, as if that alone were its seat or as if without the latter the former were deficient. To make this point more clearly, we must turn from creativity, in which there is undoubtedly an intellectual element, to responsive receptivity, where its introduction, commonly demanded under rationalistic dominance, is positively injurious.[13] Sensuous response is essentially spontaneous, and to lace it with clear thought is to corrupt its virtue. This is not the occasion on which to elaborate on this point. For at once it is enough to note that refinement is properly sensuous and the basis of all true culture, when that term is removed from its common association with intellectuality and recognized as having a universal bearing. It is societies that produce and foster the growth of culture; and intellectual achievement, which is essentially personal, must be absorbed in the greater whole to have its most fruitful meaning. This thought is not intended, then, to discredit or belittle intellectuality, though aspects of it have been glorified unduly – and so for two thousand years in the West, as if it were even required in ethical and artistic response, to vitiate both as a consequence[14] – though it is now placed on the defensive and required to examine itself more thoroughly than has hitherto been the case. Nor is it to call into question its undoubted virtue in other, more generous forms. It is simply projected to show wherein its limits lie, that it is not the paradigm of human power and excellence, but simply an aspect of that power, which has its proper place. That should not be overrated nor unduly delimited, but must be seen in its proper role, as a power that is contributory only in certain ways. For, if it is regarded as supreme without reservation, that can only be productive of grave misunderstanding of man's relation to the world and of his latent capacities, which have other forms when seen in a universal sense.

*

Whereas intellect as a term is a relatively late formation, mind is a derivative of a very ancient word, which intellect does not supercede but rests on as an extension, a power developed to carry response, under some penalty, further. Since mind is not a compound but a single world, it is fairly assumed that it preceded or predated any composite formation; and that is quite certainly the case. With earlier words, however, a difficulty arises, in that pristine meanings can never be firmly known, although it is surely a just assumption that initially they had a concrete or vital reference and related directly to basic human needs. 'Mind', or its antecedent form is a term of great antiquity, which is evinced by its variants in most, though curiously not all, Indo-Germanic languages. This suggests that it was in use prior to their split into Eastern and Western forms, prior to the dispersal, that is, of the Caucasian peoples. There is reason to think that its root was *man*[15], since its first recorded form was *manas* in the Sanskrit of the Vedic era, probably late in the Second Millennium, though the dating of the Vedas is as yet an unsettled question. But indeed, a long period must have elapsed between their composition and their committal to writing, so that what the words used originally meant might have undergone change. As a prime meaning, however, is not now accessible, that reference must be judged on the evidence available and on reasoned speculation. It is then known that in Western forms changes of vowel sounds took place, from 'a' to 'e' and 'i', apparently long, and 'u', to produce such forms as *menos, mens* and *mente, gemund, gemynd, mynde, minne* and so on, surviving with modifications into modern languages.

All refer to some form of thought, thinking or mental action, sometimes with a tincture of verve or spirituality,[16] which is of special interest because that is highly suggestive, referring as it does to something other than rationality. For surely thinking has other forms than ratiocination, and even in modern times may mean more than conscious deliberation. The days when animals were supposed to be no more than automata, driven solely by 'instinct' – a term that was grossly abused – have happily now passed, though determinists implicitly apply that also to men, governed to exclusion by ostensible causal laws. For it is not now to be doubted that animals think in some sense, study given conditions, weigh possible alternatives, if in a dimmer sense than humans with better equipment. That early man had the acumen of the modern intellectual is not sensibly surmised; but his powers were doubtless keen enough when he was tracking or hunting or when he had to devise some means of self-protection, and later means of tending the land for the nurture of his dependants when he settled down as a farmer. His thought in those earlier times was to presumption directed towards the advancement of concrete ends, and in that sense mind was an instrument deployed in the service of living, at base of staying alive, much as it is with animals. Mind then, or its root precisely, was an early word with essentially concrete meaning, formed as man realized that he had a power which was other than that in his limbs; and to that, as something he noted, he gave a generic name.

That mind acts on subconscious levels as well as on those of dim perception need not now be dealt with at length, as it has already been discussed in an earlier chapter. But in so far as the present concern is to distinguish mind from intellect and to show that the first performs quite a different function, which in a vital sense is even more important to men. For, without its prior activity, intellectuality cannot be developed, a slight elaboration seems to be to the point. As organizing nervous response to external stimulation, and thereby rendering it possible to act with some precision, to escape the confusion that would ensue were we conscious of every stimulus playing upon the receptors, its function is quite decisive. Perhaps the intellect plays some part in this process of ordering, in that memory certainly enters into this action, though that is rather in this field fed in from a store as in a computer, than evoked by the intellect at this lower level, which has as it were through past action made its material available. The same applies to intention which has an intellectual history, that is to say, is rooted in earlier conscious experiences, which were, it would seem, internalized, such that fully conscious goals, of which so much is made by empiricist psychologists, constitute but a fraction of what are more suitably called 'drives' made in response to the complex in which needs have to be met. Conscious deliberation is a time-consuming activity, and very often involves a degree of falsification, because it entails detachment from the flow of events. It is often supposed that impulse or, better said, spontaneity must be unreliable. But that is a rational prejudice, which is plainly mistaken, inasmuch as immediate reaction to conditions – witness the jumping cat – is related to vital need, as is instanced in flinching, to give a rather lowly example, when what is really of moment is the whole range of direct response. That is infinitely richer than simple reflex reaction, which is stereotyped and so knowable, though its finer forms are obscure because they are not detectable.[17] It is justly to be contended in fact that all delicacy, all refinement, all grace of manner indeed, as in rhythmic response, have their seat on this plane, not on that of conscious thought, which renders them artificial, even self-conscious and false. And this is stressed because, with emphasis on the rational or, otherwise said, the subjective, there has been a coarsening and corruption of manners, a weakening of the social 'sense' in which the self is lost, not in some conscious effort of repudiation, but naturally and simply without any thought of effect. Subconscious mental states, and even those that refer or relate to the realm of dim perception, are in their ease and naturalness the keys to courtesy and refinement; and their neglect by thinkers because they cannot be rationalized, has been one of the major causes of the present malaise.[18] Happily, these forms of response are so deeply rooted that neglect of or contempt for them as other than intellectual cannot scotch them completely; for certain attitudes of mind are resistant to such pressures. But thinkers, as they set the tone and influence postures adopted, cannot escape the onus of giving thought to these matters, even though they do not fall into the rational net.

That early man was aware of the mind's subconscious action as that is now understood cannot be maintained, since that is recognized but by few even to this day. Further, that he distinguished between clear and dim perception, distinct and tacit knowledge, is not sensibly contended. That he was, none the less, endowed with a power with which to conduct his affairs with a greater efficiency must have dawned upon him as he attained humanity, as his brain grew larger and as he developed language to name what had significance for him. No one knows how language arose or how it evolved in its various forms in distinctive areas. But doubtless words were first applied to things and simple relations, since those are less ambiguous than subtler forms of relationship, such as those that referred to what did not directly affect him, which were later developments. Initially, he must have named his limbs and certain internal organs, of the presence of which he became aware through the dissection of animals and the killing of men in war, noticing particularly those which were more vulnerable and called for special protection when he was engaged in fighting. And since it was through his eyes and his ears that he received impressions, the ideas that those were somehow registered internally, apparently in his head, gave ground to the further notion that the powers that we now call mental were seated there and probably, since a blow on the head impaired them, linked to the brain, as in animals. Hence *man* referred to that given power with apparent physical base. When all this took place, over long stretches of time, cannot now be known, unless through cranial measurement referred to the size of the brain. But it is tolerably certain that language was developed, first for simple naming and later for relationships, long before historical times in fact as need arose to specify vital interests.

Later, with the emergence of self-consciousness and self-knowledge, mind took on further meaning, as the seat of thought and conscious deliberation, to complicate its reference.[19] And so the need arose to distinguish thought applied with apparent detachment and thought applied in action, whence *noēsis* and *intellectus* were formed, as refinements, so to say, on *nous* or *menos* and *mens*. It is pointed, then, to remark that mind had also the meaning of 'spirit', in one of the uses of *manas*, in *menos*, its form in Greek, and with preference for *esprit* in French, which has no other term for mind in the sense of it as that with which we relate ourselves to the world, though the adjective *mental* like mind reflects the Latin *mens*. It would then be obtuse and against the cast of much early thinking – for *purusha* provides an exception – to suppose that spirit was seen as transcendent of nature[20] when it was rather held to be immanent in vitality. This is clearly shown in animistic thinking, but it is just as clearly evinced in the sophisticated thought developed in early times, which was far from animistic in a superstitious sense – though 'animistic' is used pejoratively to condemn or dismiss thinking which is other than sufficiently rationalistic. The notions of *tao* and *logos*, and also in some sense of *vāc*,[21] which undoubtedly predated any reference to them in writing, show that a 'sense' of the hidden, absurdly called superstitious, was present in early times in philosophical thinking. And if that sense has now been lost – though it reappears in Marcel – or rather has been subjected to scorn in philosophical circles, not unjustly, of course, when it has superstitious forms, the reason is that some thinkers are blind, as their predecessors were not, to any sense of indefiniteness in that which is confronted. And this notwithstanding that science becomes increasingly conscious of it as present in many aspects of what constitutes its interest. And this applies not only to worlds explored in subatomic physics, but even in those at one time supposed to have such regularity as to allow of firm prediction. As neurologists, physiologists, bio-chemists and physicists probe into matters more deeply, they become more and more aware of how complex relations are, of how little is constant and regular. For characteristics vary not only between members of a given species, but even in conditions in a single organic structure, for reasons that are puzzling, quite apart on a human plane from the added complication produced by admitting a psychical factor. This is superficial and very much too abrupt, for continual fresh discoveries illuminate what is not clear, only to raise new problems in the process of so doing. It is sufficient, however, to show that much indeed is obscure, which means beyond the reach of the analysing intellect confined to the world of observables.

If the nature of life or vitality defies exact definition, both with respect to its origins and to its actual working,[22] that spirit as one of its facets does so is not surprising. For its psychosomatic character introduces complexities which are the more acute in degree as its psychical component plays a greater part. But that any movement whatever is purely psychological would be a mistaken view, as ordinary language evinces. We speak of 'nerve' or of 'guts' when we refer to courage, to give a sufficient index that in one of its forms at least spirit is seen as bodily, as having a nervous base. That *man* in such forms as *menos* has reference to something with corporeal affinity tends to confirm this reading: that it has a functional as distinct from an intellectual meaning, which has no such association unless in an indirect sense. Mind clearly has wider reference since it engages actuality. That such distinctions as these have passed into desuetude with the rise of modern philosophy and its weakened links with life is an unfortunate consequence, since then it detaches itself from real issues. For, when it is asserted that ratiocination has replaced or should replace all other forms of thinking, held to be inferior, emotional or unscholarly, severance from reality can be the only outcome. Hence guidance for life, which involves relation to that reality, is in effect abandoned – though that is but one attitude adopted by philosophers. Others are more sensitive and recognize that the problem of spiritual involvement has a further dimension. This need not suppose a transcendence, for the noumenal as related to *nous* rather than to *noēsis* refers to what is extra-phenomenal, underlying reality which has influence on the psyche. Allowing for the misuse of a term, which should have read the 'intellect', a saying of Hartmann reflects this: "The mind divides, the spirit unites",[23] which may be read in two ways. First, that analysis dissects the complex which is presented; and second, which is more pertinent, weakens and corrodes what is implicit in spirit, its power to unite society by touching common chords. Mind, the power in one of its aspects to be reasonable, balanced in action and judgement, is, potentially at least, a universal endowment, related not to abstract thought but to the conduct of life.

*

Repeating that confusion between these two responsive terms involves not merely a failure to grasp their distinctive meanings, which is excusable in the face of traditional usage, but to understand what signifies in life, which is less excusable, there is yet an aspect of this which has to be further developed to show what is lost in their conflation. It is well to stress, accordingly, that mind as a term has reference to two phases of response and the values pertaining to them, which is what is really at issue. This does not so much refer to its action on two levels, that of subconscious screening and that of dim perception, both of which of course relate to actual living, as to something more, which is obscured when approaches are idealistic only. When Aristotle, then, defined man as a species, which was uniquely gifted with exceptional capacities, as a 'rational animal', that is fairly read as 'one with the power to reason', which is a generic characteristic. *Homo sapiens*, furthermore, also with generic meaning, seems to imply that man has power to attain to a measure of wisdom, of balanced understanding, which is not to be identified with knowledge, but which at best may strengthen it. What exactly 'wisdom' means, as apart from exceptional insight, is not easy to determine.[24] Its definition, however, as "soundness of judgement in matters relating to conduct in life", shows, with stress on the last, that it means something more than 'validity' or 'cogency' in a propositional sense. That man is potentially wise, as distinct from invariably so, is a proper qualification, in that it is then generally applicable, may be ascribed to every man, to every human being, regardless of whether he has acquired intellectual power. This has some importance because undue stress on that power, developed in the schools, as opposed to a natural endowment given with the genes, cannot but conduce to an élitist outlook, which, if too diffuse, leads to mediocrity, as if the possession of knowledge implied a greater understanding, which is by no means the case. The realm of mind, in other words, is fairly held to relate to a general human capacity, such that its neglect or a failure to

76

understand that the power that it represents is other than intellectual means that subjective involvement overrides the general interest. Idealism cannot comprehend the general, except in the rather dubious form of subjective generalization, which presumes, and has presumed since mid-classical times, that all men should aspire to deliberate in the manner of intellectuals, with the consequence that their latent powers are in some sense warped, as they either strive uneasily to attain to that exalted status[25] or, as is more commonly the case, reject it out of hand and instead adopt attitudes opposed to all that it represents. If a refinement which is latent in the human make-up is eroded or replaced by boorish approaches to life because standards are wrongly interpreted, that is a serious matter. To be general they must rest on a mental, or sensuous, plane; and the recognition of that gives this distinction its warrant. To urge the 'higher values' in a Millean manner[26] is paradoxically to be blind to where the real interest lies when it is seen as social, as referring to men in general.

This is not to condemn those values, which would be absurd, barbarous, uncouth. It is simply to state that if they are extolled as the acme of quality, as if all else were secondary, misunderstanding of what is at stake cannot but be the outcome. Clearly there are limits to this idea of quality, if it presumes approaches unaccompanied by insight or a proper 'sense' of value, of priorities of importance.[27] For, without that leavening, attitudes tend to become abstract and academic, and with prejudice even divisive. Further, a human potential, to be balanced, sane and sensitive, is at times, because it lacks rationalistic standing, regarded as prosaic, banal or commonplace, at least as without the adventurousness of "piercing the veil of truth", advancing to yet greater conquests. And it has to be admitted that it is not 'progressive'. But at least it seems to offer a rather more promising aim than that of the mere increase of knowledge without clear understanding of what it contributes to life, which is more than the augmentation of material power and control. Moreover, as has already been said, it is the key to culture, that is to general refinement as contrasted with the sublime and esoteric achievements of self-centred individuals, which too often affront the norms of human sensitivity, brash as they sometimes are. It would not be fitting to press this point too strongly, as if to deprecate what the intellect achieves; but, even so, what it implies merits consideration. Those whose intellectual

77

powers are weak in a relative sense may yet have other powers, which have been undervalued when the first have received such limelight as to throw them into the shade. A change in the notion of value, then, might give them greater status, very much to the benefit of social relations generally.[28]

The second of these aspects of response to actualities is that mind in this sense has affinity with spirit when that is seen as immanent rather than as transcendent, linked that usually means to intellectuality. We speak of 'spirited horses', vibrant with nervous energy, without in so doing suggesting that reasoning is a factor in such a display of mettle. But, bearing in mind that man has specific characteristics, produced through evolution by the growth of his brain, that a similar term is used to refer to equine and human capacities, horsiness and humanity, confirms the idea that verve is related to vitality. This does not lower man, as if his characteristics, other than those that relate to his patent power to rationalize, were necessarily bestial. It merely attests that he shares some attributes with animals, which is scarcely remarkable when he himself is a mammal. But that need not be pressed. For the interest in this is simply to escape the idea that human specificity, of which an aspect is sensitivity, is something removed from nature on to asomatic or supersensuous planes. That is today interpreted as essentially intellectual, as if the idea of 'original sin', which afforded a check on arrogance, were no longer operative.[29] But indeed, with the weakening of the belief in something greater than man, which in other cultures is not conceived of as a personal or a personified God but as "the spirit over the waters", the power that underlies movement, nature in a word, tends to render the intellect not only supreme but divine, or quasi-divine at least. It is seen as a power that man alone is able to exert – although it is all too evident that it is frail and flexible, swayed, for instance, by fashion.[30] And speaking in generic terms, it is to the point that 'humanity' hs a double meaning, as referring at once to the human race and to some of its finer traits, benevolence, compassion, charity, feeling for others. That it then has a spiritual meaning, with little relation to either to logocentric involvement or the accumulation of knowledge, scarcely needs to be emphasized. But to say that it was 'mindless' would be an absurd mistake. Thus mind and spirit are allied, since both have a nervous base.

Exactly where spirit resides is a very difficult question, rendered more so by the thought that what it involves is not amenable to analysis, which depends on objectification, phenomenal observation. It operates circumstantially and is not exerted, it seems, unless some concatenation of challenging conditions calls it into existence, so that it has its being invariably in a complex, the complex of events, and cannot be considered in isolation from them, as something standing alone. Names, even so, are given to its various manifestations, in so far as those are distinguishable from a tone which is present or latent, a propensity, that is, to behave in terms of what it implies. Considering it in benevolent form rather than as verve, it presumes understanding and sympathy referred to the needs of others.[31] Those features, it is to be noted then, are deployed, like grace and courtesy, in the main spontaneously and certainly presuppose a measure of self-forgetfulness. But that does not imply that they must then be 'mindless', a term that rather applies to acts that are inconsiderate. It rather means that they are undertaken directly, without conscious deliberation or subjective premeditation. Somewhere in between simple reflex reaction and ultimate intellection, the area, that is, in which mind is active, spirit has its seat. And plainly it is exerted as sensuous or nervous, not as noetic or rational, though of course it can at any time be brought up into consciousness and in that way be subjectivised, when its virtue may be impaired by the introduction of some personal interest, rectitude, self-image, desire for repute and so on. To stress its spontaneity, then, as in generous impulse – to which the alternative is a measure of calculation – is at once to establish its character as disinterested action, free from *arrière-pensée* or ulterior motivation, and to link it to nervous response. Nor does 'nervous' in this sense mean timid or excitable, or physical to exclusion. It rather means sensitivity in the face of prevailing conditions, a finesse which is inhibited by rational intervention.

In conclusion it might be asked whether 'mind', as a single word, can carry the weight of meaning that has here been placed upon it: as the controller of innervation, as the source of intuition, as the key to sensitivity, and so to cultural growth, and as the seat of reasoning when that is directly applied. The making of gestalten marks a line between subconscious and conscious response which is other than intellectual, not detached, that is to say, from direct involvement with the dynamic flow of events. But though in theory sharp enough, in practice this division is rather more opaque, as if some fluctuation took place to generate much overlap. It seems then to be the case that response can have two forms simultaneously, as is indeed suggested in the notion of tacit knowledge.[32] There is much that is affective, influential that is to say, which remains unrecognized, even though fragments of it may well up into consciousness, in a manner that seems to lack for immediate causal warrant, since the outcome is often unforeseen, apparently without precedent. Some cause, or rather some conglomeration of causes, was undoubtedly present, though it was certainly not overt. And any attempt to infer it in a retrospective act, could only misinterpret it, since that would be to apply categorization to what had no discernible parts. In sum, there is a sphere between initial stimulation, which is certainly not singular, and reception in clear consciousness, which presumes particularization or the gathering of particulars into intellectual groupings, a dimension of response that defies examination in other than physical terms, and so for the simple reason that it cannot be reached by analysis. What takes place within that sphere is, speculatively considered, a dynamic process without detectable features, such as are discernible in neural, synaptic activity, which permits some insight into the physical aspects of response at this 'lower' level. Although these movements undoubtedly have a psychical aspect, then, empiricist psychologists are powerless to engage them, inasmuch as they confine themselves to phenomenal presentations, whether those be overt, as in response to figure and ground, or hidden from the naked eye and thus accessible only with the aid of instruments which can record no more than physical characteristics. That they are psychical, however, or rather psychophysical, has to be acknowledged once it is accepted that intentionality plays part in such response; indeed, since all action is purposive, as related to vital interests, even dictates its character.

This justifies the idea that mind is active in this sphere, that it informs response below the level of consciousness, which, without its intervention, would indeed be merely physical, to confirm the ancient dichotomy which has proved so much an obstacle to deeper understanding. In view of associations that cling to the term 'the mind', as to the adjective 'mental', it might perhaps be better to have two terms at disposal, suitably to distinguish between response which is subconscious, which might be labelled 'sensuous', and response which involves awareness, which might be considered 'mental'. For neither, evidently, is fittingly termed 'intellectual', when that defines a form of response which has been distinguished as one dependent on analysis, and so presupposes detachment. As a proposal this may not be wholly satisfactory. But if, as seems to be the case, there is an intermediary process taking place between the somatic and intellectual, to distinguish that as a factor in response to externals is more sensitive than to cling to the crude dichotomy which allows of but two spheres without any relation between them – psychical or physical or, more commonly, mind and matter.[33] Once that point is made, the consequence is apparent: that there is an aspect of response that cannot be detected in the form that it actually has, but only inferred for the reason that a psychophysical process cannot but take place to convert raw stimulation into conscious response; and the problem that that raises cannot be disregarded. And let it be clear that it is not one of explanation, which is clearly not available on such a plane as this, but rather one of a better and deeper understanding of how man responds to reality.

In fine, we return to the question, apparently unanswerable, of how consciousness comes to be active against the physical world, which is otherwise to say: what links it to physicality? No answer is here provided which is other than suggestive. But such a reading as this is surely a little deeper than the superficial idea – an even embarrassing legacy – that mental activation and physical occurrences are absolutely different and apparently unrelated, except in so far as some 'mystic' force intervenes to bring them together. This theory may be speculative, and nothing more is claimed for it. But it is not metaphysical in the sense that it disregards any empirical evidence, scientific findings, which may themselves be speculative, as they bear on what is discussed. Nor is it materialistic in a reductionist sense, projected as an all-or-nothing explanation which, as paying no attention to extra-material factors, must always leave something out of account which is certainly of importance. But, that it does not aspire to rank as an explanatory theory is perhaps its virtue, based on the idea that all is *not* explicable, though all that happens in response is undoubtedly influential, that is, value-laden in some sense or another. In short, by placing the stress decisively on value when giving thought to the nature of response to actualities, or to the terms that refer to it – which are surely too personalized in idealist thinking and too deterministic in materialistic readings – a fresh and perhaps a more fruitful approach is developed in this projection. That, to this thinking at least, renders it philosophical, concerned with evaluation that is, with its own peculiar difficulties, rather than with scientific explanation, where the difficulties encountered have quite a different character.[34] This distinction is doubtless deplorable from a rationalistic viewpoint, tied, as it seems, to the latter, to explanation or explication, and demanding, in the name of truth, irrefragable answers. But as rationalism is powerless to provide a better solution to this perennial problem, that is scarcely a matter on which tears are suitably shed. A distinction between terms which are used uncritically, thus to hamper or delimit a better understanding of what response entails, is justly made if it conduces to a greater insight into man's relation to what he in depth confronts, the dynamic of becoming.

Chapter Four

Subject and Object

Of all the terms discussed in this book, these two, and the first especially, stand in most urgent need of closer examination. For their meanings in epistemic and evaluative discourse are so different that to confuse them is to misunderstand the nature of involvement, as when the first is supposed to be applicable to the second, as if the knowing self were one with the active agent. Once it is accepted, then, that the prime concern of philosophy is general evaluation and thought is directed towards an important question that raises – as to whom value in general accrues, which admits of no easy answer – it is incumbent to clarify what these terms refer to in their most meaningful senses. If value is the concern, it is its recipient only who constitutes the subject irrespective of what is meant when reference is made to the object, seen as that against which he reacts, to which he is subjected in any form of response. Nor, when so considered, need the object be the epistemic object, something clearly defined; and it may be something so different that the use of a single term to refer to it merely confuses. Both terms now being considered have a Latin origin, though of course as they refer to the recipient of impressions and to that which gives them substance, and words with similar meanings are found in every language. But 'similar meanings' is certainly too simple an expression, for neither word has one or an unambiguous reference, despite the idea that both should have unequivocal import. During the course of their histories, particularly in the West, meanings have undergone considerable modification, such that they have been taken at times to be interchangeable, as when such expressions as 'the subject of a science' and 'the object of enquiry' are considered together. In fine, both terms are enmeshed in a tangle of ambiguity, which makes their essential meanings difficult to determine, unless contexts are first defined or the purposes they serve are clearly understood. One thing, however, may be said to be sufficiently constant: that the subject is whoever is subjected to some pressure which is felt internally, as affecting a sentient being, and that the object refers to what is taken to be external, broadly something assumed to be outside the recipient who is subject to its influence. And 'assumed', as will be seen, is a fitting term in context, since that the object is wholly external is to some readings debatable. But, apart from this broad and somewhat indecisive distinction, which is too simply seen as that between passive and active entities, unequivocal usage is not readily attainable. The antithesis between these terms may be variously envisaged, so that it is requisite, to avoid misunderstanding, to refine ideas on their references in the present sphere of interest or as they are differently used.

If, discounting earlier origins, we consider the Latin etymon of the term 'the subject', a fairly clear meaning is given, since the ambiguities produced by later accretions are not present to render its pristine import obscure. The term is then derived from a prefixed verbal form. For *jectus, jactus* in earlier forms, is or was the past participle of the infinitive *jacere*, with root, it is believed, in the Sanskrit *ja*, 'to go', which itself has several derivatives. In this, its Latin form, it means, with other later meanings, 'to throw', 'to cast against', to which the prefix *sub* was added, to give the further meaning 'to throw or cast or place under', of which an interesting cognate was *subere*, 'to submit'. *Subjacere*, with its genderized past participles, *subjectus–subjecta–subjectum*, was a post-Augustan usage, referring to the status of the governed under the rule of the Imperial jurisdiction, who were required to be *subjectivi*, obedient and submissive to the dominant authority. In that sense the term survives into modern times, as in the expression 'British subject' for example, referring to a person who is subject to the Queen or, rather more precisely, to the British constitution and the law that it imposes. Carrying this further, the 'subject' also means one who is subjected to certain pressures or influences,

84

natural or social as the case may be, as when it is said that 'men in general are subject to hunger' or, in a social form, that 'they have obligations to society at large'. And all men, in the words of a well-known apothegm, are implicated in or subject willy-nilly to "the slings and arrows of outrageous fortune". From pressures such as these no one can escape, and such vicissitudes indeed strengthen our awareness of our common humanity, in that with maturity we recognize that others bear the burdens that we do, though with sufficient courage they are not exposed. And, even though some may seek, sometimes with success, to override those pressures which have social form, none without disaster to himself and at times to others, can go completely against those imposed by nature, which are what determine the very conditions of life in all its vital forms and dimensions.

Confining thought at once to pressures in social forms, we must see that those are almost as compelling. There is no need to appeal to Hobbes in order to confirm that the ordering of affairs is essential for civilized life, that a lawless, unruly, undisciplined mass would not long survive. And if bands of outlaws do so by escaping into the forests, the mountains or the swamps – today into 'no-go' areas – even they must have their leaders to control internal disputes, over booty for example, to decide on tactics when raiding and to secure some order and discipline in otherwise turbulent groups. But anarchists and freebooters are happily exceptions to the general rule that would-be stable societies must organize themselves in some acceptable way, establish legal procedures and hierarchies responsible for making firm decisions on matters affecting the whole. The point, then, as to how far legal systems alone are sufficient for holding societies together is one that might be debated, though not to much effect since it is widely recognized that something more than those – meaning the acceptance of ethical obligations, which do not depend on the tacit threat of coercion that underlies statute law – is also a requirement. When thinking of social pressures, then, both must be included, although the second must surely be seen as the more fundamental and the first as an auxiliary power which is called upon to support it with recourse to force, as a last resort when more subtle and sensitive means of holding the structure in balance have been defied or affronted.[1]

It is not at once to the point to discuss how far structured arrangements, under which perforce some are subject to others, are required for sustaining order in society; although it is plain enough that any enterprise whatever has to have direction, presuming the acceptance of final responsibility for the conduct of affairs and for the making of decisions. Even in sport there have to be captains and referees, even in academe there are ranks which imply that someone, by whatever means appointed, is ultimately responsible for seeing that all is in order. No claims to personal liberty, demands in every aspect of life for democratic procedures, can wholly disregard this as a requirement: that some kind of pressure, happily persuasive, has to be exerted when there is occasion for it. Freedom is never absolute, unless in a trivial sense, since even those in higher station bear the burden of obligation, not only with respect to those on whose behalf they act but to society generally, in that any decision made has some effect on its interests. Taking the professor, in one of the freest roles, his ultimate obligation is, through students, to society, to ensure that those who benefit from higher education receive it to the end of contributing to the community and emerge as mature and capable members of some profession, to justify the system in which he plays a part. But indeed, in all departments of life some discipline is the onus of those in charge, from parents to prime ministers.

All this is plain enough, since it is directed essentially towards the securing of efficiency, broadly the material welfare of the community, whether that be a primitive group dependent on hunting and fishing for its simple survival or the most advanced of civilized societies. But, seen in that sense alone, it gives but a limited notion of what the requirement really comprises. For if the man who holds a given responsibility, to whom, that is to say, his subordinates are subjected, carries it too crudely, thinking only of efficiency, value may be attained but so perhaps at penalty, since in such a case his 'subjects' may be restless. Hence he must also know how to exert authority, without humiliating those who are under discipline, without affronting their dignity and so arousing resentment, such that subordination is rendered unendurable. Obligation, then, does not merely consist in the act of performing competently. It has a deeper meaning, and in that sense refers to something to which everyone is properly subjected, the call to behave towards others in an acceptable manner. This raises further issues which have philosophical bearing, in that they are not, unless with insensitivity, amenable to enagement in scientific terms. And indeed, to suppose that they are so may have something to do with the confusion into which vital meanings have fallen, as when the subject is seen as the mover, the 'I' who knows and controls, rather than the moved who acts in quite a different manner. Courtesy, grace and delicacy are recognized as values only in their absence; and yet they are the very lubricants of life. They have their meaning and value in interrelativity, in the network of social involvement, and so cannot be viewed inductively, as if they could be objectified. Nor is anyone conforming to such modes as these subject in any legal sense to those to whom he relates, even to those who are senior to or greater than himself. But all are subjected to certain norms which cannot precisely be specified. Nor is this a matter of fashion, transient and ephemeral, even in any measurable sense of cultural conditioning, since it relates to something in the human make-up, developed through evolution perhaps but certainly not imposed;[2] it is a 'sense' in depth of what is appropriate in behaviour. Respect for women, whose needs are generally more subtle, differs, for men at least, from respect for other men, which is more closely aligned to age and responsibility, as carried in whatever sphere it is properly exercised.[3] To distinguish between the sexes thus does not here imply thought on relative status. It merely makes note of a difference with respect to need, which is less definable on these *social* levels than it is often taken to be. And if distinctions such as these have not always been observed – or rather, if men have sometimes been unduly arrogant or exploited their greater strength – they have nonetheless, as in respect for age, formed part of the normative structures of human societies generally and have constituted refinements which were external to legal codes.

The social pressures to which people are subjected, at deeper levels pervasively, are almost as great, as has been said, as those imposed by nature, and so for sufficient reason. For, if there were not a measure of trust and mutual understanding, social, communal life could scarcely be sustained. That balance depends on observance of certain unspecified norms, to which children have to be trained,[4] mainly by checking failure to comply with implicit requirements, should be plain enough, since with their disregard or abuse life would indeed be limited, "poor, nasty, brutish and short".[5] Insofar, then, as all the members of society depend on their observation for fulfilment in life, they are subject to them simply as social beings. Doubtless, the pressures of nature are more exigent than those that are social. But the difference between them is very far from absolute, though the penalties of defying those that nature brings to bear, as in refusing to eat or sleep or unduly abusing the body, are evidently greater. The obligations of parentage are, for an obvious instance, both natural and social, although the latter predominates as civilization advances. And other obligations have this dual character, insofar as norms are innate and have their seat in nature. Savages, even animals, observe certain rules of behaviour, accept that certain acts, such as killing those who have already surrendered, should 'not be done', though nothing clearly determined forbids their perpetration. All societies have developed certain gestures to show that advance is not aggressive, and all warm-blooded creatures respond to a genuine caress, formalized into bowing, raising the hat, and so on. How far these are natural to the human species as opposed to conscious acquirements is a question not easily answered;[6] and yet some form of respect for strangers or acquaintances is a common characteristic in all human societies. And indeed, inasmuch as such acts refer to basic social needs, for confident reciprocity, they plainly have very deep roots related to felt requirements. *Tao*, it is to the point to note, has both ontic and ethical meaning, to imply that what is appropriate in social interrelationships is what is in accord with the harmonies of nature. If good manners, then, are considered 'natural',[7] 'easy' as is said, that involves an insight into the human condition of a form that analysis cannot further specify – for 'natural' means more than 'physical'. And if defiance of these norms is now indulged quite freely, apparently without pain to those who adopt such stances, without scruple discomforting others, that is an act which constitutes a 'going against nature', which may and probably will have long term effects, the corroding of society. As free, it is contended, man is not subject to norms and is empowered to disregard any possible consequences. But consequences should surely be of some interest to philosophers, once truth in respect of what is the case has been shown to have limited bearing, and is replaced as the central concern by one that is rather deeper: man's relation to a world to which truth does not apply.

*

So much for the basic meaning of the term 'the subject', a meaning that it has retained into modern times, and one which may accordingly be regarded as fundamental. In the course of time, however, several other meanings came to be attached to this word. These do not surmount this import but they tend, none the less, to blur it, in respect particularly of what it should mean in philosophy when that turns its attention to evaluative problems. Some of these further meanings are in that sense innocent, in that they refer to 'things' or to notions of them rather than to persons in the role of responsive beings. Thus when we speak of 'a subject' meaning 'some subject matter', called *tema*, *thème* or *thema* in other European languages, reference is to what is being given attention, subjected to our interest. Extensions of this are to be found in such expressions as 'subject-heading', 'subject-index', 'subject-catalogue' and so on, reflected in grammar in which the subject is that about which something is written or said. But with that use of the term we arrive at a more equivocal meaning. For, if in a grammatical sense, the nominative is taken as referring to a person acting in some way, that he is subject to an accusative does not of necessity follow. When Balbus built a wall, it was the wall that was subject to the action of Balbus not Balbus who was subject to the action of the wall, which would only have been the case had the wall collapsed upon him. Subject is then an ambigious term when symbols are given meanings, in part determined by the verb, when they cease to be strictly abstract, formal terms in propositions.

Grammarians distinguish between active and passive verbs, with reference to action by or against the substantive word; and the form of the verb that is used determines this 'by' or 'against'. This is seen in such sentences as 'the fireman broke the window' or 'this stone submits to polish' – when the fireman is the agent and the stone is the recipient or the subject of possible polishing. However, it could be said, without grammatical error, that 'polish could be applied to that stone', when polish becomes the substantive, or that, no less correctly, 'the window was broken by the fireman', such that in either sentence the first word, or the subject, is in the nominative case. Sentences can then be framed so as to eliminate any ambiguity with respect to the term 'the subject' – the fireman was responsible – by the simple expedient of changing their constructions. For grammar is a flexible tool giving power of adaptation to meet whatever the requirement; and, apart from a number of rules that cannot be disregarded, it allows of alternative forms as circumstances demand them to reduce any tincture of doubt. This is not the case with syllogistic logic which permits of one form only and cannot handle tenses, or prepositions comfortably, unless with circumlocutions of rather clumsy forms, since its formations are rigid and effectively unchangeable. In so far, then, as it dominates philosophical thinking, its use of terms for its elements, 'subject' in this context, dictates the meanings that terms receive when other interests are paramount, when logic as a discipline on statements, positive statements, is in effect ancillary. The term, the 'subject' has in this way been tied to its meaning in logic,[8] and thence in epistemology, even though what it might fittingly mean when concern is neither cognitive nor alethic, may be very different, even antithetical. That the effects of this are delimiting scarcely needs to be stressed.

Once we pass from the basic meaning of this term, defined as a relation to influential structures, to its current meaning in logocentric philosophy, we find ourselves in difficulties, for the question then arises, what precisely is under review? What, or better who, is under influence or pressure, the sway or the authority of nature or some system political or social, and is properly as a consequence to be designated the 'subject'. Or, to put this another way: Is the subject subjected to the forces playing upon him or are they subjected to his investigation? These questions have been present implicitly from the outset, from the time, that is, when need arose to give names to the components of that structure called 'the syllogistic formation'. Premisses apart, which mean simply 'puttings forward', it is to the specific parts that attention must now be turned. For something was put forward, 'set up' if that is preferred, of which something else was said, in a statement which was for conclusiveness to be affirmed or denied. This last was called a 'predicate', *praedicatio* in Latin, *kategorēma* in Greek, which meant a 'laying down', originally a charge or an accusation, something publicly proclaimed by a plaintiff against a defendant in a court of law. If a man was subjected to an accusation, spoken against so to say, some doubt of the suitability of this choice of a term is not wholly out of order. However, if it is simply taken to mean an attribute or a property of what is under review, no suggestion of a charge, a legal accusation, fairly attaches to it.

Initially that of which a predicate was to be made was designated the 'substance', *substantia* in Latin, *hypokeīmenon* in Greek, in which it had several meanings further to complicate issues, though at once it may be considered, employing simple language, as that which is presented for consideration, that which is to be subjected to attention. Meanwhile, if it is thought of as 'standing under', its literal meaning, difficulties arise, with respect especially to its use in metaphysics, though not quite so acutely as when it came to be called the 'subject', even should it be so in the sense that it is that which is to be subjected to what will be predicated of it.

These original terms in the discipline projected by Aristotle continued to be used as the standard terms in logic throughout the middle ages and even later when interest in formal logic declined. During those times, however, their ambiguity was recognized, with respect to the subject especially, by realistic thinkers, Scotus, Ockham, Gerson, Cusanus and several others,[9] noting the difference between the logical and the real, the internal or the ideal and external actuality as affecting the human soul. For the subject in the latter sense was subjected to natural forces, interpreted as God's ordinances, whilst the subject of the former was something about which an abstract statement was made. But usage was by this time sufficiently well-established that such 'loose' or concrete comment could be comfortably disregarded, since rationalism was dominant and doubts about its reach, though not without effect, could not undermine its authority. "The medieval philosopher" – though this is a rather broad statement – "thought of the mind as conforming itself to objects rather than of objects as having to conform themselves to mind for logic to be possible":[10] and logic had to be so. Thus the mind, the intellect in the present context, was subject to the world, regarded not so much as objective as the creation of God, in respect of Whom men were, as sentient beings, creatures. In that sense there was no essential conflict in usage – for the soul and not the subject was the centre of interest – even for those who commented on the lack of sensitivity in rationalistic approaches.

Descartes did not diverge from this scholastic heritage. But, in regarding thought, the ego, as pre-eminent over that to which for knowledge it turned, 'matter' in his language, he intensified ambiguity. For implicitly matter was then subjected to the mind, the self as thinking and knowing, whilst the mind, correctly the intellect, was the subject in logic, either as the thinker or that to which his thought was addressed. The question then, although it was not immediately raised, was which of these two meanings, the logical and the cognitive – roughly the internal pitted against the external, that engaged or confronted in the pursuit of knowledge – should override the other? As philosophers, even idealists and those now known as epistemologists, chose in the following years to use the term the 'thinking self' for what Descartes called the 'ego' rather than the 'subject', which they left to school logicians, no serious conflict arose until the time of Kant, who raised it even acutely when he "was woken from his slumbers". The story then becomes so complex and involved that his thought, which certainly bears on this matter, cannot well be epitomized without doing it some injustice. But, concentrating interest on this semantic issue, certain points are suitably made, even if superficially.[11] The salient points in his doctrine, as they have present bearing, may then be taken as these. First, there is the distinction he made between what he called *sensibilia*, the passively received, and *intelligibilia*, certain forms of structuring imposed on those by the agency of the transcendental ego. When the ego is called transcendental that does not imply that it is transcendent of nature, since it was for him a natural mode of approach to given presentations, given the constitution of the human reflective capacity. This means that the intellect acts, so to say from above, on perceptual response, taken as intuitive or simple 'sense-experience'. And if 'sense' is in this an ambiguous term, when its reference is to perception, his wording must be used.[12] The ego, the intellect, then, brings its concepts or categories – the forms that it must use to comprehend this material – to bear on what is thus intuitively recorded, apply *a priori* concepts, concepts developed, that is, in independence of that experience, on what has been received. To that he gave the name *a posteriori*, which may be taken to mean 'that received in experience', what emerges as the outcome of initial stimulation. It has to be noted in this that the subject, though that term is used in traditional logical sense in the *Critique of Pure Reason*, was not yet employed in such a way as to generate serious ambiguity, as it was later to be. For that was only, decisively, the case in his moral philosophy, where its meaning was personalized and given a dominant role and where it was presumed to act on an extra-rational plane. This exercised an influence on thought on moral issues, now deployed outside the range of formal logic; and such was its influence on that thought that morality thereafter, at least as this doctrine held sway, became increasingly subjective. Yet, despite this Kantian appeal to intuitive powers, to conscience, theoretically rational – exploiting, innocently no doubt, the equivocacy attaching to that adjectival form – moral philosophy did not readily relinquish its tie to formal logic, so that it rather became a concern with the acts of the *rational person* as an autonomous agent. The further effects of this will be discussed in a later chapter. Meanwhile, it is enough to note that now the subject had at least two divergent meanings: that which it had traditionally in propositional logic and that which it now acquired in a wholly different connection.

Let that pass at once, however, whilst a further point is considered: that Kant's critical philosophy is of additional interest in context because of its relation to a distinction already made, that between mind and intellect. For it seems to confirm that the way in which the intellect acts is other than that in which the mind, responding to *sensibilia* intuitively and directly, performs in its own sphere. A divergence from his thought resides in what is taken to be subsumed under *sensibilia*, in that herein, with the insights which gestalt psychology now makes available to us, though not of course to Kant, they must be taken to be effective not on one but at least on two planes. It is only then on the level on which they are perceived, as is shown in what the expression 'sense experience' meant for him, that they can be known or engaged by the transcendental ego, that is to say, the intellect acting in full consciousness.[13] But, by positing the 'thing in itself' – the plural is not appropriate with a holistic ontology – as "thinkable but not knowable", he plainly acknowledges that as their source, linked, as it is now believed, through various stages of response to ultimate conscious reception. For initial stimulation is directly induced by changes in the external world, fairly to be equated with the *ding an sich*. Hence it might be said that the mind is subjected to impressions, whereas the intellect, although dependent on them for knowledge, indeed for the power to act, imposes its categories on them in order to gain that knowledge, when it is effectively active rather than passive. If intellect is the subject, then, as it is in modern philosophy tied to formal logic – though the ego and what

93

it addresses are surely not the same – and if those have been confused since Kant in effect identified the knowing and moral selves, the question is how far this applies in epistemology. For knowledge is derived from interpreted phenomena, regarded as externals, and not from propositions with linguistic reference only. But generally the 'knowing self' rather than the 'subject' is the expression preferred in epistemological discourse; and that is wisely adhered to to avoid yet further confusion.

Hence, to discover the cause of this essential change in the reference of this ambiguous word, we must turn to Kant's moral philosophy, to the *Critique of Practical Reason*, a very much easier text. As more readily comprehensible, then, this book has exerted great influence in this field of enquiry, which for him was fundamental. Indeed, he held this aspect of his thought to be more important – and rightly so if morality takes precedence over cognition, the spiritual, seen realistically, over the material – and in that sense laid stress on the primacy of practical over theoretical reason. For the first, and this is significant when thought is turned to the general, is something with which all men are naturally endowed, whereas scientific enquiry is the interest directly of relatively few and does not in the deepest sense have similar social consequences.[14] But this interest in the self is already evident in the *Critique of Pure Reason*, where in an elaborate argument he relates the subject, therein called the 'soul', to substance, hitherto regarded as a category of relation, and finally to the 'I think'.[15] He thereby changed its meaning from that which it had in traditional formal logic, as that to which thought was referred, to that of the thinker himself. There is a sense perhaps that that from which a start is made, Descartes' 'spiritual substance', may be held to have priority; but, if so, there cannot but be ambiguity and confusion. For, if a precedent allowed that the subject, the self, and substance could be taken as interchangeable – though the knower and what he attends to are certainly not the same – the outcome can only be that terms have lost their basic meanings, with unfortunate ethical consequences.

It is his moral philosophy, then, with the will as practical reason, or rather the power to exert it, taken to be the rational mind acting in absolute freedom, that equivocation really comes up for review. But why its possessor should then be designated the 'subject' – and so without a precedent in this field of interest – when he, as the rational self, is apparently subject to nothing, unless to the dictates of conscience planted in his soul by a benign Divinity, it is difficult to see. This usage seems to involve a shift from the rational to the moral, when response to the imperative might even be deemed irrational, as if the subject in the guise of the transcendental ego were fittingly carried over into a realm which is surely rather that of the 'soul'. The rational self and the moral self – long supposed to be rational though its acts are largely spontaneous and questionably deliberative, as 'rationalization' in ordinary language shows – were to be equated, given a common name. That use of the term the 'subject', with its logical connotations, could only lead, as indeed it did, to grave misunderstanding with regard to man's relation to the world by which he is encompassed, wholly, inextricably, a world which is neither rationally or cognitively constructed in its actuality.

Kant himself was sparing in his use of this term, since the transcendental ego or the conscious self were the terms that he preferred as alternatives to it. And so it was left to Fichte, to Schelling and to Hegel to make use of it more extensively. For they aligned the subject firmly with the Spirit, equating it with the Intellect, acting either in independence of or as dominant over nature. Or, if that is not quite fair, the thinking self, specifically designated the subject, assumed a kind of mastery over everything else, as the creative principle, or the agency of creation, as the ultimate cause of the world, indeed as one with Being.[16] The Intellect or the Spirit, for these terms were now interchangeable, was paramount over all else, an outcome of which is that what is now called the 'object' becomes that which the dominant intellect, subject itself to nothing, brings to being or controls – a further elaboration of Cartesian duality. How far this type of thinking was developed under influence of the Romantic Movement, turning on the self, is a question for historians. Enough to say that once this meaning of the subject had been firmly established and generally adopted, it penetrated every field of philosophical thought, thus to render it blind to what signifies in ethics: that man is subject to social pressures. In the two centuries prior to Kant, thinkers who devoted their attention to moral questions were concerned, at least in principle, with social conduct *in general*, with how far, for instance, the passions and the emotions affected moral action, with how far reason might be brought to discipline and to control them,

95

rather than with questions of personal motivation. Kant, it is true, placed moral choice entirely on the person, the autonomous individual, in general a little obscurely. But it was not until that personalized involvement – always an attractive stance with appeal to the individual, and with the added virtue of being rationalizable with individuation – became the only interest that received attention, that failure to consider any general social issue characterized approaches in this important sphere.[17] The knowing self and the moral self, 'subjects' both of course under this new dispensation, were aligned to serve a common philosophical interest. That stressed the power to act in a wholly rational manner, regardless of the fact that human action generally has quite another character. Hence the 'subject' is now pre-eminent, the creative, controlling force; but so in a strange perversion of terms, which left its basic meanings to such lowly spheres as politics, with the consequence that it lost its really significant reference in philosophical discourse. It is for that very reason that this changed use of the term is now called into question, regarded indeed as improper, as an impediment on clear thinking.

*

As idealism in various forms dominated philosophy, centred on the 'subject', what this new use of the term involved as a restriction on thinking when that was realistic was not seriously examined. If a start is taken from the self, the knowing self precisely, any idea of externals as other than phenomenal can scarcely be envisaged.[18] For that is surely to posit a world that is unknowable, beyond the reach of cognition, essentially inexplicable. And if that could not be rationalized, rendered comprehensible, then it was either taken as "a blooming, buzzing confusion" or, in existential thought, as something even menacing, which was to the reflective mind a source of acute anxiety inspiring men with dread, *sorge* as "the essential structure of human consciousness".[19] That it could be something of which man himself was part, in which he was en-meshed and, wisely for peace of mind, accepted as the given, as that indeed which endowed him with life and with vitality, was foreign to that form of thinking. It did not think of nature as itself the basis of consciousness but only for its supposed effects on the supersensi-tive self. And if aspects of it could not be cognized or tamed by explanation, then to cognitivists they were 'mystic', to be dismissed as something scarcely worth attention or, from the morbid viewpoint of existential philosophy, features which threatened the self, the almost cowering subject. With such ontologies as these, deterministic or personalized, men, as they accepted them, were alienated from nature – with all the problems that that raises. For they do not provide a foundation for saner ideas about life, and none for the understanding of man's real or basic relation to the truly external world, that is, to actuality. They rather render man either unduly arrogant in his essay to ride above nature or pathetic in his fears as he faces it alone. A doctrine, in some sense Hegelian,[20] of continual progress, holds out hope, of course, that the troubles that passion generates – not excluding selfishness which the cult of the individual cannot but encourage – will in time be overcome. Unhappily, such passions render this notion utopian; and, as materialistic, as they tend to be under that cult, make greater refinement, a sensible aim, more difficult of attainment. For as long as the self, the 'subject' in this new vocabulary, is valued above all else, with failure all too often to recognize its limits – that it is subject to conditions and so is only free in a limited sense – for so long will confusion reign, since it is that recognition alone which provides a means of escaping it. If we cannot distinguish between the subject as a free agent, which is nothing less than a contradiction in terms, and the subject as one who is placed under pressures and obligations which he is never quite free to escape, we can scarcely be surprised that thought, philosophical thought specifically, is, as a guiding influence, generally ineffective.

In this tangle of ambiguity, in which the real and the ideal are scarcely to be distinguished, unless the first is considered as the interest of the second, a question plainly arises: which of these two meanings is to be preferred or which, as is rather better, has the greater significance from a philosophical standpoint? Perhaps an accepted meaning should be retained in formal logic, though the ancient 'substance' is surely a more appropriate term for that to which predicates are applied. But, as that is an abstract discipline confined to linguistic usage, in which the subject may be anything about which something is said – Socrates, horses, grass, machines, or whatever it may be, if it is not merely a symbol – its relation to actuality is tenuous, if not specious. It could of course be contended that this is the usual form of a sentence, in which the subject, commonly designated the noun, plays the part of the substance or the subject in formal logic, that of which something is said. But, as logic grew out of language, classical Greek precisely, that it reflects its structure is scarcely very remarkable. And that certainly does not justify any identification of the noun, with its multiple references, with the transcendental ego. As there are, moreover, many alternative terms for the subject in this connection – the 'I', the 'ego', the 'thinking self', the 'seat of thought', and so on, its use in other fields than those of formal logic may be said to be optional, as is indeed the case in philosophy itself as it enters wider spheres.[21] Accordingly, a use of the term which obscures its deeper meaning cannot really be justified when it so delimits other, more fruitful readings. If it is strictly confined to logic no great harm is done; but, if it is carried over into fields where the subject has an entirely different, even contrasted meaning, then certain forms of relationship of very much greater importance than the attainment of logical rigour are simply misunderstood. A derivative, however, seems to have some value, since there is no other word with completely equivalent meaning. 'Subjective' defines a state which is not otherwise suitably specified. For it has come to mean something other than 'egoistic', 'selfish', or 'self-centred', forms of apperception; and it is freely and valuably used in disciplines other than logic, where it is not applied. It rather then refers not to the thinking subject deliberating clearly, but to psychological states, introspective, imaginary, or those that are even deeper, quasi-conscious or subconscious, invariably related to pressures on the psyche. Its retention, therefore, does not entail that the 'subject' in an idealistic sense is applicable any further than in logocentric discourse.

Interest then turns on its meaning in a more far-reaching philosophy, which, to be far-reaching, has to be realistic. Man is a subject, then, not as a knowing self, dominant in principle over that of which he has knowledge,[22] and with it controlling power, but as one who is subjected to the pressures that bear upon him, irrespective of whether he is conscious of them or not. That subject is only master of or at one with his situation in as far as he can adapt to it. And if he is able so to adapt, often with greater finesse as reflection does not intervene to introduce complications – for 'mastery' means no more in this sense than ability to adapt, to achieve harmonic rapport with nature – so is he one with becoming. Further, since a man, for all his special powers, responds for the most part subconsciously, aided, it seems, by memory, that he should be deemed a 'subject' in a logical sense constitutes a misreading of how he normally performs. Man is a subject essentially, to this deeper reading, in the sense of being "thrown under", subject to whatever affects his nervous system through stimulation directly. This, we repeat, does not lower man, as if he were one with 'brute beasts', who to appearance largely lack his powers of sensitivity. It merely states 'what is the case', which is forgotten at penalty. It is all very fine and consoling, flattering indeed, to suppose that man, as self-conscious, is infinitely superior, the highest form of being when, with the power to reason, there is nothing above him, or when, with the notion that he alone is endowed with a 'soul' – though *anima* originally meant simply the breath of life, which is certainly not unique to him – he is especially graced. But that can be overemphasized. Undoubtedly, he has power to act with nobility and refinement; and to recognize that as commendable, since it puts a pattern before him to which he may aspire. And all thought urging that throughout the course of history, at least from the time of Phahhotep,[23] has served an invaluable function in raising the tone of society from lower to higher levels. But valuable though it has been, that idea can be abused, as when for hundreds of years exhortations to noble living have been correlated effectively with the exercise of the intellect, with intellectual power, to reach a point of absurdity when in moral philosophy that power is wholly personalized, to render the knower the paradigm at expense of the simple or ignorant. It is not knowledge as rational, or even as revealed, that makes for natural nobility; and the idea that it does so is especially deplorable when sects hold those who do not strive to cultivate that lofty power to be quite beyond the pale, damned today as 'outsiders'. Only the elect are saved, to evoke an ancient notion, raised to higher planes; though that as an end is not noble, since nobility supposes some riding above the self or strictly personal interest, such as personal salvation or intellectual eminence. For that is not only divisive, with unhappy social consequences; it involves a failure to comprehend the real nature of the problem.

If philosophy claims to be general, then, its concern is with men at large and with the conditions they face as involved or sentient beings or, otherwise said, as subjects. In fine, there is a danger with undue stress on rectitude, logical or moral, both of which are conscious, even self-conscious states, that norms will be overlooked. And as the pursuit of ideals, popularly regarded as raising thought to sublimity, may and often does involve a scorn for 'bourgeois' life, viewed with a certain disdain as banal or commonplace,[24] that in effect degrades it, and certainly inhibits the prospect of its refinement. Thus, on an intellectual plane, a preoccupation with logic, seen as pure and free from any ulterior interest, often implies contempt for more flexible approaches, which have yet to be adopted if real problems are to be met. It may be a little unorthodox, then, to hold that virtue rather resides in the acceptance of life and in the recognition of the problems that that raises, when those must be seen as *general*, as having their seat and meaning in an interrelative manifold. The subject, viewed in such terms as these, is the ordinary man, continually subject to pressures the sources of which are obscure. As those are natural, of course, science may to a degree do something to delimit them, though it cannot do much about the abuse of bodily powers, which it itself augments by removing man from nature. "Moderation in all things" still stands as an admonition of philosophical origin and in that sense shows that philosophy also has something to say on the matter of confronting the pressures produced by nature. As these pressures are rather social, then, and thus have a spiritual meaning, it is that discipline alone which is potent to consider them, or rather the consequences that ensue when they are affronted. That men should learn to cultivate a saner and more mature view of their situation, to acquire a more sensitive attitude to the conditions in which they live – a more adequate ontology in philosophical terms – cultivating attunement in place of attempted mastery of the world and of other men is, or certainly should be, the concern of philosophy. But it can scarcely be so when the subject is taken to be the master of all he surveys, the dominating force, consigning sensitivity to the sphere of vapid emotion and linking the thinking self to the autonomous individual, aspiring, at times with frustration, which aggravates his restlessness, to dominate his environment.

Man, though not alone, is capable of love, that is to say, of feeling for his fellow men. It is of interest then to note that, though for the early Christians *agapē* was interpreted as 'love in its most intense form', for the classical Greeks it rather meant 'general affability'.[25] The trouble with the first of these two senses is, as Hartmann drily observed when contrasting it with justice,[26] that as a strong emotion it is not unrelated to hate, as history clearly demonstrates. Conversely, if love is taken to mean a sense of our common humanity, all men, unless they abuse the trust presupposed in this, merit respect, or love in this form, and considerate treatment, honouring each for what he is given his conditions. That 'all men are brothers' is not unique to Christianity. It is a common acceptance in many other cultures, in which it has the meaning that all, and so without exception, are subjected to pressures that can only be met with difficulty. And if those are greater for some in a social context, or even in one that is natural – as when harvests fail or illness has to be borne – others for whom they are less severe are under obligation to recognize these more burdensome obstacles to fulfilment. In so far as they are social, answers may be political, though solutions such as those are open to abuse[27] and cannot in any case relate to more than material problems. Hence, this concern with the easing of human interrelationships may be more deeply related to something rather more subtle, less oriented towards a theoretical equality, which, even if attainable, could doubtfully be sustained, than to latent potentialities, to something that overrides differences in position without weakening or destroying what may be of value in them.[28] That men are subject to pressures over which they have little control – for control can only be exercised, unless in a spiritual sense, over what is measurable – has then some bearing on this, since it is a spiritual factor that then becomes the salient interest. Understanding of what this implies is a matter for philosophy, turning on the idea that, as what is entailed in that is more widely developed, life may be rendered more tolerable. It is sometimes said that philosophy 'teaches men how to die', but perhaps it is better directed towards teaching them how to live, to live with grace and courage, which was the classical view. If man is then the subject of the pressures that bear upon him, a fate that he cannot escape as a sentient being, it is not the subject as the knowing self that should be the concern of philosophy. It is the subject in a deeper sense, as a being involved with reality, whom, in its preoccupation with abstract formulations, it has tended to neglect.

*

101

Let us return, however, to the strictly semantic question of the most valid meanings of terms, when 'most valid' is taken to mean those that are most fruitful in thought of what is under discussion. It is not in ordinary language the case that a word can have one meaning only, as it is in formal logic, which admits of no divergence from an established definition. It is a matter of suitability, of meeting the occasion. Moreover, it is the meaning that counts, not the words used to convey it, which do but direct attention to what comprises the interest and are certainly not definitive.[29] There are in English several words which have in the course of time acquired two quite different meanings, of which 'cleave' affords an example. But that divarication seldom renders them ambiguous, since their meanings are given in contexts or can readily be clarified by sentential reformulation. Puns seldom deceive, for if they did they would lose whatever their point. But 'subject' is a particularly difficult word because, even when used in its basic sense, it has several shades of meaning which are sometimes contradictory. The thinking self, for instance, is both subject to impressions, in want of which thought processes could scarcely be developed, and subjects them to attention. Yet is the subject as thinker different from the subject as a sentient being, in that he is self-aware and conscious of what affects him, though that to be so received must be given objective form. Unless under obligation to obey the laws of logic, he then ceases to be a subject in a basic sense, since he now subjects whatever he has selected for closer attention to investigation or scrutiny. But mastery in that form is not in the same sense available to the sentient being, who, faced with the stream of events, is rather subject to them. Under threat from an approaching car, instinct demands avoidance, immediate counteraction, which is not contemplative. And if that as an instance is rather extreme, it none the less reflects the compulsions attaching to many aspects of life which call for instantaneous action, spontaneous adaptation. Should this still be thought to turn on lowlier forms of response, its meaning may be raised if such acts include more refined forms of empathy, in respect of suffering, of need which is other than obvious, of the mere dictates of courtesy, which need not involve conscious thought. All those, though they presume a measure of awareness, tend to be impulsive, as 'generous impulse' implies, free from deliberation and thus instances of rapport.

102

A question then arises as to whether it is in order to consider the subject in this sense as a representative figure, as having on this 'lower' plane common characteristics. For, considered philosophically, this idea might be questioned as claiming a generality that is insufficiently grounded. For to generalize, or such is what we are taught to believe, is the function or purpose of theoretical thinking, seeking a general truth, whereas, as if in contrast to that, the responses cited above seem to be incidental and are seldom or never repeated in exactly similar form. Thus, they cannot be generalized, since they are nothing more than circumstantial instances. Though this may be true as we think of them as isolated events which cannot be clearly defined, it is certainly less so as clear definition, permitting their relation in intellectual terms, is not the interest at issue, which is rather more subtle. The point with immediate bearing, then, is that reference to them does not involve analytical thinking, which isolates to generalize, to bring particular instances under some general rule, but to discern resemblances as they refer to needs in the complex of reality. These may have universal forms of quite a different character, not as ideal and definable but as real and in that sense implicit. Such responses as these, as they are indeed spontaneous, probably, almost certainly, have something common in them – with roots in innervation. And though that as a characteristic is not immediately evident, there is reason to believe that on these lower levels, on which the differentiations that conscious thought produces do not play a part, responses tend to be similar, which need not mean identical. If the interest is logocentric, it is in the last analysis, claims to the contrary notwithstanding, essentially self-centred, as the expression the 'thinking self' evidently evinces, as is seen in the idiocyncrasies of rational debate, which depends on disagreement to warrant its continuance. The projection of truth claims is surely an intellectual act, in that they are put forward by their upholders in full consciousness. Conversely, a concern with men in their relation to actuality – which rather involves proposals of a tentative type and in principle a desire in view of the importance of what is under review to come to some agreement, provisional though it may be – seems to presume what is later to be distinguished as 'understanding'. That is not directed towards a particular conclusion but towards a more general interest, which is necessarily vaguer: the service of society envisaged as a whole. And if this in so far as it involves thought is itself subjective, its end is certainly not so; for, in referring to a general, the interests of society in a realistic sense, thought is directed outwards. Something must be envisaged as its common characteristic,[30] notwithstanding that that cannot pretend to certitude.

This does not, of course, affirm that common characteristics are present in nervous response: indeed it simply assumes it. But once the conscious self passes out of the picture, so that individuation is not a separative factor, it is likely that response does have common features. In any case, however, as in the example of the threatening car, reactions are broadly similar; and if on more refined planes variants occur, a latent potentiality may yet be a prevalent factor in the human make-up, notwithstanding that it is obscured by the cult of self-assertion. Finally, if the interest turns on the general in actuality, rather than as at present on the logical universal, the supposition that it exists is reasonably adopted as affording a criterion when deeper needs are considered. Like any other species, the human species has features which distinguish it as such, not only in a physical sense, which is sufficiently obvious, but in manners of acting when responses are direct. And if this is not fully detectable, but only so in part – all societies, for instance, have developed ethical norms and certain strong inhibitions – when we speak of 'human nature' we are in effect attesting it. There is something that renders us human, even perhaps humane, and that is more than the power to reason. In some sense, no doubt, for otherwise it would be meaningless, rational, explanatory, truth-determining discourse does relate to life, even if, like science, it affects to be value-neutral.[31] But, unless with some distortion, in that it is filtered and in that sense indirect, that talk does not refer to general evaluation in a way that relates it to conditions in actuality. Indeed, it cannot do so, since it presupposes detachment and thus severs itself from contact with what is actually taking place in the dynamic complex, which cannot be stilled for inspection.

This is not to deny, of course, that values are given by science – and perhaps in that connection by formal logic too – though those are properly weighed against the disvalues that it may perpetrate.[32] It is merely to state that the values that may in this way be given have to be judged for their worth by criteria other than those that rationalism adopts. For the only needs to which those refer directly are heuristic. The criteria, then, that must be observed in a general judgement of value are those of the needs of the subject, or rather of subjects generally, which cannot of their nature be specified precisely or clearly understood. And if, as a consequence of this, they are not to be rationalized or defined with any show of precision, the problem that that raises does not reside in trying to overcome these weaknesses by attempting to refine analytical procedures but in developing ways of approach more suited to what is involved. Hence, if value is viewed in this general interrelative sense, as opposed to any idea of it in some isolated form, the problem it presents is not a rational problem but rather one that calls for more sensitive procedures, with power, if not of producing total understanding, at least of avoiding the pitfalls of blind misrepresentation. For the subject, and so his needs in this deeper sense, is indeed misrepresented, and his needs misunderstood, if he is confused with the subject as the detached and self-centred thinker, whose interests are quite different.

The obvious final question, then, is which use of the term the 'subject' has the greater significance from a philosophical standpoint? Or what, in other words, does this term most fruitfully mean when the concern is evaluation in a general sense? And the answer of course depends on how the role of philosophy is to be seen when science shows that what is confronted in depth is a dynamic complex. Given acceptance of that, there seems to be no alternative if real problems are to be met – and all without exception finally turn on human value – than to agree that the 'subject' should mean what it initially meant. Even so, to be firmer, further comment is fitly made: and that might suitably be done by applying Ockham's razor as a principle of economy in extra-explanatory discourse. If entities are not to be unnecessarily multiplied, this doctrine might apply to words as they refer to meanings, and fittingly so if conflict is produced by redundancy. There is no pressing reason why the term the 'subject' should be used in formal logic, when 'substance' better represents Aristotle's *hypokeīmenon*. And in any case, if reference is to the thinker rather than that to which he addresses his thought, there are several alternative terms which are more appropriate, of which the 'thinking self' – the normal usage prior to the time of Kant – or the '*ego*', which was used when discourse was in Latin, afford sufficient examples. This principle also applies when this term is

105

used in its basic sense, where its philosophical meaning ought to be distinguished from its other, subsidiary senses. 'Citizen', 'vassal', 'liege', 'subaltern' and so on, and even such ghastly concoctions as 'experiencer' or 'testee' – which are not acceptable English, albeit that 'sufferer' is – though all of them are subjects in this basic sense, are not synonymous terms, since they refer to specific forms of dependence or subordination. As the concern of philosophy, the 'subject' is not the 'sufferer', but someone, or rather everyone, under pressure of general conditions, which do not pass, as suffering may,[33] but persist throughout active life. There is nothing specific about the subject in this sense; and hence he is properly the concern of a generalizing philosophy, and not of any other discipline, law or whatever it may be. If then this meaning is blurred or rendered almost unusable in a philosophy narrowed to rationalistic enquiry, uncalled-for ambiguity and confusion is engendered, and Ockham's advice is not heeded. It may be rather late in the day to urge that thought be given to this matter of verbal usage and the need for its clarification. But the warrant for this advocacy is to free the vital meaning of this significant term from the associations which obfuscate its import, so that fuller and deeper attention may be given to what it refers to in its most pregnant sense: man's involvement with the world which he confronts directly. For that is very surely the fundamental problem once it is accepted that there are other interests than cognitive explanation.

*

Before this matter is left, a comment might be made about the term the 'object', a word which is not so much misused as to occasion confusion as given a special meaning in cognitive engagement, such that its use in other forms of philosophical enquiry may lead to misunderstanding. And when that interest is dominant, with the outcome that its vocabulary is absorbed into other spheres, certain effects may follow which are far from happy, as with the idea that all externals are objects. This term is not, to confine critique at once to its cognitive usage, the antithesis of the subject considered in basic sense, but only of the subject in the sense of the knower. And that is indeed a restriction which leads to misinterpretation. For it would be absurd to hold that the world in its entirety, that with which the subject has to contend in aspects, constitutes an object when that means something knowable. If the world is called 'objective', because it is external from a cognitive viewpoint, that is a very loose usage, since the world that is then referred to cannot be objectified, unless in such vague concepts as the One or the Absolute, which are properly without substance. If then the world is defined simply as 'all that there is', as an all-embracing complex, then man, as a mode of that complex, must be seen as someone who cannot stand outside it, as if by an act of detachment he could set himself apart from it. Only that can be objectified which can be gathered phenomenally, which is certainly not the case for the world as a totality. Nature, furthermore, another name for this totum, is not synonymous with the physical defined as what is material, since it plainly subsumes psychical forms of being in men and other creatures.[34] Those are only phenomenal which are exhibited physically, in which sense the behaviourists, recognizing that knowledge as strict refers only to phenomena, used certain terms correctly and were consistent empiricsts. Hence, if the term the 'object' is referred to all that there is – or more precisely to partial reflections of the physical – that is a misuse of terms. The 'object' has meaning only, then, when knowledge is the interest and can only be referred to what can be objectified, separated out to permit of cognitive engagement.

'Object' is a word derived directly from the Latin, in which *objectus* meant a 'lying or placing before', 'something set against'. In an elementary sense, it is that which the subject confronts, against which he must act, a barrier, an obstacle, a given state of affairs. In a deeper sense in which the subject is considered as a sentient being,[35] that against which he reacts is the complex of reality, nature understood as a dynamic continuum, to which he has to adapt as changes occur within it. And that, as has already been said, can scarcely be called an object in the sense in which that term is used in cognitive enquiry. For to use it so would be as crude as it would have been in scholastic times to consider God as an object when His creatures were held to be subject to His ordinances. If there is ambiguity, then, not to say grave error, in regarding externality as an object or objective, that is because of a failure to recognize cognitive limits, that objects refer to singulars and not to relativities. Forgetting original usage with its reference to concretes, things against which the subject is thrown, placed, positioned or set, aptly called 'situations', let attention now be turned to the modern use of this term, linked to sophisticated forms of cognitive enquiry. Objects, then, are not things as such, as they are in ordinary language reflecting ancient usage, they are rather conceptions of those filtered through analysis. The knower, strictly considered, is confined to the world of phenomena, from which he abstracts what he refers to as 'particulars', elements of wholes received in gestalt presentations. For gestalten received directly, as in dim perception, plainly embody more than that which is given attention in concentrated focussing, as is seen in tacit knowledge. The act of separating out is the act of objectification, a necessary preliminary to the process of analysis, loosely identified with it. It is a means of dissecting an object so distinguished into its parts or properties in order to categorize them, in that manner transforming them into intellectual concepts related to other concepts similary so formed. An object in such sense as this is an intellectual construct with a phenomenal base, formed by an aspirant knower in a selective act. It is not something in the world, for phenomena are appearances, but only in the intellect, which so to say creates it. It is an abstraction further from the phenomenal world, which presents itself more widely to perceptual response which is not delimited in this way and which effectively has no bounds. For even that world is a complex when thought of as it is. Thus, though there may be a 'modes', to use Spinoza's term, there are no objects in the world, even when viewed as phenomenal, since 'objects' in a cognitive sense are conceptualized perceptions brought to being by the intellect.

When thought is turned to the subject in that word's basic meaning, it is not against such objects that he is projected, nor is such an object that to which he is subjected. It is fitting, then, to abandon the subject-object dichotomy, which is appropriate only in a cognitive context, since it has no meaning and merely confuses issues when attention is addressed to evaluative problems. It is not denied that the subject can be a conscious being, as when he responds to what is presented in dim perception. He may even be a subject in this basic sense in a cognitive capacity, or so at least before he indulges objectification, since he has to respond to impressions to gather knowledge at all. But as soon as he brings analysis to bear on what is received, applies transcendental categories in strict and rational form to objectified particulars, in principle he is the master, subjecting what concerns him to examination and scrutiny. He aspires to dominate and control what he regards as 'mere matter' – though that as an idea is now a little outdated when matter itself is in question as the ultimate form of nature; so that, whilst still a subject in a vital sense, he wills to be quite other, the detached and prepotent knower. It would be invidious to deny his claim to this power to exercise a measure of control, a power at the disposal of everyone in degree as he is obliged to cognize in the process of taking action. But that is still a limited power, with a precarious outcome, inasmuch as the process of filtering removes the cognizing agent from the world he seeks to engage. Moreover, it is not and cannot be the approach when man as the subject in this vital and basic sense demands philosophic attention with respect to his deeper needs, his real relation to nature.

If, then, the subject is taken as set against the object under the logical precedent of that of which something is said, near relation incidentally to the object of cognition, and if the use of this term has no extra-logical bearing, there is an obvious failure to recognize realities, since the term must then have idealistic reference. The subject is then the subject in an ambivalent sense, both as one subjected to the pressures bearing on him and as one subjecting these pressures to investigation. What logic ordains may be sacrosanct, not to be gainsaid, since truth is established as absolute. In principle, then, its vocabulary is improperly put to the question, which means that, if it is indeed the backbone of philosophy, all other forms of that discipline must conform to its rulings. To that the only fitting response is to question its reach, for only thus is it possible to escape from its limitations, in context from its privileged and restrictive use of terms, 'subject' in particular. "Logic", said Heidegger acidly, "is regarded as a court of justice, established for all eternity, whose rights as first and last authority no rational man will impugn. Anyone who speaks against logic is therefore tacitly or explicitly accused of irresponsibility. And the mere accusation is taken as a proof and an argument relieving one of the need for any further, genuine reflection."[36] But it is just such reflection, disciplined by logic in its role as a critical instrument – very different from its role of establishing absolute truth – on the word the 'subject' which is now incumbent if the problem presented in general evaluation is to constitute the concern of a serious philosophy, which is the only discipline really equipped to deal with it. It is not necessary, then, to relinquish its traditional employment in formal logic, notwithstanding that 'substance' might be a more appropriate term. For all that is required is that it be acknowledged that 'subject' used in that sense has a limited reference, which, if extended beyond its own sphere, confuses all further entries and thereby disallows of a proper understanding of what 'subject' most fruitfully means in realistic thinking.

Chapter Five

Ethics and Morality

*Before Socrates there was no morality in Greece, only a
sense of propriety.*   Bury

It was not without hesitation that this pair was included, not
because it lacked the importance of the others or was related to
something more concrete, but because it has been discussed in
greater fullness elsewhere,[1] in which sense it might seem
redundant. But indeed, so far from being a topic to be omitted for
that reason, the making of a clear distinction between these terms,
commonly used synonymously, is even a matter of urgency, since
failure to differentiate them with sufficient sharpness may have
unhappy consequences for present-day society and inhibit
understanding of the problems it confronts. There is further reason
for thinking that the distinctions made between the other terms in
this study have their ultimate warrant, which renders them more
than verbal, in allowing the present pair to be seen in its real
significance. The meaningful *reality*, metaphysics apart, is that
reality which is confronted in normal life, the reality with which
we as sentient beings are vitally involved, here and now or, to
stretch a point, in the foreseeable future in which our descendants
will live. For the balance of society, its sweetness and refinement,
depends on the recognition by man of his relation to nature, to
which he has to adapt himself to live in a sensible way, broadly to
be at one with himself and with his fellow men. Unless it is

111

understood that the greater part of response takes place on subconscious levels, on which grace and refinement, culture seen without pretension, have their proper seat, we shall continue to be trapped in the cult of cognition, with its base in subjectivity and so in individualism, which is slowly corroding society. *Sensation* plays a part in life, when its modes are harmonic, which is infinitely more basic than that of phenomenal perception, which in fact depends upon it, such that its understanding in a philosophical sense must be seen as an essential preliminary. There is a grave imbalance when thought referred to reality is effectively seen only in cognitive terms, as something to be brought under maieutic control as contrasted with something to which we have to adapt. And this has to be rectified, or seen in better proportion, if man's involvement with reality is to be seen correctly. Roughly the same applies to thought about the nature of *mind*, which has in every sense a more important function in the process of living than the categorizing intellect. For it is the instrument with which attunement is effected as contrasted with the intellect, aspiring, all too often with erroneous conclusions, to total domination. Its attempt to exert control over the forces of nature can, unless conditioned by sufficient sensitivity, lead to grave disasters, perhaps to the destruction of our balance in the environment – *nemesis* as the outcome of a blind and unbridled *hubris*.

With the meaning of the *subject* a vital point is reached: that, if that term is interpreted as the knowing self, and thereby in effect confined to comparatively small groups as if simple people's interest were without significance, understanding of man's relation to what encompasses him cannot be grasped as it is, with all the implications that that understanding involves. The subject in any vital sense is one subjected to pressures to which he must adjust. And to interpret that word as if that which bears upon him were of no concern to philosophy, or as if adjustment could simply be made by adopting and applying rational procedures, is to lose all sense of what normal life involves, even when that life is shared, once they leave their studies, by dedicated cognitivists. In fine, when the interest is value as contrasted with knowledge, all the salient terms in this list, the last of them especially, have to be understood in their essential meanings, which have been obscured to serve the limited interests of cognitive enquiry. The outcome is that society is seriously disturbed, lacks firm ideas on value, or the priorities it supposes, since it is without proper guidance from those who should attend to these matters. What has real priority is neglected or forgotten in the interests of control, which, since nature is not amenable to ordering on the part of a few whom she has gifted with certain powers, can never be complete. Natural interrelationships are infinitely too subtle to be comprehended fully by the categorizing intellect,[2] notably as they are taken to be inclusive of psychical factors playing part in human, and in animal, life. Value, understood as accruing from successful adaptation to the pressures that nature and society together bring to bear, as attunement to their rhythms, as balance in conditions, is fairly claimed to have the ultimate priority, since without it life is jagged and far from what it might be. Nor is this a value for the person only; it is one that redounds to the benefit of his fellow men, to the quality of relations in society generally.

To elaborate on this: if the ultimate interest is value, it is well to understand what, in philosophical terms,[3] that word properly means. As philosophy then lays claim to be a general discipline, to be concerned, that is to say, with what is common to men and has universal bearing, its thought should be addressed not to the desires of the individual person but to the quality of the whole, the frame in which he lives and in which those desires are met. In so far as the values at which individuals aim are attainable internally, regardless of the milieu on which many of them depend, they are his personal affair and do not concern philosophy, unless, as is often the case, their attainment interferes with the basic needs of others. If they are not achievable, because circumstances are unfavourable, every man must learn to accept a measure of frustration, which he can only do with grace when he understands – in which philosophy might help him – that the world is not 'his oyster' and that there are limitations, the interests of others, which have to be respected. In any philosophical sense, value is therefore general, tied, that is, to the social frame in which it has its meaning as accessible universally. And if this has been forgotten or has never been considered in sufficient depth under a tradition in which self interest is paramount, philosophy fails to understand in what its role consists: the attempt to render relationships more favourable to fulfilment.

For reasons to be considered, the relation between the two terms now brought up for review has supreme importance, inasmuch as it turns precisely on this question: what should be considered the ultimate ground of value? In as far as value, then, is the aim of all enquiry, for even knowledge has to be seen in terms of the values it gives, for otherwise it is simply an academic interest, philosophy should consider it in its basic nature, as a matter which is properly outside the province of science. Value in its general form, as present or accessible to all men whatsoever, is something very different and altogether more meaningful than value seen, as it usually is, in subjective forms. The quality of society in which it has its ground, with its ultimate roots in nature, the harmonizing force of which society is a reflection, is, or rather should be, the prime concern of philosophy. For that constitutes the frame of life in its human form, as distinct from the sphere of abstractions, of interest to metaphysicians perhaps but with little bearing on life as it is actually lived. Ethics, as will be seen, constitutes the study precisely of this form of value; and morality, which relates to it, for both are concerned with quality in social interrelationships subsisting between persons, is an aspect of it, which is mistakenly studied in isolation from it and without the recognition that it is properly subordinate to this greater interest. But that, which might seem outrageous were it not considered in rather closer terms, requires a fuller development, which must now be undertaken.

The aim in drawing attention to meanings that have been veiled to serve the special interests of rationalizing thinkers, is not analytic, notwithstanding that it is semantic. It is to restore or reaffirm earlier vital meanings. In so far as the forms of all words are conventional, as their references are not – which the different sounds of the first in distinctive tongues evinces – the interest might then be seen as a better relating of conventions to real needs, to needs as they relate to fundamental interests as distinct from those which are rather academic, which have tended to sever themselves further and further from them. The relation of formal logic to the ordinary use of language, developed to meet the requirements of normal communication,[4] is not easy to discern, although it in some sense exists. Enough at once, however, that people do not normally speak in its stilted, pedantic manner – which does not necessarily issue in perfect agreement – even when discussing important public affairs. At best it provides a training in critical verbal powers, so that flaws in statements may more readily be detected.[5] But that is its negative function, which is certainly different from its assertoric aim of establishing absolute truth, which is only attainable on an abstract plane. This is not the place, however, to elaborate on that matter, when the salient point is rather that, if it claims that its usages, its terms and its procedures, its conventions that is to say, have universal bearing, that not only renders all further thought inflexible, it deprives it of the terms it must use if it is to refer, as it must, to volatile actualities. Subject, one of its own terms, has already been discussed to demonstrate this point. But, under this dispensation, several others terms, although not part of its own vocabulary, are none the less delimited as their references are related to the procedures it demands. Ethics is in such sense conflated with morality – which has, as will be seen, quite a different reference – and so because the latter is believed to be amenable to rational enquiry, inasmuch as it turns on personal motivation and choice, both deemed to be fully conscious, and accordingly analysable. Thus, in this case we do not have a blurred or a dubious reference, in effect we have none at all, since the word is merely used as a substitute for morality, or rather for moral philosophy, and is in that way personalized. This is unfortunate in the sense that what it once referred to, and might again refer to were it understood for itself, is lost to view when the word is applied to something, of undoubted value as a special study, which in its own meaning does not comprehend its references. In short, the coalescence of these two important terms effectively obscures what might otherwise be apparent: that there are two interests in the field to which both words refer which are quite distinctive with regard to what they mean and to the functions that they serve. Hence, if one of the two, clearly the more important in terms of social interrelationships, since it covers a wider sphere, has been neglected or overlooked as the consequence of a failure clearly to mark a distinction, that is surely a matter that merits closer attention.

Despite this identification, a difference between their meanings is dimly, if no more, recognized as subsisting, less by rational thinkers, it seems, than by ordinary people involved in action in the world and accordingly caught up in the mesh that that world comprises. But this differentiation, in as far as it is noted, is insufficient to set apart a fundamental interest from that which it is not. It is not required at this juncture sharply to distinguish between a general or social interest and one that is in principle incidental or personal, or rendered general only by the dubious application of subjective generalization. But it is to the point to remark that when this distinction is made in rationalistic terms the tendency has been to consider the first of these interests, in the manner of Hegel, in political terms.[6] The effect has been to overlook a meaning more closely related to deeper or spiritual needs, which politics and law, and sociology for that matter, are ill-equipped to deal with in a sufficiently sensitive manner. And indeed, when that aspect of life which is distinguished as 'spiritual' is presumed to be tied to consciousness, as in idealistic thinking, it is difficult to see that it more meaningfully resides in something which is general, not ego-bound or subjective. It is immanent in vitality, as has already been said,[7] and that must be understood if the role or meaning of ethics is itself to be so. Just, then, as the subject is other than the thinking or knowing self, and is more suitably seen as a sentient, sensitive being involved with a world to which he is obliged to adapt to sustain his very balance, both physical and psychical, so his ethical relations presume a similar involvement with the process of becoming, the world that is about him. The social complex is as much a dynamic, indivisible, interrelative structure as is the external world. For, though it is man-made in a sense, it is not a conscious construction but a development out of conditions, the outcome in effect of an evolutionary process produced by adaptations to circumstantial changes. Unlike morality, then, which, in principle at least, aspires to absolute standards, forms, attitudes and prescriptions which will stand for all time, and accordingly suppose a measure of finality, ethics must take this dynamic fully into account and so give scope for generalized responsive flexibility.[8] The need it mets is more opaque, subtle and elusive and cannot as a consequence involve objectification; for, as apart from anything else, what it is concerned with is not directly observable. This necessarily makes for a rather different approach, which underscores this divergence and the requirement to mark it clearly. But all the implications of that are not fitly discussed at once; for they suppose a relinquishment, or at least a modification, of traditional procedures with their turning on the self. And that raises a host of questions.[9]

*

The first requirement is then to show that these words do have different meanings, even though they have been employed without discrimination for a very long time indeed. In fact, such usage is nothing new, a recent or modern development – as is the specialized use of the term the 'subject' – which might be taken to justify a clinging to such an entrenched and widely accepted employment, were it not that this difference seems to have special significance in the present state of society. That is even undermining itself by failure to observe what it means when traditional norms, which sustained the structure in balance, are apparently losing their power to hold the social fabric together. This synomymous usage has been a feature of Western thinking for at least two thousand years, though precisely when these two terms were first used coincidentally is not at this distance in time easy to determine. For documentary evidence does not clearly reflect it and is in any case sparse. Later translations, as that of the *Nicomachean Ethics*, may not, as terms have changed their meanings over time, adequately render what Aristotle meant when he used the substantive *ethikē* to describe what he was discussing. For it doubtfully had the meaning that 'ethics' is given today. He certainly used the word; but it is fairly to be asked whether what it meant for him is to be identified with what it now refers to in the expression 'moral philosophy', which involves, and even demands, conscious deliberation. For it seems that his use of the term referred rather to dispositions absorbed or adopted subconsciously, inasmuch as he sometimes spoke of a 'second nature' – *to ĕthos oīon phŷsis gīnetai*[10] – an innate or an inbred tendency, something quite different from what concerns the modern moralist, at least as he invariably appeals to rational powers.[11] But to understand this more fully, it is well to refer to etymons, since those show that these two terms had very different roots and originally referred to quite distinctive interests. To use them interchangeably, then, is to be blind to the meaning of either one or the other; and, as will be seen in a culture devoted to autonomy, it is the first that has been eclipsed with certain unfortunate consequences. Reference to etymons then allows of some recovery of distinctive meanings, hidden in effect since the advent of Christianity, concerned with the immortal soul of the individual, or even further back to the

117

time when an unhappy transliteration from the Greek to the Latin linked one idea of a relationship, itself in some decay, to another with a different origin and history.

Ethos, of course, is Greek, in which language it had two meanings, an earlier and a later, the first of which is now, by a curious twist of fate, best represented by 'morale' as used in modern English.[12] Whether 'ethnic' has the same root is not fully determined, although that seems to be likely, which is of interest in that it suggests relationship to groups, to peoples with common customs. However that may be – for it has not been studied closely – the idea of collectivity has some bearing in context as aiding an understanding of what *ĕthos* initially meant. The primitive Greeks – for it was only later that they came to be known as Hellenes – were almost certainly nomads in the plains of Scythia, whence, for reasons that are obscure, possibly desiccation, they emigrated southwards into the Greek Peninsular and the coasts of the Aegean. These overseas penetrations, like those of the later Norsemen, were probably for the most part undertaken by sea from what is now Bulgaria in waves across the Aegean into Greece and Ionia, where they impinged upon the indigenous Pelasgians. And it is of some interest to note that cultures often arise, to account for the Greek achievement, from the contact of different peoples, when the less advanced are influenced by the existence of a more mature development, which seems to inspire a creative thrust, as if in emulation. But that is by the way, for what *ĕthos* then implied related to the lives of these invading groups rather than to those who are settled in their traditions and satisfied with their lot. Its reference then, it seems, was to the attitudes required of those who dared to penetrate into foreign lands in relatively small parties, who in these adventures were dependent on each other and on loyalty to their leaders. If anyone failed to play his part, 'let the side down' so to say, the result could be disaster, since what the invaders confronted were larger local forces fighting on their own ground. What *ĕthos*, in contradistinction to the later *ēthos*, appears to have implied was a spirit or disposition, its usual translation, of freely accorded co-operation, which was less deliberative than subconscious or inbred, instilled perhaps by training, as is morale today. And this spirit, later conducive to considerable bickering, in the absence of latent threat, distinguished the Greeks in later times from the more impassive Romans.

This seems to be in tune with Aristotle's 'second nature', reflecting, though its meaning was undergoing change, the earlier import of *ĕthos*. And indeed, that a change was taking place with reflective thinking about how one ought to act, called in distinction *ēthos*, a change from an internalized, spontaneous disposition to conscious deliberation on what attitudes were required of the thinking agent, is shown in documentation. This is well brought out in a later book, entitled *Magna Moralia* - Latin not Greek terms - probably compiled by one of Aristotle's disciples, in which a pertinent passage reads: "Everybody knows that *ēthos* comes from *ĕthos*",[13] fairly interpreted to mean that thinking about behaviour was a later development on simple adaptation to the conditions prevailing. Bury, in his *History of Greece*, illuminates this passage when, with considerable insight, he writes: "Before Socrates there was no morality (*ēthos*) in Greece, only a sense of propriety (*ĕthos*)".[14] This, it is noted in passing, relates to the distinction made between *yi* (the conscious cultivation of rectitude, required of the Ju especially) and *li* or *tao-chung-hsin* (an innate or inbred ethical 'sense') in classical Chinese philosophy. Aristotle, following his immediate pre-decessors, Socrates and Plato - of whom the former appears to have been steeped in the ancient tradition, as his acceptance of death evinces - represents an evolving movement from *ĕthos* into *ēthos*, from simple adherence to what was taken to be proper to thought and discussion about it.[15] However, the earlier attitude seems to have persisted, and almost certainly did so in ordinary public life, although that is not now firmly to be established, much as those in the future may have difficulty in grasping from recorded statements made in the mass media that the notion of honour lived on in present-day society despite an apparent contempt for it displayed by those whose views enjoy the widest publicity.

It was not until the time of the later Stoics that a stress on personal virtue, cultivated consciously, fully emerged as an attitude. And it is not without bearing that Zeno, the father of Stoic philosophy, was of Semitic origin, heir to the notion of guilt rather than that of dishonour, a principle with greater appeal to the classical Greeks. The first could be forgiven or assuaged by genuine penitence; the second, once committed, could not, with the upshot that there was no real recovery from it. This afforded a strong deterrent, leading at time to self-destruction, practiced even more vigorously in the cultures of the Far East. And this of itself suggests, and Roman stances confirm it, that the notion of *ĕthos* in some sense persisted, even though, as with Cicero, or later Marcus Aurelius, *ēthos* or *morālis*, to give it its Latin name, constituted the interest of the thinking classes, of the Stoics and Academics at least, if not of the Epicureans, who cultivated attitudes which were more or less spontaneous. Both Stoicism and Epicureanism might faily be regarded as personal religions, or ways at least of conducting life on the part of the individual. They promoted their philosophies as 'medicines for the soul', so that they were general or social only by courtesy, in the hope perhaps that what they proposed might in time receive universal acceptance. As practical regulations for life they were in fact addressed to the faithful, though with a clearly marked difference between them.[16] Polystratus, for instance, criticized the Stoics for their contention that moral demands were conventional in origin and accordingly rationalizable, stressing by implication that norms were rather natural and in that sense linked to *ĕthos* rather than to *ēthos*, or the later *morālis*.[17] Indeed, referring to rational thought in a later book, Lucretius sought to liberate the soul from what he stigmatized as 'superstitious madness'; and what he was urging was in effect living according to nature, notably with respect to the calm acceptance of death.

The point at once, however, is less to stress that attitude than the persistence of the idea of a fitting disposition, not so much within oneself as in relation to others, *agapē* in classical meaning. But with a gravely disturbed political situation, which continued for several centuries – from the Peloponnesian Wars to the end of the Republic – and with the collapse of the *polis*, replaced by large Imperial States, this disposition became increasingly self-centred. The idea of a natural social sense gave way before another, one that militated against all that it represented, turning interest inwards, rather towards the attaining of some form of personal balance than the balance of society, which was now sustained by political, military means, Roman administration and law, with *Pax Romana* behind them. The upshot was that an *ĕthos* spontaneously maintained, resting for its fulfilment on co-operation, allegiance, implicit accord and loyalty, ceased to exert its erstwhile influence on society.[18] Thus, the individual effectively stood alone, seeking means, adherence, for example, to a faith, which, as giving promise of personal salvation, offered him a form of psychological balance. It was that essentially to which later thought was directed, first by thinkers conscious of unsettling conditions and later by people at large, as personalized religions, the mysteries and those which emerged in the time of the Empire,[19] made themselves available – to the neglect and so the weakening of the deeper idea of a social or ethical sense. In this way the ethical principle was engulfed in or replaced by personalized moralities, claiming to be identical with what that principle represented, which was certainly not the case.

*

The Latin term that referred to social cohesion was $m\bar{o}res$, the plural, which is significant, of the singular mos, which may be translated in various ways but suitably in context as 'custom', 'lore' or 'wont'. Hence $m\bar{o}res$ may be taken initially to have meant a body of lore or custom, on the observation of which the State, originally the tribe, effectively depended. It may then be compared with the bodies of lore which controlled and conditioned the lives of primitive peoples in many parts of the world up to modern times, and still, where life is primitive, continues to be operative, through taboos, initiating trials, appeasement of the gods, ritual sacrifice, and so on. The Hellenes were, of course, originally primitive peoples; but, for reasons that are obscure, they had by historic times already developed a freer attitude to life than the more conservative Romans, who remained attached to their traditional tribal customs, as the Vestal Virgins evinced. And if the Greeks also did so, as indeed do modern societies, that was in a more relaxed and generally sunnier manner. Rigorous conformity, together with grave penalties attached to any failure to act in the manner that was required, characterized the Latin, specifically Roman tradition, which doubtless accounts for later military achievements, dependent on strict discipline rather than panache. Roman life was distinguished by a hierarchical system incorporated into law, gradually refined, and by patriarchal rule, which was initially absolute. That only later gave way to more tolerant, freer attitudes, confined in the main in Imperial times to the wealthier classes, who long resisted challenge to their hereditary privileges on the ground of established custom.[20] Hence $m\bar{o}res$ certainly meant something different from *ĕthos*, and is rather to be seen as a quasi-legal system to which compliance was enforced than to one that called for free co-operation, spontaneously accorded.

How far the tradition enshrined in the idea of *mōres* influenced later Roman attitudes is not easy to determine. For, as Rome expanded, very great changes took place, especially with the turn from the Republic to the Empire, founded in part to accommodate them. Forgetting for the moment the influence of Greek thinking – to be discussed in the sequel – attention may be turned to other operative factors. One was very certainly a vast increase in wealth and an upsurge of indulgence, one of the effects of which was a growing disregard for the ancient idea of virtue and of public duty as an aspect of it, which did nothing to promote the idea of a social sense but rather undermined the notion of obligation. That was further reduced as the State took on the role of administrative leadership once performed by the ruling classes, compelled in that sense to act in a responsible manner. Another was the great influx of foreigners into Rome, in the main of lower types, bringing with them as they settled their own modes of life,[21] thereby to undermine the old Roman idea of purity, sustained in principle at least by the leading families until they became corrupted by the luxury wealth produced. Thus, the notion of virtue, manliness, decency, honour, very much a feature of the ancient dispensation, ceased to have the influence that it had had in the past, to give a warrant to leadership, the idea of 'the noble Roman'. Later this influx combined with the growing infertility of the indigenous Romans had consequences which profoundly affected Roman society and were in no small measure causes for its decay. Colonials came in time to form the bulk of the army, which, if not less disciplined, lacked the same sense of loyalty to the spirit of Rome, which had characterized its armies in the time of the Republic and the earlier Empire, made up not then of mercenaries but of independent farmers from the surrounding hinterland proudly serving their fatherland. But what was yet more significant was that these immigrant peoples brought their religions with them, in that way to undermine traditional Latin cults which had held society together: for it was such cults as these, with the rituals they involved, that unified the community.[22]

It was not, however, to challenge these ancient modes, some of which exhibited considerable resilience, that foreign faiths were accepted when they were introduced. For, with this great expansion into further worlds and with it loss of a sense of a common heritage, such that the titular gods no longer exerted influence and such that Mars became too remote to inspire a sense of loyalty. For the Roman Pantheon seemed to represent a power far greater than the deities with which men were familiar, a kind of malaise set in. *Panem et circenses*, a materialist narcotic, was scarcely an adequate answer for those who sought for something deeper. Hence a readiness to accept alien religions – and even thaumaturgies – which held out hope of something to which adhesion could be given, together with a promise of personal salvation and so of psychical balance. How far this was related to *mōres* or *mōralis*,[23] in so far as those referred to the needs of the individual in tightly-knit communities, is an open question, possibly to be answered by drawing a comparison with the degeneration of traditional tribal peoples when they abandon their ancient customs, feeling a loss of protection without anything to connect with, for them at least, a formless modern society. As the Romans developed no *ĕthos* with which to bind society, unless in their fighting forces – whence the modern word 'morale', likewise confined to a group – the principle in effect of co-operating voluntarily, the road was open to searching for alternative means of fulfilment, which were necessarily personal.

*

Whether this comparison between two kindred cultures should have been made so sharply may perhaps be open to question, although it is not unfairly said that there was a difference between their attitudes to life. And that was not unrelated to the terms with which they defined the relation of men to society, one of which undoubtedly gave greater scope to freedom, freedom of the spirit, at some expense perhaps of rectitude within the frame of a hierarchic ordering. *Mōres* is not a term that allows of easy definition; but it certainly seems to refer to something bearing more heavily on the members of a group conscious of their status and of the obligations it carried. No doubt, it should be granted that the Romans were more responsible, at least in the times when that principle dominated society. But this raises a delicate point, as to how

123

responsibility involves the evoking of consciousness linked to a sense of the self,[24] and how far it should be spontaneous and in that sense internalized, based on innate dispositions? It is part of the Western tradition that it ought to involve cogitation, an idea with roots in the change from *ĕthos* to *ēthos* and *ethikē*. But that might be said to be a doctrine adopted by thinkers endowed with intellectual powers, even one imposed on those who lacked the required equipment. It then remains a question as to whether a rational attitude can be operative universally, as democrats now suppose; or, otherwise said, whether it is not a rather more sensible doctrine to stress a natural potential in men, discoverable in courtesy, which certainly does not exclude an onus to feel for others, which need not be wholly conscious. For then the subjective or personal scarcely intervenes, as if to inhibit natural grace, which relates this mode to *ĕthos*, or to ethics correctly so called, rather than to morality in the form of something demanding conscious deliberation. But that does not resolve the problem of what *mōres* actually meant in its pristine sense, unless it is seen as a system imposed by a dominant class on others who had to submit to it. All that can firmly be said is that it produced a form of society which, prior to its expansion and consequent decay, was distinguished by its rigidity, by pressure placed on the person, who, as acting under this pressure, tended to be more self-conscious. This is not wholly adequate; but, for the immediate purpose, it helps to mark a distinction between what is meant by morality, which is clearly related to what is required of rational agents, and what is implied by ethics, which refers to relationships of more general bearing in which everyone is involved, regardless of whatever their intellectual powers.

Reverting, then, to the period when these changes first took place, that of the later Republic, it is of some interest to study the philosophical origins of the linking of these two words, ethics and morality, and the consequent coalescence of what they represented. Their roots may be insignificant as compared with the great events that more decisively brought about such momentous changes of attitude. Even so, what thinkers think – though their thought in the following years was not distinguished by creativity – does exert some influence which seeps down into society.[25] Thus, if the importation of later Greek philosophy had a decisive effect only on the scholarly or educated classes, it was not entirely confined to that relatively small group. It is known that paganism died hard in the rural areas; and there is evidence that some of its forms had considerable influence. But all that we have to guide us in this is surviving documentation, the remnant of what has not been lost in the process of natural decay or was not destroyed as heretical by fanatic Christians. Enough, however, remains to permit of certain judgements, specifically on the matter of the linking of these two terms. That almost certainly had its roots in Cicero's translation of the later Greek *ethikē*, for which, naturally referring to his own tradition, he chose or rather invented a term of his own *mōralis*, thus relating it to *mōres* and so to all that that term implied. And since from the earliest contacts with the thought of Greece, introduced by an embassy led by Posidonius – a Stoic and a Monist, advocating vital force – Stoicism proved to be its most attractive form, it is to the point to consider the relation that that had to the ancient Roman heritage. It was not this pantheistic theme, which was too impersonal, that the Roman thinkers took up, but rather the idea, then prevalent in Greece, of Stoic self-sufficiency, the duty of the person cultivated consciously, as if obeying a law devolving on himself. This is rather superficial, inasmuch as Stoic thinking had several variant forms.[26] Nevertheless it suffices to show, in however broad a manner, that concern with self-cultivation was its later characteristic. In fine, in the climate of thought that was then developing, to reach its culmination in the second century, interest tended to become increasingly subjective, concerned with the destiny of the soul rather than that of society.

With the further emergence of salvational religions, notably Christianity, which developed their own philosophies, a concern with obligation tended more and more to lose its public meaning, since one's duty now referred to God rather than to the community. It is easy to understand resistance to this teaching on the part of those who took a larger view.[27] But as the social interest became increasingly legalized, a bureaucratic concern, much in the Latin tradition, and as responsibility passed from the private citizen to the public authority, the remnant of a social sense was lost in what became a cult of personalized morality, linked to sin and guilt instead of to something nobler, honour and propriety. Thought on what should be done under the dictates of conscience, always highly subjective, tended to replace a sense of the public interest.

125

The last was not forgotten, of course, though by degrees it passed into the hands of the law – where it largely resides to this day – which became increasingly civilized under the later Empire, until overthrown as a system by the invading barbarians. Thereafter public spirit almost ceased to exist in any form whatever and chaos ensued for centuries, held in check to some degree by the dominant Church. But religions stress morality rather than an ethic[28] – and to speak, as scholars do today, of the ethos of a group, is to misuse the term, which must, to have real meaning, have social or general reference. They urged conduct in relation to God, Who is loving at once and fearful, rather than to society, which in any ordered form scarcely now existed. Order was slowly restored, in the main by military means; and that law, the basis for it, was gradually re-established, did not mean the revival of an ethical sense – unless in the highly specialized form of aristocratic chivalry. It meant that the morality sustained by Christianity, which rationalized its form more tightly as time went by, dominated attitudes, as it did until quite recently, such that its weakening poses a serious social problem when nothing exists to replace it. For, whatever its limitations, it afforded a check on assertion and secured a measure of decency.[29] Hence, the implicit criterion behind all moral thinking, the general or social interest – for that is the form it must have – has since then been regarded as a politico-legal concern, calling necessarily for rational procedures, which cannot properly engage subtler psychical needs. As an approach this is far removed from what *ĕthos* meant when it was active in ancient Greece and it has the effect of blinding thought to these deeper interests, now considered as spiritual in a transcendent sense and so dissevered from reality, and to the proper meaning of the general in actuality, response to which is sensuous and in that sense spontaneous, quite other than ideal.

*

Given that the aim in discussing words used in philosophy, as those have been allowed to lose their fundamental meanings, is to rescue them from the restricted interpretations that they have been given in the interests of cognition or of ideal modes of approach, what this aim implies must now be considered more closely. Of all the misreadings projected, then, none is more unfortunate than that applied to ethics, which for these reasons has ceased to have a needed distinctive meaning. And it has never been more urgent that that should be restored. Assuming that philosophy has a vital function in relation to normal life, distinct from that of science, religion, law, or politics, the interest is then to determine what that most fruitfully is and how the meanings of terms essentially relate to it. Nor is an answer readily or simply to be stated, since the name by which it is known, unlike the names attached without exception to other disciplines, itself affords no index of what its purpose might be. The Greek *philosophīa*, 'love of wisdom' in English, means nothing at all precise. For 'wisdom' seems to be a word steeped in ambiguity, ranging from profound insight or understanding, which need not be strictly rational, through identification with truth in its logical meaning, to prudence or common sense, which is how it is used in life as it is normally lived. It is accordingly obscure and not confined to philosophy. As for 'love' as an attitude, that is an emotion which is essentially subjective, and so is a very odd word to apply to what purports to be a wholly objective discipline, detached from, even scornful of, emotional involvement. As a consequence of this vagueness with respect to its appellation, philosophy appears to embrace a multitude of interests, supposed, a little loosely, to comprise a consistent whole. But the only force that links it, or so we are urged to believe, is abstract formal logic, itself a power that is almost uniquely evoked in the West.[30] Science may have many forms, but all have this in common: the augmentation of knowledge. That that is the end of philosophy is very far from certain, though some would contend that it is so, despite the restricted knowledge it gives in the form of abstract truth. This raises a pertinent point with respect to what it in fact contributes as a serious discipline concerned with vital problems, such as priorities of importance, which refer to life and not to simple verbal abstractions.

It is true that its various branches do have descriptive names – logic, epistemology, ontology, axiology and in recent times analysis, which, since its interest is predominantly precision in definition, is presumably to be seen as a form of the first. But the status currently given to these various studies under idealist rulings, which is broadly the order in which they are set out above, is undoubtedly mistaken and should rather be reversed. The value of formal logic, which is accorded primacy, or so at least today, is certainly overrated, since it is merely abstract and has little application when discourse is turned, as it should be, to real or pragmatic affairs. For it is too restricted and rigid to engage vital or practical problems, quite apart from the limitations – now recognized by logicians[31] – which plainly delimit its reach. Precision is an ideal, which well may be misplaced when it is not correctly available. This is not, of course, to gainsay the value of natural logic, commonly used by philosophers when their thought is developed more freely, nor that of negative logic, seen as a critical instrument, though neither of these is acknowledged as the powers that they actually are. But further discussion of that must be left for a later occasion: the immediate point is simply to challenge the pretensions of a strictly formal logic. As for epistemology, it is, as tied to cognition, restricted to the plane of that which is cognizable. Hence if any relation is not, and that must surely include many vital concerns – which, as Foucault observed,[32] may well be misunderstood if that is the only approach to them – its excessive cultivation may actually be obstructive. If knowledge is regarded as the only end of enquiry – a peculiarly modern prejudice – philosophy either assumes that it is guiding science, which is surely capable of weighing its own procedures, or trespassing on its ground without contributing to its aim.[33] Such disciplines as these are largely academic, and nothing would really be lost did interest in them diminish. Rather the contrary since, with the freeing of thought from the restrictions imposed by rigidity or confinement to cognition, which is the province of science and not of directed philosophy, real problems could be approached in a realistic manner. And dangerous though that thought may appear as opening the door to indiscipline, it may be the key to reviving powers of creative thinking and of overcoming the crisis produced by a growing sense of futility.

Ontology in certain forms is a much more meaningful discipline. For, disregarding those forms of it which are better called 'metaphysical' – the study of being *qua* being, causality, and so on, the distinguishing feature of which is that, despite interminable debate, no conclusive answers are finally produced – ontology is concerned with a very important issue, and so because further discourse depends on what it evinces. That is thought on the assumptions that are suitably made with respect to the nature of reality. The point to notice, then, is that there is not, as idealism supposes, but one presuppositional set which is properly adopted, and oddly believed to be provable, since any assumption made in respect of what cannot be taken as given has to be related to what is under review. Under the cults of cognition and of truth as an end, that single presupposition has been deterministic in the absence of any alternative that is rationally acceptable, that is, that nature is uniform and regular in action, in principle predictable. That certainly works for science, which cannot with ease abandon it, even though it is recognized now that the forces it confronts are rather more subtle and complex than was once supposed. For even though aspects of it appear to be quite regular, it is a mistake to assume that that as a finding can be generalized. But it plainly does not work when other aspects of life have to be considered, of which the most obvious is the need for responsible action, ungrounded if the doctrine is that everything is determined. Another presuppositional set is evidently required, the more so as the bulk of response to the external world, and through that world to others in the social complex, is subconscious or internalized, that is, unobservable, beyond the reach of cognition; and, as psychical, far from regular. That the world that man confronts, for the most part in that manner, is, or is almost certainly, a dynamic, indivisible, interrelative complex, both in a social and natural sense, that it is fluid and ever-changing, is plainly a sounder assumption when man's relation to his world and to his fellow men is the subject of attention. A determined and, in principle, a controllable reality, which, as a bye-product, grounds social engineering, constitutes an idea that has led to even gross mistakes and could even be one of the causes of the present unrest, as if man at all resembles what appears to be malleable. Science has never proved capable of engaging psychical problems, of those of any depth, without insensitivity, and so because it rests on unsuitable presuppositions – not to mention procedures – and so cannot take account of a force such as intentionality, which is certainly more subtle than projected goals or drives.[34] The spiritual, in a word, is other than material, and plays a more significant role in the lives of human beings.

That aspect of philosophy distinguished as axiology constitutes, as its name implies, the study of value or worth. The telling point is, then, that that is beyond the range of science, which can only evaluate in particular terms, and so is impotent to judge the value

129

of any act in a general sense, that is, in terms of its greater or repercussive effects. Indeed, its contribution, knowledge that is to say, has, properly speaking, itself to be judged by some external standard, and the more particularly so as it is but material, which is certainly not of itself sufficient as a criterion. What is of value in life comprises very much more, the meeting of deeper needs, which are not really submissive to material definition. The problem that value presents is other than scientific, to mean that it is philosophical. It is, indeed, the paramount problem faced by philosophy as it aspires to deal with real or vital issues. Thus, whereas formal logic and epistemology can only be regarded as ancillary disciplines, and as ontology when concerned with the presuppositions most suitably adopted in any form of enquiry is also so, though undoubtedly in a more significant sense, axiology is beyond all question fundamental. In the last analysis all enquiry is directed towards the securing of value in some form or another, that is, with the enhancement of life, however that is viewed. In that sense everything falls within the purview of axiology, to be judged in terms of what it contributes to life and its meaning or in terms of the degree to which it frustrates or delimits it. And if frustration is part of life and has to be accepted with courage and equanimity, it is relative to value and may be preliminary to it, in which case the problem is one of priorities of importance. Something must be sacrificed, abandoned or overcome in order that something more worthwhile, which might involve the reduction of excessive desire, may be developed as a means to a better balance, psychical particularly. Thought on such matters as these receives too little attention when the prevailing doctrine is one of an unlimited promise. For that can only lead to frustration and disappointment, a failure to understand the limits of possibility. Thought is certainly needed, then, to guide people now confused by mere material expectations, as if those comprised the key to quality of life. If this is the role that devolves uniquely on philosophy, which deals with greater issues and concerns itself with value in a general and deeper sense, taking all factors into account as they bear on what this involves, then that study called axiology makes an important contribution and accordingly has primacy. For all else is subsidiary to it.

*

Axiology, however, is a field that encompasses a number of different interests, which are not of equal weight, since they vary in the significance that should be attached to them. It is roughly divisible, religious and other special interests apart, which are not the concern of philosophy,[35] into divergent interests, which are, philosophically speaking, aesthetics, morals and ethics. Though not entirely so, since the quality of the environment is a matter of public concern, notably as it has effects on those on whom it impinges, aesthetics, better termed 'artistry',[36] is in the main a field in which satisfaction is personal. "The world", it has been said, "abhors a mediocre poet"; but, if his work is abhorent, that is of little moment, for no one is obliged to pay attention to it. The same applies to works, however fine and noble, of painting, sculpture, music, ballet, drama and literature: that there is no requirement to see, to hear or to read them. For what we choose to enjoy is simply a matter of taste, and tastes, or conscious tastes, evidently differ.[37] However enriching the arts may be – and it cannot justly be doubted that they are a civilizing force, in which sense they certainly have a public meaning – it remains the case that, since the values they give are personal, they do not have the standing of morality and ethics. Were it possible to determine what exerts a debasing influence and so vulgarizes life, aesthetics as a discipline might be said to be concerned with general evaluation.[38] But, as it is usually referred to individual works and to the subjective effects that they have on the critic, not infrequently conditioned by the fashions of his time, it remains a subsidiary form of private evaluation, general only by courtesy.[39]

Moral concerns, meanwhile, have undoubted public importance, for the way in which people behave has profound effects on others and the quality of life. A society may survive without cultivating the arts; but it would soon fall into chaos without a moral structure, some general acceptance of norms or rules, prescriptive for the most part, needed for sustaining its continued stability. The rulings accepted may change over time, but not as they are basic; and failure to distinguish those that may be modified without occasioning the disruption of those that as vital are absolute, by no means an easy task, is unhappily characteristic of much modern moral philosophy. The reason for this would seem to be the want of a firm criterion, when the 'rights' of the individual to 'express his 'personality' – even when what is said or done is publicly influential and has an effect on attitudes – apparently take priority over social need, which is often unrecognized. An even deeper reason is that, as it is now developed, in part because of a heritage steeped in subjectivity, moral philosophy concentrates on personal motivation, that is to say, on the causes of acts rather than on their effects.[40] This may be rather sweeping, since that is not always the case. But with the cult of the individual and a failure to distinguish between ethics and morality, there is more than a little uncertainty as to where the real interest lies. Moreover, with the dominance of idealist thinking linked to logical procedures, it is plain that what is cognizable, the motivated act undertaken consciously, is amenable to its approach. That it is favoured as an interest is then quite comprehensible. Thus, when the real end of giving thought to moral action is grasped, if dimly in the main, the cult of the knowing self is too strong and the logocentric tradition much too firmly entrenched to permit an escape from subjective involvement into a greater breadth of outlook. Virtue is seen as personal, only to be acquired by means of a conscious effort, as if it were a matter of deliberate cultivation, as in the call for self-discipline, magnificent as an idea but rather too demanding. Hence, it is not surprising, since that power is relatively rare and difficult to acquire, that its advocacy has little effect on *le moyen homme sensuel*, who is seldom given to reading edifying texts and who acts, as he acts well, because the presence of a legacy of almost irrational norms, decency, honour and so on, conditions him and not because of admonitions projected by earnest moral philosophers. In fine, there is a 'sense' of seemliness and propriety, which is innate or internalized, latent if now overridden, and which in the last analysis lies behind motivation and gives it its meaning in a form that is only dimly perceived. Rationalism, moreover, is certainly double-edged, as the popular use of that term sufficiently evinces; since finding excuses for what are recognized to be improper or vicious acts is a conscious or rational attitude.[41] Concentration, accordingly, on the rational agent, the conscious knowing self in idealist philosophy, may even be said to obscure our notions of the purpose behind insistence on moral behaviour, as if that were related to incidents in effective disregard of their further repercussions. For those plainly cannot be cognized, since they are both unobservable and are plainly more complex and diffuse than are any effects which are manifest overtly.

For ethics, in contradistinction, personal motivation is not the primary interest. Not that that lacks for importance – for it is the warrant for training, as related to attitudes that have to be instilled in the earlier years of life to ensure the acquisition of a fitting approach to later social involvement – but that that is rather the concern of moral philosophy. It might, if a little cynically, even be suggested that the act required in a given situation may be undertaken with dubious motivation,[42] as when the agent acts with indifference or detachment and yet performs quite fittingly, whilst others, full of the right emotions, prove incapable of decisiveness or misdirect their sympathies. "The road to hell", it is said, "is paved with good intentions"; and egoism in this sense may even be altruistic. But it is made to counter an implicit weakness in excessive rectitude, righteous indignation for instance, which can cause considerable damage. No, to urge the ethical interest does not of itself imply any depreciation of the study of motivation, an interest that cannot be faulted, since without its cultivation anarchy might ensue. But conscious motivation – for, of course, all acts are purposive and could not well be otherwise – is not a matter with which ethics are fitly concerned, since that is not its province. And this point must be firmly made. For when morality has priority that detracts from the general interest: the consequence of actions as they affect the body social. Nor can that be overstressed; for, unless a clear distinction is made between ethics and morality and the distinctive functions they serve as studies related to conduct, we are continually thrown back into the confusion which obscures an understanding of the essential issue: the vital reason, that is to say, why any thought should be given to behavioural issues at all.

Proper motivation undoubtedly plays a part in securing suitable conduct. But it is the effects produced, directly or indirectly, and the last are certainly not in strict sense conscious or knowable, amenable to analysis, that really have social significance and constitute accordingly the ultimate criterion. One way of putting this is to say that, whereas moral philosophy is justly and properly concerned with the problem of personal virtue, the integrity of the self as a free-acting agent, ethics is concerned with the quality of the society in which he is enmeshed. And that, or such is the aim in that discipline, should itself be so constituted as to provide an adequate frame in which his latent powers may be developed and deployed. When, then, the expression the 'free-acting agent' is introduced into discourse turning on this matter, it has itself to be understood since that brings out a salient point. That, as a social being, a man is no longer free in the sense that his actions are unlimited. For he is in that role caught up in a network of obligation, of implicit responsibility, in which in some sense the self is lost, such that acts are largely impersonal.[43] All this should be tolerably obvious to a little thought; but, with the dominance of the cult of the individual, sustained by idealist thinking with its stress of the knowing self, it is very largely forgotten. And if, by placing emphasis on this difference with respect to involvement as it bears on the socialized individual, attention is directed to what has real priority, that itself is of value. Concentration on the self exerting free will correctly may be a noble aim in theory, an idea with a strong appeal to those already inclined towards it. But when its practical consequences as a general counsel are self-assertion, competitiveness and materialistic rivalry, personal virtue, although it may shine in contrast to these attitudes, is more difficult to sustain without verging on pretension or adopting what appears to be a posture of self-righteousness. Happily current society is not so far sunk in depravity that decency is exceptional, self-interest the only criterion. But as, with certain trends, a general decay of quality becomes a possibility – and history shows that societies have in the past decayed through a lack or a gradual weakening of a social sense – ethics, the sustaining of which should be the primary interest, then constitutes a vital study in itself.

*

It should now be clear that the need sharply to distinguish between ethics and morality, between the public interest and that referred to more personal involvement, has to be recognized because it relates to vital issues. For if the general and so the greater problem is overlooked, not deliberately, of course, but in a failure to mark in what it properly consists, concern with the effects of acts on society at large, whose members naturally tend, when this point is not sufficiently stressed, to concentrate almost exclusively on their private affairs, then sense of the general interest is very largely lost. The reason for making moral demands is even itself obscured,[44] which is a serious matter when their ultimate warrant is social. It is little surprising, then, that much confusion ensues, since, with this failure to distinguish priorities of importance, countenance is given to egoistic acts excused on various pleas. 'Anything goes', as the saying is, anything is excusable or can be defended by argument, carried to the point where those who find certain acts deplorable are dismissed as illiberal, void of a sense of modernity. Thus, the individual, when he alone is the judge, is entitled to do as he sees fit, regardless of the consequences. That as a stance can only lead by way of social disturbance, contentiousness and bickering, leaving an ugly residue, which is growing and proving increasingly difficult to control, to social disintegration, though that to the unthinking is not considered a possibility, notwithstanding that history shows that civilizations have declined for not dissimilar reasons. Failure to maintain a measure of symbiosis, adherence to tacit norms, has social repercussions which may not be readily recognized, although their effects resemble any failure to comply with the requirements of nature – as in omitting to water plants, which shrivel as a consequence, or abuse of the physical system in the human species. And if the outcome is not immediate in terms of social effects, it bears on our descendants, on future generations. Law, of course, can be evoked as a means of stemming the tide. But that presupposes coercion, which must become increasingly harsh as it is extended; and it is scarcely an adequate substitute for civilized maturity. Nor, with increasing corruption, play on the edge of legality, is it easy to distinguish truly criminal acts, still relatively rare, from those which are disruptive in a more subtle sense. The growth of near-criminality, of anti-social attitudes, though this is admittedly speculative, may well have roots in a growing contempt for traditional norms. For those, since they cannot be rationalized or defined with sufficient precision, are readily shown to be without rational authority, even as inflictions on individual freedom, supposed to be exercised rationally. And as this dubious doctrine of the liberated self effectively rides unchallenged, because there is no developed sense of any greater interest, social modes are corroded to mean that the need to apply coercion becomes increasingly a requirement.

Thought of the general need is never entirely absent – unless among logicians – and it is, of course, the basis of law and accordingly gives coercion, authority exercised justly, its warrant and justification. Nor is it entirely forgotten by those concerned with morality; even though they do not see as clearly as they should how it bears on their rulings. Thus, moral philosophers commonly speak of 'subjective generalization', showing with the second word that they are well aware that it is incumbent to generalize. But that, as the first word indicates, is a rather specious doctrine, based on what amounts to a dubious use of induction. For though on a rational plane – with logic as the criterion but also a genuine effort to establish universality – there may be similarities and constancies of relation, it is clear that with subjectivity interests vary widely. It is only on subconscious planes, where self-involvement has no place and consciousness does not enter, that responses have something in common, which, though that cannot be clearly defined and is therefore not rationalizable, must be recognized as present, inasmuch as nervous systems are broadly structured alike.[45] In fact, were there not resemblances on this responsive level, grounding most of our relations – courtesy, for example, is largely deployed subconsciously – life would be chaotic; for if we had to rely on rational agreement, notoriously hard to achieve even on logical planes, we could scarcely make links with each other. Difference or disagreement, which is of its nature detectable, as a standing out against a circumambient harmony, only comes to being with the evoking of consciousness, the emergence of subjectivity. In other words, subjectivity is even improperly generalized; and may, if it is so, often involve the imposition on others of what a thinker himself, or a group of thinkers, deems to be the pertinent interest – idealist thinking, for instance, to challenge which is heresy.[46] It is not to be denied that there are universals on a conscious plane, such as the laws of logic or, in the moral sphere, the repudiation of clearly deplorable acts, murder, blackmail, and so on. But if those, or acts which are rather less heinous and depraved, such as failure to keep one's promises, are the only ills to which thought can be applied, its reach is plainly limited. Many disruptive tendencies have more subtle forms and cannot so simply be categorized. But in a general sense it is those with which ethics is concerned in terms of their effects, leaving the more obvious forms of anti-social behaviour, to the attention of those whose disciplines, law and moral philosophy, can properly engage them.

In the last analysis, then, ethics is concerned with the general acceptance of what is needed for social quality: the sustaining of dignity, its protection against abuse, and other forms of relationship which are less easy to specify. That morality must be fostered, a sense of duty internalized, so that it is generally present and properly applied, cannot be disputed. But 'internalized' is the key word here, in contrast to 'subjectivity', seen as a conscious state, since only that can be generalized in any effective sense, and only so if what ethics involves is properly understood: as the discipline that refers to what is, or is potentially, common to humanity. If this sentence is paraphrased by reference to a potential, that is for the reason that what is apparently latent in the human make-up has been overlaid, blunted or corrupted by the propagation of questionable ideas, placing undue stress on the interests of the self, as though there were nothing higher than the desires of the individual, the rationalizing agent. The virtue of sensitivity, which is a latent human capacity and in that sense universal, has apparently been degraded into sentimentality, such that it is viewed as emotional or inferior. Notions such as honour, which is surely one of its forms, are only so regarded by those who do not understand what is implicit in it and who seem to think that it is a cultivated acquirement, notwithstanding its presence among the most simple and primitive peoples. A 'sense' of what is required in a given situation does not mean the weighing of the advantages of behaving in an acceptable manner. It means an innate and implicit sense of what is at once appropriate, related, without calculation, to the general state of affairs. If this sense has been lost or allowed to fall into decay, that is a serious matter, injurious more particularly to those in weaker positions, who do not have the power to reject what amount to forms of patronage. A sense of the general must be instilled, or perhaps restored is better when reference is to those with the onus for setting the appropriate social tone, of releasing a latent capacity from what inhibits its flowering. And it might be remarked in passing that its weakening or absence makes for greater difficulty in achieving balanced forms of personal fulfilment. But this faculty cannot be fostered by admonitions addressed to the 'rational' individual, if only because adults resent correction from above, as if they were devoid of a natural sense of propriety – to show that that is latent and woken by challenge to it. If this appears to ride against the deliberative tradition that dominates philosophy, it is time that it was recognized that a clinging to postures derived from casuistic reasoning is not the way to proceed, since that is all too plainly tied to the self-centred prejudices of the now dominant class. Thinkers, of course, are responsible for the influences they exert; but if those are bound to narrow beliefs and unfitting presuppositions, taking start from the knowing self and incapable for grasping that there are more sensitive entries, they are either misplaced or malign. The problems in this field are very much more subtle than cognitivists can grasp.

It is tempting to align the two terms under review too closely with the abstract terms the general and the particular, but that would be too simplistic without some refinement on it. For, though the bearing of ethics is general and morality refers rather to personal acts, all social behaviour whatever has repercussive effects and so an ethical dimension. There is a point in this, however, that merits closer attention, since it tends to be neglected when the thrust of thought is rational. And that is that the particular is rooted in the general, indeed is abstracted from it in order that what is collected may be subjected to definition, distinguished from all else. When the general can only be seen as the product of analysis, as the logical universal, as the correlation of abstracted particulars synthesized by the intellect, the tendency has been to discount the underlying complex, *the general in actuality*, which cannot itself be rationalized and is thus misunderstood in its form as an interrelative whole. The logical universal is compounded of particulars, which have being only in the phenomenal world. The real world, which is the world to which ethics has to relate, is not composed of objects or things, but of changing interrelationships. The point is then that whilst moral acts may be viewed in isolation, as observable phenomena – though motivation is surely more complex and indeterminate – what the ethical interest refers to cannot be so seen. It is the social complex, reflecting that of nature, as dynamic, indivisible and in process of constant change, that constitutes its field. Hence, if moral acts are seen to have a social bearing, that is, in terms of their effects rather than their causes, they have ethical implications. In fine, they are more than moral, since their ultimate meaning is ethical. This confirms that ethics is a distinctive discipline, calling for different approaches than those that apply in moral philosophy. Those must plainly be sensitive, penetrant and flexible, since what they refer to is the general in actuality, the interrelative whole, constituting a field of very much

138

greater complexity. And that necessarily raises a methodological problem of even acute dimensions, though this is not the occasion to discuss what that implies.[47] Enough at once, accordingly, that ethics and morality, ethics and moral philosophy, are seen as discrete disciplines which should be distinguished clearly, if only to ensure that the basic or general problem shall be given proper attention, which it cannot receive when interest turns essentially on the self, as if the greater social need were effectively forgotten or given but passing thought. What ethics involves must be studied in its own, its specific terms, which are very different, both in respect of ends and the procedures needed to reach them, from those that apply or are at least accepted in moral philosophy. As particulars, then, are properly aspects of the general, extracted from it for the purpose of acquiring positive knowledge, a general which in itself has to be thought of differently, so morality falls within the general frame of ethics, inasmuch as that affords its ultimate criterion, the justification for thinking about moral action at all.

Chapter Six

Understanding and Knowledge

Nature we explain: psychic life we understand.
                                                    Habermas

Although there is ample precedent for adopting such a view as
scepticism in respect of the reach of rationalism as such – not to be
confused with reasoning justly so called, of which it is fairly to be
regarded as a class – to do so is quite certainly to raise a host of
questions. These refer to the consequences of taking such a stance.
For when consequences are considered, those must surely embrace
rather more than the questioning of pretentious claims, appropriate though that may be, and must show that the door is in this
way opened to something meaningful. In other words, deconstruction must pass into reconstruction, that is to say that positive
benefits must accrue. But it does not at once appear that the more
penetrant sceptics, from Gorgias, through Pyrrho, Sextus,
Autrecourt, Cusanus, Glanville, Cournot and Sigwart, to Adorno
and Derrida, answered this demand with any show of sufficiency or
even indeed attempted to confront it properly.[1] It is all very well to
decry strict rationalistic procedures, to declare that they establish
no contact with reality; but that is little more than a preliminary
manoeuvre. It is effectively barren if it bears no fruit. Many
thinkers, even today when logic and all it implies is so much in the
ascendant, are conscious of the limits of an idealist approach and
recognize that it is impotent to pass beyond an ideal or subjective

140

plane. For the interest is then essentially, if not exclusively, verbal, such that by contrast action receives but little attention. It is true that we cannot communicate unless by using words – though logicians and mathematicians appear to do so with symbols,[2] fondly in the first case believing that those refer to events in the actual world. But it is no less true that words are ideal and external events are real. Between strict definition and the employment of suggestiveness, to refine on the relation of speech and what it refers to, there is surely no small difference. For the latter permits the hearer a certain scope, based on experience no doubt, but formed, since that means more than the meaning that empiricists give it, of past impressions which may not be perspicuous and precise. And the fact remains, however we try to disguise it, that the gulf between the ideal and the real, if not complete or absolute, has never yet been bridged to total satisfaction, notwithstanding attempts persistently made to do so.[3] It is thus that scepticism has the leverage that it has. But merely to be sceptical is not to face the real problem: namely, what procedures have to be adopted when thought is directed to what is beyond a rationalistic reach and cannot be comprehended in idealistic terms.

The problem in question takes many forms; but the matters of greatest concern are those that refer to life and action, especially man's relation to the world of dynamic becoming, which is plainly not to be reached by means of analytic procedures. For those can only refer to what can be particularized, and that does not include relations in the complex, the interrelative whole that characterizes quite clearly both nature and society. Yet, with these limitations and with increasing recognition that what is confronted is indeed a dynamic complex in its various aspects, the only respectable end is assumed to be cognitive explanation and the only acceptable disciplines are those devised to serve it. As a consequence of that extra-cognitive problems, such as those of evaluation, can only, if taken seriously, be engaged in a rational manner, which, as sceptics have shown throughout the course of history, is a clumsy and crude approach leading to grave mistakes and even gross misunderstanding. Rationalism has been triumphant in the West because of a long tradition of seeking conclusive answers, a passion to elicit truth as irrefutable, though sceptics have frequently pointed out that truth is not available in respect of external being or, more precisely, of becoming.[4] And so far has this passion been taken that a thinker has found it possible to declare that Heraclitus, who undoubtedly held that nature persisted in a state of ever-changing equipoise, "foreshadowed the modern conception of the uniformity of the laws of nature".[5] But that nature obeys invariable laws discoverable by reason, the power of the human intellect categorizing its forms, is surely a misreading of the thought of that ancient author. Flame, to which he compared its thrust, is too volatile and mutable to be submissive to measurement, albeit that we may know the causes of combustion; and it was plainly intended as no more than a metaphor for a continually changing structure, which, though it conforms undoubtedly to underlying laws, is constituted so subtly that those are not accessible to rational enquiry. Human action is also no doubt conditioned by certain norms, to carry this point further; but it is even notorious that no rational laws are discoverable on psychological planes, unless in such simple forms that they scarcely touch the question of why men behave as they do.

If this appears to go against the achievements of modern science in cosmology and physics, purporting to have discovered or to be on the way to discovering the ultimate forms of nature, the open-minded scientist knows that that is far from the case, that many such findings are speculative and likely to remain so because the means of making such discoveries as these leave much to be desired. Big bangs, black holes and the movements of sub-atomic forces can only be projected as findings of limited character because mathematical revelations are supported by minimal evidence, which depends on the employment of restrictive apparatus, with which isolated incidents are taken to reflect a whole in which forces are acting freely. A philosopher makes such points as these with the utmost trepidation, since he lacks the equipment to discuss such matters adequately. But with respect to the first at least he should not be overawed by such marvellous projections – such as a gravitational tension of a thousand million million million million million tons, 10^{39} – but should see them in proper perspective, that is, in relation to what really counts in life. For, even supposing these findings are true, that a big bang in fact occurred, that the universe is expanding and may in the distant future contract, "to bring time to an end or reverse it",[6], their bearing on human life as it is actually lived is surely far to seek.

Physics has to be considered rather differently, since, even in more arcane forms, it plainly has bearing on life, as atomic power makes manifest to everyone; though that is not fair if it suggests that the knowledge it provides is destructive and no more. Other aspects of its findings are evidently more fruitful. For what it affirms, which is undoubtedly of value, is that nature must be seen as an indivisible whole of which man himself is a mode and not a being standing outside it observing it in detachment, as the mind–matter dichotomy most improperly held. And, of course, in its more immediate forms, it conditions all that we do, all that underlies and sustains our modern activities, as in our dependence on electric energy. Finally, biology, and with it biospherics, constitute forms of science that bear directly on life, and are bound to the criteria that life itself imposes. Experimentation, then, has a rather different meaning, since its end is not so much to explain as to deepen understanding of what conduces to health, such that the tests its theories face is less veridicality or proof in intellectual terms than assurance that applications shall be beneficial and free from harmful effects. Moreover, it is recognized that what is under study is better described as the finding of working or practical principles than of veridical laws, since it is understood that those render the free-flowing rigid, as that no organism studied exactly reflects another.

These thoughts might be extended, but that is not now a requirement once it is accepted that a sceptical or, otherwise said, a critical philosophy does not sweep the board to throw doubt on all employment of reason – and that must include itself – but only on certain forms of it, choosing its targets discreetly. It is well to remember, indeed, that it was primarily directed against rationalistic pretentions, claims to establish truth, which it shows to be abstract or verbal. It accordingly distinguishes experimental enquiry – a questioning of nature directly as it were – and abstract explanation, insisting that the final test is not verbal or alethic, but vital, that is to say, effects on human life. To a superficial view the achievements of modern science tend to be related to what is most remarkable, inspires the simple with 'wonder', to use a Platonic term, even worship of the power of the human intellect, its apparent control over nature. But this is a dangerous attitude, and so for a number of reasons, one of which is that such control, on the part of a small minority, can all too readily lead to control over other men, to social engineering. And apart from that, such extensive powers, which tend to be exerted without real responsibility when the only check is internal, generate unhappy divisions in society, between the god-like knowers and the unenlightened majority. Knowledge *qua* knowledge is not necessarily good, though uncritical thought accepts it on its own evaluation. It has to be judged for its effects by some external standard, ultimately qualitative; and that is not a matter with which science is fitted to deal. Hence, the exaltation of cognitive achievement, admired without qualification, is justly subjected to question, the more so as there are aspects of life that cognition cannot engage, which may be more significant than the augmentation of knowledge for ends that are often obscure and seldom given very deep thought.

This brings up a salient point which tends to be overlooked when cognition is taken to be the only essential end, the only acceptable warrant for disciplined enquiry. And that is that all knowledge, using the term strictly in a scientific sense, is and cannot be other than material or quantitative. It is derived from measurement of what is presented phenomenally; for, though experiment questions nature and touches it directly, observation can only be of what is recorded consciously. This means and can only mean that what is not cognizable, recorded in that manner, is either denied attention or left to what are regarded as undisciplined approaches, held to be subjective, personal and emotional. Thus an essential aspect of responsive life, commonly called the spiritual to distinguish it from the material, lacks intellectual standing,[7] whatever virtue that may have when seen as something that permits power and control over nature. And to confuse the issue further, associations of terms, the identification, for instance, of the intellect with spirit, *Geist*, in idealist philosophy, renders comprehension of realities more difficult. 'Spiritual' is again a term which, under the dichotomies that rationalism indulges, is referred to transcendent, other-worldly spheres as if it were above and beyond the arena of the physical, taken itself to be synonymous with nature, though that is surely inclusive of everything that there is, psychical no less than physical relationships, a point that particularly signifies when psychological studies are restricted to the empirical. An alternative reading of it, accepted in other cultures, is that spirit is rather immanent in nature, that is in vitality, as various words, such as *anima*, effectively confirm. Given this, it is clear that it is related to nervous response, which, though some of its processes plainly have physical features, and may be studied accordingly by cognitive procedures, evidently has other and richer characteristics. For instance, the as yet mysterious coming to being of consciousness and other more subtle by-products, grace and sensitivity, cannot be so discerned, as if physical facts revealed them. In fine, there is a sphere between initial stimulation and fully conscious reception that science cannot engage, but which is yet the seat of highly significant aspects of life, life in its deeper meaning.

All this is said to show that a cognitive entry alone has very serious limits, since it is powerless to engage much that conditions life in its more subtle forms. Another approach is clearly required if those are to be considered in a proper manner, when proper implies that what is discerned shall be more than simply subjective, essentially personal, and constitute a form of public, open disclosure submissive to critical comment. The argument, then, which might still be raised, that if findings are not objective in a rational sense, then they must be subjective as if there were no alternative, is easily met by stating that all reception is subjective and could not well be otherwise. What renders it public is that it is stated openly and so invites critique, which is justly required of any statement made, whether that be factual or in this case evaluative. The only difference resides in what is being reviewed and in the means whereby findings are elicited. Hence, if the second is other than a claim to establish facts, in which case discernments can be judged by known techniques, checks must be devised which are no less effective, to ensure that no statement is made which is improper or inept, likely to be confusing. If no such methodology is at present available, as a result of which serious errors are made and dubious ideas are permitted to pass unchecked, the time has come, particularly with the recognition that it is not particulars or objects that are confronted but complex inter-relationships, to give further thought to this matter.[8] Scepticism, therefore, of the reach of rationalism, extended to cognition as that amounts to a form of it, is justified if it does no more than bring this point to attention. But from that we must go forward to consider its several consequences, ultimately the need to devise a further procedure with which to engage those interests that given methodologies are plainly powerless to meet. Finally, if cognition is the only valid terminus of disciplined enquiry and is shown to be but one form of reception, another end must be considered and projected. That is here called 'understanding', seen as something other than 'knowledge', and to the distinction between them attention must now be turned.

*

To discriminate between the terms 'understanding' and 'knowledge', or rather to show that the first has a distinctive meaning as a terminus of response, is perhaps the most difficult task confronted in this book. For in this appeals to science or to etymology, which give substance to what is said, are not available as they were when other terms were discussed. Moreover, further to complicate the problem it presents, the two terms now exist in an intimate embrace, such that knowledge seems to involve some form of understanding and understanding some form, however vague, of knowledge. But that very sentence shows that there *is* some difference in their meanings, for otherwise why should two terms be used when one would be sufficient to refer to what is intended: a product of knowledge perhaps or something rather different. But indeed, that there is a difference between them is widely recognized,[9] felt perhaps if that is allowed when discourse must be verbal, though the problem is to determine wherein it most fruitfully lies. To steer a course between the Scylla of strict cognitive assertion and the Charybdis of suggestive or allusive expression, which may involve awareness, is certainly not easy. And it is rendered more difficult when strict rationality, and the methodology so fully developed to serve it, has to be challenged to do so, thereby removing the basis on which thought is supposed to depend. All thinking referred to worlds beyond the reach of cognition is assumed to be subjective, that is, personalized and involved with the ego and its interests rather than with an objective, and in principle a detached, address to what is external, so that it lacks the requisite breadth and impartiality. That may be a rational prejudice; but it is so deeply entrenched that the idea of a *via media*, of a means that permits of a disciplined grasp of more subtle and complex relations, which is open to check, is almost inconceivable. It is important, then, as a preliminary to considering any such possibility, to recognize what is intended. Indeed, to accept that, though concerned with the extra-cognitive, interest does not turn on esoteric experiences, claiming a certain immunity, but on real and vital issues with which everyone is involved. If reception is subjective, as it is in whatever form, it is not its subjectivity that is of moment here; it is the manner in which response has greater or public effects, other than those that are obvious and in that sense rationalizable. All reaction is not explicit, conscious and cognizable, nor is it otherwise solely concerned with what affects the self. Without meaning to do so perhaps, it has external influence, which, though theoretically public and so open to definition, is too diffuse and elusive to be submissive to such treatment. It is such aspects of it as these which constitute the interest of this further form of enquiry, which so presumes another end than cognitive explanation and thus calls for a different approach.

To clarify this further, a distinction made needs sharpening, for rational dichotomies tend to lump together all that is extra-rational as subjective or emotional,[10] even as superstitious. But that is plainly too crude. It is scarcely to be denied, then, that though some may lack that character, certain mystic experiences are undoubtedly real, actually occur as psychical events, possibly as deeper contacts with reality than any that are available to ordinary response, which does not take one out of oneself or the sphere of normal living. But in so far as they are, they constitute peculiar, exceptional experiences confined to very few, those who are either gifted with special psychic powers or develop special techniques in order to acquire them.[11] Thus, they are plainly not common forms of response such as are general and undergone by every sentient being as he adjusts to the pressures brought to bear upon him. The techniques employed by mystics are indeed intended to discourage ordinary persons from entering closed circles without due preparation, so that they cannot be regarded as coming within the sphere of normal human involvement, which, as a further point, presumes association with others and not separation from them. As the interest here is responsive meaning as it bears on normal lives, it is to the point to make a clear distinction between the mystic, or fully subjective, and the general with social commitment, which, if also subjective in part, is so in a different sense, as it were incidentally. The aim is then to distinguish that

147

form of response to pressures which is extra-cognitive but not for that reason personal in any peculiar sense; in fine, that form of response, for the greater part subconscious, which is common to all men, including intellectuals as they are enmeshed in the process of living. For, even if all conscious response, implicit in discussion in any field of enquiry, presumes some form of knowledge – where, for an example, the light-switch is to be found – that need not mean knowing in a scientific sense. It presumes a more subtle relationship, which need not be overt.

Between the esoteric and the scientific, there is a sphere of interest which has no firm name. Hence its product is often called 'knowledge' and commonly regarded as an inferior form of it, as if that term embraced all forms of reception, to be rated in terms of prestige as they are rationally developed. The consequence of this is that an aspect of responsiveness is either misunderstood or gravely misrepresented, notwithstanding that it refers to the very substance of life, in that it is linked to relationships of significant social form.[12] Somewhere in this neglected zone lie interests of great importance, which can scarcely be held to have a secondary status, to be a field of impression devoid of intellectual standing. They must then, if findings referred to them do not take rank as rational, be seen to have a character and significance of their own, to which the only relation may be some form of 'understanding'.

However, before discussing what that term most fruitfully means, it is necessary to comment on a commonly held idea of it. For, to add the difficulty of distinguishing clearly between these two responsive terms, the case is that both are extremely fluid and ambiguous and are likely to remain so unless deeper thought is given to meanings as they bear on life as it is actually lived. As they have been so long employed in equivocal ways, it is idle to suppose that that can be overcome with the mere observation that there is a difference between them which is obscured if it is not recognized. But this vagueness about their meanings does not permit philosophers, experts in verbal precision, to exploit these ambiguities as they often do; and notably so as the case is that their proper separation would itself give scope for a better grasp of relations in and with actuality. This is seen when they themselves, to give it rational standing, purloin the term 'understanding' to serve their cognitive ends; or, as Gallie expressed it: "... the way that A knows that p is true involves 'A understands what p

148

means'".[13] For in this sense, assuming that what scholarship holds gives the standard, the term is shorn, unless that still counts, of its wider meaning, and thus is its significance delimited unduly. No doubt, that is itself a form of understanding, a grasp of relations as might be said. But, if it is regarded as the only respectable or acceptable definition, it is clearly a narrow one, inasmuch as such a grasp is intellectual only, of related symbols or objectified phenomena. Understanding also refers, and so beyond question more pertinently, to a wider, more general experience, of which this, as a rather specialized reading of its meaning, is no more than an aspect, and apparently a derivative.

*

The difficulty in distinguishing the most fruitful meanings of these entangled terms is compounded, as has been said, by the fact that both are ambiguous and that neither can be related firmly to classical etymons to give a measure of clarity. For both terms in effect have Teutonic origins going back to a time when precision in the use of words was confined, if developed at all, to those employing Latin as a medium of expression, and was not characteristic of speech in the vernacular. When they in fact came into use in Germanic languages cannot now be established, except in so far as it is reasonable to suppose that it was in early times, when languages in use today were in process of formation, in the south at least, from an amalgamation of popular Latin and local dialects. In as far as it is possible to elicit their roots, that can only be done by considering each term separately. For confusion between them seems to have occurred at an early period, and almost certainly took place before their commitment to writing, in which the need to distinguish between them was seldom clearly recognized, even if different meanings were rather vaguely attached to them. So let the basic reference of each term be considered in the meaning that could be unique to it, less as defined in dictionaries, which tend to be cognitively bound,[14] than in what is rather implicit, enshrined in common usage referred to contact with the world, the needs and actualities confronted in ordinary living.

The English word 'knowledge', to deal with that first, has at least two features – quite apart from the fact that no other language echoes it – which render it distinctive. One is that its suffix is peculiar to it and unexplained with respect to its root, which was in earlier times written 'lunge' or 'lech', neither of which can be related to any known word in modern or ancient languages. The second is that its prefix, or rather its main component, appears to come from words of primitive Aryan origin with roots such as *gno* and *jña*, giving *gnōsis* and *jñāna*, both of which, at least later, referred to esoteric insights rather than to knowledge rationally acquired. *Gnōsis* and *jñāna* have plainly the same root as 'cognition', since *cognoscere* is certainly a development on (g)*noscere*, meaning 'to be aware of', 'to be acquainted with', with the additional prefix of *con*, originally *cum*, to carry the idea of 'thoroughly', 'in depth'. For such a term was needed in the Courts of Law, where it mean 'to investigate', 'to examine closely'. Thus are such forms as *connâitre, conocer, conocere* found in Romance languages, though by this time these terms have ceased to be clearly distinguished from others, *savoir, saber, sapere*, derived from the Latin *sapĕre*, with its correlate *sapiens*, which at first had different meanings, ranging from 'to taste', 'to discriminate', to 'to be wise' in the sense of exercising prudence. In English its form is 'to savour', though it is of some interest to note that the slang expression 'to savvy' has been introduced to fill an apparent lacuna, in order to refer to something rather more subtle than strict rational knowledge, 'to know' by applying analysis.

The consequence of a limited vocabulary in this sphere is that the English word 'knowledge' – for 'savvy' is also a noun – is called upon to serve a variety of functions, to refer to simple awareness – 'acquaintance' in scholarly language – to the registration of precise or rational findings, together with a range of intermediary meanings, not caught in Russell's dichotomy.[15] As the word is so ambiguous, philosophers have been conscious of the need to sharpen distinctions between exact and looser knowledge, and so have introduced the scholarly term 'cognition', with its verbal form 'to cognize', in order to differentiate between these two forms of knowing. All other forms of knowing, or grasping of relationships, are justly then entitled and distinguished as 'extra-cognitive', a usage that will be maintained throughout the rest of this chapter, and so without any suggestion that that means mystic or emotional. In addition to *gnōsis* – in respect of which *nous* and the later *noēsis* may have a common root – there is another Greek term *epistēmē*, which seems to have developed no later or modified

150

forms until its conscious reintroduction in the Nineteenth Century, when it was adopted in academic circles to refer to strict scientific or to theoretical knowledge.[16] This was one of several Greek terms referred to the act of knowing, which came in time to have an essentially rational meaning while *gnōsis*, which began its life as a generic term, came in the course of time to have a rather specialized import, that of esoteric, revealed or mystic knowledge. A point of some interest in context, then, is that whereas *gnōsis* in earlier classical times seems to have had the meaning of 'knowledge consciously recorded' – as *gnothi sauton* instances – which could be interpreted fairly as 'knowing that', *epistēmē* rather referred to 'knowing how', that is to say to loose and even subconscious knowledge – 'savvy' in modern English – which was for the most part internalized. It would have applied to the acts of pianists, dancers or horsemen, who, though all rely on memory, subconsciously evoked, do not calculate or ponder what should next be done but perform spontaneously, lest otherwise their acts should be clumsy or inept.[17] Accordingly, like other later adaptations, it lost its pristine meaning in the act of relating it to cognitive enquiry, as if that were all that counted.

What emerges from this is that philosophers in the West have sought to find words with which to distinguish knowledge rationally acquired from knowledge as that word is used in common everyday language, knowing that from knowing how or having mere awareness. Thus in English we find, as in related languages, recourse to words that are little used except in learned discourse or by pedantic persons: 'cognizance', 'apprehension', 'intellection', 'apperception', 'percipience', 'introspection' and others derived from Latin, all of which refer to forms of conscious response.[18] With this even extensive vocabulary lying at their disposal, it is a little unfortunate that the loose and equivocal 'knowledge' is yet so freely used by philosophers to refer to what is quite clearly received. For then there is no scope, with claim to verbal authority, for discussing forms of knowledge which do not have a rational or scientific grounding. Indeed, unless with the adoption of a qualifying adjective for differentiation, as with the expressions tacit, revealed, intuitive or professional knowledge, or with the slangy 'savvy', thought, disciplined thought that is to say, on certain aspects of life is effectively inhibited. This is the price that has to be paid with an idealist heritage, with concentration on truth or total explanation, as if what is not to be interpreted in such terms were of little moment and had no real significance.

Of all the terms referring to the acquisition of knowledge, 'science' is plainly the most precise and freest from ambiguity. For 'truth', apart from being ambiguous itself – for moral truth, of which the opposite is lying, and logical truth, to which the foil is falsity or error, are plainly very different – is of little moment if it is simply abstract or verbal. With roots in the Latin *scire*, 'to know', with the nominal form of *scientia*, said to have even deeper roots in the Greek *keāzein*, meaning 'to cleave', 'to split', 'to separate into parts', in other words 'to analyse', this term is entirely appropriate as a word referring to what science does. Though that is open to question once holism is accepted as the characteristic form of that which it now confronts. That its approach is only inductive should not however be stressed, since its investigations have, as is well enough known, been illuminated at times by subconscious intuition, so that scientists who are not dedicated rationalists acknowledge that as a mystic factor in their enquiries without compromising what constitutes their essential purpose:[19] to know in greater depth through whatever means are available. But any finding made must yet be subjected to testing, which is the ultimate discipline that science as such accepts. In fine, it is with relations in underlying reality, subsisting beyond phenomena, and not with verbal relations that science is concerned. And so it may fairly claim that whatever the means it adopts, the end in view is 'science' in its proper meaning, only abused when findings are not submitted to adequate testing, which alone gives confirmation.

Science then stands as a term with an unequivocal meaning, which is not the case for knowledge, whether that is derived from the manipulation of symbols or from any other procedures which afford information. But, as science is now as a term referred to well-defined forms of knowing, those specifically derived from empiric investigation, it is not a term applicable to all forms of strict knowledge, those acquired by means of rational procedures. A more comprehensive term is required adequately to cover what, using that expression in its modern sense, may be designated 'epistemic knowledge', knowledge which is defined as true and systematic. If 'cognition' is then accepted as an appropriate term for knowledge acquired intellectually, though in a wider sense that too is dependent on physical testing, that is now to be taken as the word most aptly contrasted in the present context with other forms of gathering, which may be systematic but do not involve analysis or claim to be alethic. For in this way, by securing an exclusive use of terms, other forms of reception may be distinguished from it as external to it, as having their own characters, to be met and to be disciplined in a more appropriate manner. If this is a little arbitrary, its warrant resides in this: that, if 'knowledge' has no strict sense, since it has several shades of meaning, such that it may even be equated with 'understanding', any attempt to elicit a distinct and more fruitful reference for the latter must be abandoned. Knowledge in this context means 'cognition' and nothing more, 'intellectual knowledge', which is how 'cognition' is defined in professional dictionaries.[20]

*

'Understanding' as a term is no less ambiguous and its origin seems to be even more obscure. It has some affinity with the French *entendement*, which is derived apparently from the Latin *intentio*, taken in one of its senses to mean 'directing the mind towards something'. But this relation, if more than one of simple association, lacks for justification. Another source must be found. It is not to be doubted, then, that the prefix 'under' is cognate with the Latin *infra*, and that 'standing' has its roots in or roots at least that are common with the Latin *statio*, of which the basic meaning is that now given to 'station', so that the whole might be taken to signify 'standing under' – an idea that is difficult to relate to any modern meaning. Though structures of parallel form are found in other Teutonic languages, which substitute *ver* or *for* for the English 'under', that is not very helpful if those mean 'remote' or 'distant' and have other roots than *infra*, to complicate the issue. For even if 'stands' means 'stands for', to admit the interpretation of 'representing under', that is more related to the conscious formation of concepts than to what 'understanding' is commonly taken to mean. But perhaps it originally meant a form of 'undergoing', that is to say an experience which was not as of need fully conscious, though that is stretching a point and seems to be rather tenuous. In short, the matter is open, when this alone is certain: that the term came into use at a very early period, possibly before Germanic speaking peoples with their many dialects –

related without doubt to primitive Aryan ways of speaking – made contact with classical cultures.

If its etymon is obscure, the meanings of 'understanding', or of correlative terms in other European languages – some of which have evident roots in classical Latin – are open to inspection as parts of the living language. What that reveals is that they are distinguished by a variety of associated references. For, quite apart from the cognitivists' 'final grasp of facts', already briefly mentioned, this word carries such imports as 'agreement', 'convention', 'harmony', 'like-mindedness', 'knowing how to deal with', 'taking something for granted', 'native wit', even 'wisdom', 'empathy', 'rapport', 'tolerance' and 'sympathy', tacit in most applications. And in so far as such meanings are not experienced overtly, they are beyond the reach of objective investigation. But, despite this limitation, they as accepted meanings are of no small interest in the present context as suggesting that there are other forms of responsive termini than those that involve clear consciousness. Nor have philosophers always been blind to this as an aspect of life, even as one that is deeper than that to which rational thought applies. And Aristotle's 'second nature' seems to give an instance of this. However, as that may be questioned or otherwise interpreted, let attention be given to some modern forms of thinking.

Discounting at once that this was implicit in the idea of revealed or intuitive knowledge, as in all sceptical thinking as that raised questions in with respect to the reach of rational entries, interest may be turned to the thought of those who, when deeper issues came up for review, felt the need for a term that referred to something other than strict epistemic knowledge. Reid, Hamann, Herder and Jacobi, omitting later thinkers, Rickert for example, may not by present reckoning have been thinkers of the first rank. But they undoubtedly influenced Kant, whose use of the term *Anschauungen* merits some attention, even if it was not related to *Verstehen*, translated 'understanding', but rather referred to a form of intellectual grasping. Schopenhauer's *Wille*, which is obstinate, blind and impetuous, is scarcely to be equated with intentional understanding, when intention need not involve consciousness, though von Hartmann's later notion of *Unbewusst* (the Unconscious) seen as synchronizing, subconsciously in effect, the Will and the Idea, undoubtedly relates to it. It is not, however, until we

154

come to Dilthey and, in a rather less sensitive manner, to the sociologist Weber, that this problem of confronting more complex interrelationships was considered in real depth. The latter, in an essay entitled "Objectivity in the Social Sciences",[21] shows clearly enough in that title that understanding was for him a form of knowledge, which his idea of the 'ideal-type' evidently confirms. With Dilthey the case is different, for he makes a determined effort to distinguish *Verstehen* from *Verstand* and *Erkenntnis* as a distinctive interest or terminus of response, as a term which he referred to human or social affairs as opposed to those of concern to science. Unhappily, he could not in his time escape an involvement with the rational dichotomy long established between the objective and the subjective. The consequence was that he regarded subjectivity as the characteristic form of psychical response and could only consider that in terms of mimetic reconstruction or empathy (*Einfühlung*), the last of which is surely, except for aestheticians,[22] a largely subconscious state. Such notions as these are not to be scorned; but to label them 'subjective', as if to imply that such forms of response were necessarily conscious, was an unhappy mistake. Moreover, his doctrine of response, or his notion of understanding in this more sensitive form, is compromised by his desire to be 'scientific', that is to explain. This is implied in his employment of the expression *Geisteswissenschaften*, specifically projected as involving subjectivity in contrast to *Naturwissenschaften* held to be objective. In fine, there is an ambiguous strand present in his thinking with regard to what he had in mind when using the term *Verstehen*, if that is to be rendered in English as 'understanding'. As he was under handicap of being powerless to know what was later elicited by Gestalt psychology in its pregestalten aspect, that is understandable. For that shows that subjectivity, properly considered, comes to being only after filtering process has taken place. His significance in this context, then, is that he was the first who saw the need clearly to distinguish a faculty of responsiveness from cognition strictly so called.

Husserl's phenomenology scarcely involves a concern with understanding considered in this deeper sense, since it refers, for all its claims to explore the 'life-world' (*Lebenwelt*), to strictly ideal reception, which must be fully conscious to ground 'scientific' explanation, which he declared to be his aim. In the hands of those he influenced, the existentialist Heideger and the realist Merleau-Ponty, deeper penetration was undoubtedly achieved, with the first in a largely subjective sense, with the second in one which was rather more subtle, reaching into the world of what is here called 'dim perception'. Polanyi, again, projected what he labelled 'tacit knowledge', which has no relation to fully conscious bracketing, and which, although not called 'understanding', certainly refers to something impinging on consciousness, obliquely as it were, to exercise influence on it.[23] Whyte was also concerned with the character of unconscious – or better subconscious – response and with the subtler forms of reaction to the dynamic of becoming. However he did not discuss the expression 'understanding', since he was rather concerned with the limits of conscious involvement and with intuitive response – "indubitably...one of the most important cognitive faculties of man"[24] – which he considered had been neglected.

Notwithstanding these precedents, and there are several others,[25] it is broadly the case today that thought is concentrated almost to exclusion on cognitive concerns, forms of explanation and epistemic problems. If interest is scientific – which may or may not include the 'science' of formal logic – that is as it may be; for science, as its name implies, is directed specifically towards the acquirement of knowledge. Perhaps the pre-eminence it enjoys in an age devoted to material advance gives it such importance that it affords a paradigm. But when philosophy apes it in a rather pathetic way and aspires to be regarded as itself an explanatory discipline, it merely shows itself to be ancillary to it and incapable of adopting any alternative role and so of contributing in a way that science is powerless to do, so deeply is it entrenched in the logocentric tradition. It seems to believe that the only disciplined methodology is that of formal logic, seen – though Aristotle seems to have had scientific ends in mind when he introduced it – as its peculiar achievement, its essential reason for being, effectively unaware that science now seldom adopts it, since it too rigid for what it has now to engage.[26] But this preoccupation with propositional logic is itself a recent development, since, after a chequered history during which recourse to it even in classical times was relatively infrequent, it only really re-emerged in the Nineteenth Century, since when it has been seen to have obvious limitations. If it is then regarded as philosophy's prime warrant, its contribution to thought as that is directed towards real problems is evidently minimal, since as a formal discipline logic is powerless to deal with any vital issues, which are infinitely more complex than with its stringent procedures it even begins to comprehend. Otherwise said, as was implicit in the thought of those who endeavoured to discover alternative approaches, the interest to which thinking should properly be directed is fairly termed realistic, such that idealist procedures, difficult though it may be to find a substitute for them, are effectively outdated and in that sense impede advance.

As for other forms of philosophic enquiry, broadly called 'metaphysical', which are presumed to refer to matters beyond the reach of science – to being *qua* being, substance, causality, and so on – it is difficult to see what is being achieved by recourse to such rational means as those which it adopts. It would be most improper, of course, to deny the great discoveries that philosophy has made in the course of its history. But whether modern philosophy, with certain distinguished exceptions, adds much to what has already been said is an open question. If the problems specified in Nagel's popular text, *What does it all mean?*,[27] are taken as a listing intended to embrace what concerns it as a discipline, one wonders whether answers to such problems are available or rationally to be found. Two at least, those of 'Other Minds' and of the 'Mind-Body Problem', no longer seem to merit serious attention. And as for such concerns as 'How do we know anything?', 'Death' and 'The Meaning of Life', those are scarcely answerable with any degree of finality, as are such further questions as those of 'Beginnings' and 'Ends'. Others may be considered as having an ethical bearing – 'Free Will', 'Right and Wrong' and 'Justice' for example. But these are scarcely problems properly to be met by rationalistic means, since, if nothing else, their terms are circumstantial, so that ratiocination is a very crude technique for dealing with what they involve. One aspect of metaphysics is, however, important, and so because anxiology lacks for grounding without it: namely, the presuppositions that are most wisely adopted. And, since those should be related to what is being considered, so that there is not a unique or simple answer to this important question, as those who seek truth and conclusiveness seem to believe that there is, ontology in this broader sense calls for further thought. And this is the case especially because the idea of requirement adopted in recent times, which applies exclusively to cognitive enquiry – that the world or nature is uniform and obeys invariant laws – has to be reconsidered. It must be seen as no more than one view, if the ultimate end is rather extra-cognitive, when evaluation, that is to say, constitutes the real interest. Once it is accepted that what is really confronted is some form of dynamic becoming – which, if it is informed by laws such that everything fits into place, is so in a subtler, more complex sense than the intellect can conceive with its simple categories – approach must be reconsidered. For such are the real laws of nature, defiant of representation in conceptual terms, which are constant only in the sense that they are broadly repetitive in such macroscopic forms as are open to detection. At best the laws discovered are instrumental only; they are not explanatory in any absolute sense. Strict knowledge is subjective; it is, that is, compounded of intellectual constructs derived from objectification, in which sense it is ideal and has only conceptual character. The ideas it so projects are *not* the forms of nature, even should it seem so from the study of certain relationships, of which the movements of heavenly bodies afford an obvious example.[28] For what is 'out there' is infinitely more complex and elusive, as vitality, the power to respond to persistent stimulation, without which it has no being, sufficiently evinces. And since nature includes the psychical, for which no firm laws have been found, a deterministic doctrine is evidently limited, if only in that sense. And hence, of course, the difference between studies of matter as such – which should not be confused with the physical, the animate that is to say – and of the incorporeal, presuming intentionality. Beneath the ideal world, which is the world of the intellect, lies a very different world, one that cannot be engaged through categorization; though that it exerts an influence on the endopsychic, not to mention the physical, can scarcely be open to doubt. Another presuppositional set is plainly then a requirement, even, it seems, in science; nor is it far to seek, since science itself provides it as holism is projected. And that implies another approach, though just what that should be when distinguished as 'understanding' is a more difficult question to answer.

*

A short digression must follow here in order to clear the ground of certain misconceptions arising from the idea that the end is truth in philosophical discourse, wherein it apparently differs from the more modest aim of science, which is rather reliable knowledge. For if truth is a form of knowledge, indeed its ideal form, it is, with verbal confusion, linked to understanding, notably in the form of the last about to be discussed, such that a proper distinction becomes more difficult to establish. There is a doctrine, for instance, related to this tradition, that intuition affords "true or certain knowledge of the essences of things",[29] apparently because it presumes direct contact with reality. It certainly eliminates several distorting processes which objectification and analysis impose. But that its products are true, as opposed to freer from distortion, is improperly claimed; and certainly no such claims should be made in respect of understanding. Moreover, the equating of truth and understanding is grammatically unjustified. Truth is the end or outcome of representational grasping, achieved through objectification; understanding is rather an activity or a process, as its verbal form evinces. It too culminates in a grasping, though that does not involve analysis, so that it is rather related to knowing as an activity, expressed in verbal form, except in so far as knowledge, the noun that refers to attainment, distinguishes the end from the process that preceded it. And this may be related to the different means adopted to arrive at ends, in that one, cognition, is conscious and the other is more opaque. Such developments of language may be adventitious, and so should not be stressed. But they show that there is a relation between knowledge and understanding as responsive activities, devoid of the staticity associated with truth. Thus, knowledge may be true or, better said, reliable, just as it may be false, as truth can never be; and understanding surely has similar chracteristics: it cannot pretend to be final. When comparing these terms with regard to their most significant meanings in a vital sense, truth accordingly plays no part in discussion of them. In fact it does not refer to any form of reaction, response to eternal pressures that is, to what may be presented in the kaleidoscope of events to the nervous system – effects that formal logic affects to disregard. For now we are dealing with forms of response and not with abstract terms referring to relations which are ideal or intellectual, only by supposition referring to actualities, to what has vital significance. Thus, when

Jaspers opined that there was doubtless a truth about external reality, he added, very pertinently, that it could not be known, given conceptual form[30] – which might amount to a caution to overambitious scientists. Put in another way this means that no intellectual construct truly represents ultimate reality, notwithstanding that *ratio*, a relation between magnitudes, characterizes both planes. There are ratios in nature, but conception does not reflect them.[31]

This said, it is possible to proceed without undue confusion and to see that both the terms reviewed have reference to processes by which the brain endeavours to grasp the nature of what is received, ultimately through changes in the external world. It would be unduly simplistic to declare that whereas knowledge strictly so called is confined to the world of phenomena, understanding rather refers to that of actuality. As a statement, however, this is not wholly unjust, when the word 'reference' means, or better is taken to mean, no more than that to which attention or interest is turned. It is true that science, in contrast to formal logic, does in experimentation refer to ultimate reality, against which alone any theory projected is shown to reflect relations or conditions in it or to fail to do so. But it is to clear perception, and so to objectification, that science is confined when its end is positive knowledge. If the problem, then, is one of relations in actuality, a cognitive approach touches them only obliquely, in that findings are bound in the intellect, which is the very character of inductive generalization. For a number of reasons, then, this is inadequate as an entry. Another approach is needed if actual conditions, specifically effects on sentient human beings, are to be grasped more thoroughly and with greater sensitivity. And since such an approach cannot be 'objective', separate wholes into parts, it is commonly dismissed by cognitivists as 'subjective'. But that is a dichotomy postulated by those who are only concerned with cognitive enquiry and accordingly disregard any other interest, which, with a further dichotomy, certainly no less crude, they dismiss as simply emotional, as if any ingress other than one that was strictly rationalistic were devoid of sufficient reason. It need not be respected, then, as it was by Dilthey, once its limitations as a doctrine have been exposed. Omitting to exploit what can scarcely be denied, that the acquirement of knowledge is itself subjective, as is every conscious response, at least as that term is taken in its modern meaning, as the characteristic state of the knowing self, it is well to bear in mind that it does not apply in a similar sense to response which is direct, in which the agent is subject to external pressures, for the most part received subconsciously. All direct response indeed, whether it be subconscious or made in dim perception, is properly extra-subjective; and that has some significance as eliminating a prejudice. For if the subject is to mean the conscious, knowing self, then direct reaction can only be seen in such terms, which means and can only mean that its nature is misconstrued.

There is then a further difficulty that has to be confronted: that, unless response is conscious, it cannot be the topic of informed discussion. However, that there must be clear objectification before anything reaches consciousness certainly does not follow. A difficult field is entered here because it has long been supposed that all consciousness is clear consciousness dependent on the collection of objectified particulars related in the intellect applying analysis to them and so achieving generalization. Intuition, if this is so, though accepted by philosophers as a recognized form of reception, cannot be subsumed under any such a procedure. For what it appears to comprise is a grasp of relations which is direct and immediate and so cannot involve analysis, at least in overt form. It is recorded consciously without intervening action or developed interpretation, though that, of course, can be applied at a later stage. Though knowledge is usually stressed in definitions of intuition, that knowledge is certainly other than objective knowledge, and might fairly be called 'understanding', as if in contrast to it. And it is not without interest here that dictionaries define 'insight', which seems to be its synonym or something very similar, as "a penetration of the understanding", though that may be deceptive when the last is itself defined as "the power of abstract thought", as correlative with conception. What might fairly be said is that it is immediate inference, possibly rooted in memory, implying with that adjective – for 'immediate' surely means 'without mental mediation' – that it does not involve analysis. But here again it has to be asked whether definitions of 'inference' allow it to be subconscious.[32]

Leaving that puzzle to those who have given it rational meaning, as if there were no other, let intuition as a response be considered more closely. If we confine attention, then, to the cognitive tradition, this appears to be a rare and quasi-mystic experience, acknowledged as active by scientists, but embarrassing to philosophers – notwithstanding that they have similar experiences[33] – because it seems to run counter to all that logic involves. But it is tolerably evident, if we enlarge our perspective, that it is extremely common in normal relations in life. We do not stop to analyse the bulk of our impressions; we act in the main without reasoning when performing quite reasonable acts. We only start to think with care when pressures are more exigent, not to be met subconsciously, especially when what confronts us constitutes a threat – to give a simple example, when about to cross the street in the face of fast-moving traffic. But it is doubtfully 'knowledge', unless that is internalized, which is evoked in such cases, so that it must be something else for which no clear name exists; for 'instinct' will scarcely do if it means stereotyped response. 'Understanding', however, although it may have that form, must have a further meaning if it is to refer to the study of general relationships. Thus it has to be seen as a power which is other than that of knowledge, developed in order to engage something rather greater than isolated incidents. Perhaps it may be thought of as akin to intuition, less as an exceptional form of response to situations than as a means of grasping problems seen at large which may be cultivated by thinkers. For too close a kinship is too readily assumed, since the powers of intuition cannot be evoked at will, inasmuch as they emerge to all appearance involuntarily, 'out of the blue' so to say, and cannot therefore be a means cultivated consciously, nor one that can be conditioned by a disciplined approach. To act as a means of engaging relations in the complex, understanding seen as a more sensitive approach must constitute a consistent and systematic process which can be applied, as are rationalistic procedures, in a methodical manner and which can be subjected to proper critical questioning.

*

Inasmuch as this approach is sceptical in form, it would be wise in view of the strong resistance that such a posture arouses when more than trivial or internal to be clear about the character that it has in the present context. For, unlike other kinds of scepticisms projected, as of our knowledge of other minds or of past events,

162

which have little bearing on life, this cannot simply be brushed aside as a perverse form of thinking with rather limited interest. It is not then directed against reliable knowledge, which has meaning in that it is as established knowledge reliable, and in that sense life-enhancing. It is in this context directed, firmly and decisively, against the current cult of logically-grounded truth pretending to universality. In such a form as this a sceptical approach is entirely justified, inasmuch as it frees thought from confinement to abstractions and so permits it to reach into further worlds, such as that of man's relation to actualities, which is even absurdly assumed to be comprehensible rationally. For it cannot be so considered without clumsy misrepresentation. So far, then, from condemning this saner form of doubt, rather should philosophers embrace it as affording an opening to better understanding of what their discipline should be studying if it is to make a meaningful contribution in place of mere play with verbal interrelationships. Moreover, such an acceptance would present no threat to anyone but those who cling to these delimiting procedures, in part because they seem to give them a certain authority – as guardians of the truth – and in part because of what appears to be an incapacity to conceive of any alternative to them. And it may be remarked in passing that science now concedes that a fundamental change of conditions has occurred, such that the assumptions once made, in 'classical physics' for instance, though not entirely forsworn have certainly to be modified. This does not appear to be reflected in philosophy, albeit that the world it confronts is evidently the same, an interrelative manifold which cannot be particularized or, as might otherwise be said, given strict rational form, generalized in terms of rational modalities. This scepticism therefore implies that there are other ways of approaching the problems which should be of concern to philosophy. Indeed, there positively have to be if those are to be dealt with in a proper manner, in terms, that is to say, of what they really impose. Which said, it is requisite only, though that may be a large order, to deal with what amounts to the salient point: namely that, if rationalist procedures are restrictive, what means of disciplining discourse is to take their place or, to speak in less divisive terms, to complement or augment them? In other words, can what is here distinguished as understanding,[34] regarded as an approach that is other than simply cognitive, be applied to engage what that as a means cannot comprehend unless with insensitivity?

The problem that this presents is, if for no other reason than that even to raise it is to affront an entrenched tradition sustained by all the weight of authority, not readily considered in a sentence or two. Nor, since the immediate interest is essentially semantic rather than procedural, is it suitably discussed in the present context, even though it is clear that the bare idea of an entry which is other than cognitive poses serious questions of a disciplinary character. But in fact that aspect of it is so fraught with difficult issues that any brief discussion is bound to be superficial. Hence deeper thought on this matter should properly be the subject of a further book, in which its implications can be considered more fully and with sufficient attention to all that they involve.[35] Facets of it, none the less, must be projected here, to show that the problem presented – roughly, how to engage the dynamic of becoming – is not wholly insoluble and that there could be an alternative to an exclusively cognitive entry.

As always, the aim in the present book resides in giving thought to the most appropriate meanings of terms, immediately 'understanding', as they relate to real problems, those, that is, that refer to the promotion of value in general or social terms, from which consequences follow. Immediately discounting questions of procedure, this point may be made. A sensible, workable ethic must take man as he is, recognizing, of course, that he has finer potentialities, but not aspiring to mould him to some ideal of perfection. It must take the whole of society, not a selection, as its sphere; for, whilst heroes and saints can look after themselves and reach to the loftiest standards, humanity as a whole has rather more limited powers. But its members are involved, without exception, in society, which requires their co-operation to sustain itself in balance. What ethics is then concerned with is not some form of total redemption, some utopian paradise which has always proved unattainable, but simply continuing balance, the maximization of harmony. To this end what concerns it as a pragmatic study, though this may seem paradoxical, is not positive value directly, which is not, if value accrues from attunement to conditions, in strict sense specifiable; it is rather its protection, which is in some sense achievable. Attention has then to be given to what inhibits its attainment, that is in effect to *dis*value, to what is disturbing or

164

disruptive. To emphasize the distinction between evaluation and science, the latter, unlike the first, promotes, when its findings are benign, positive forms of value,[36] though those in the nature of the case can only be material, broadly the quantifiable, which leaves what cannot be so viewed outside its domain. In fine, the promotion of value in more subtle forms is only to be achieved as it were indirectly, which is indeed the only way in which it can be done, the only form of entry which allows the intellect, abandoning ideology, justly to intervene. Ethical requirements are constraining or interdictive and have been so throughout history from the Ten Commandments onwards,[37] and so for the very good reason that they should have general authority, address themselves to every man quite without exception, which certainly cannot be said for ideological rulings, flouted even when coercion is used to enforce them. Restraint without that pressure – the appropriate sanction of law as it deals with anti-social behaviour in its more extreme forms – is the aim in ethics, which in that sense inhibits in a gentler manner, leaving the law to attend to what patently defies the acceptances of society.[38]

Ethics, in fine, is simply concerned with what is needed to ensure harmonious interrelationships, achieved by sustaining the norms, internalized for the most part, and protecting them from abuse. It is restrictive, then, in a way that conforms with social requirements, that is with the needs of everyone who, as a member of a community, is under obligation to comply with what it ordains. It is not, however, with law that ethics must now be contrasted; it is with explanatory science, or rather with what science is organized to achieve, determinative discoveries. And if what was contended above – that scientific findings are in general at least positive and material – is not entirely just, it is sufficiently so to permit the making of a point that is operative here: namely, that the procedures which could be adopted in ethics, should not be projected as though they had universal bearing, which would be an improper claim. Thus, if science feels the need for more sensitive methodologies when a holistic ontology has to be accepted, that is its own concern and must relate to its special interests. And should it find what is here proposed to meet needs in evaluation provocative or suggestive, that is as it may be. The problem that is now of concern, with no thought that an answer to it might have wider application, is that of a disciplined approach to extra-cognitive studies, deploying understanding in contradistinction to knowledge.

Evaluative enquiry is then properly directed not towards what *ought* to be done, which may be apt in morality when it is addressed to the person, but to the study of what potentially generates turmoil and threatens social balance. Accordingly, the approach it adopts is essentially negativistic, as might be said Socratic.[39] And that is the key to a disciplined way of dealing with the problem that it properly confronts. As Spinoza astutely observed in one of his letters: *determinatio negatio est*[40] – which is fairly taken to mean that it is only that which does *not* fit into place which can be discerned, defined with any degree of finality. Nor should it be too difficult to grasp why this is asserted. When all is as it should be, properly in place, in harmony or attunement – and that is the normal relation of man to the world and his situation – nothing is suitably said. Explanation is not merely misplaced or impertinent, it is in effect impossible; or, even should it be possible, it would be redundant. No purpose is served by explaining what is adequate as it is and so of itself promotes value. Conversely, when something is out of place and constitutes a threat, if no more than to homeostasis, the conscious mind or the intellect is woken to attention, since counteraction of some sort is evidently required. What is in such cases presented is a *standing out against*, against the normal and acceptable circumambient harmony, whether it be a discord or a greater menace generated by nature or some social situation.[41] Whatever it is may then be said to *objectify itself*, that is, to present itself in apparent isolation without a prior process of interpretative analysis, or conscious preselection from the complex of events. In this, and only in this way, does the conscious self, since it has no alternative when impact is instantaneous, make contact with reality directly and immediately, no filtering process coming between contact and its effect. This is the means, the only means, by which it can get to grips with forms of actuality, reach beyond the phenomenal world into what lies behind it. If disturbance is the concern, then, this has potentiality.

There are, however, problems in this, which in the present context can only be touched on briefly.[42] There is the question, for instance, of where the disturbance resides, in the external world, in the psyche or in both with a certain nexus between them, which is not so readily answered as might at once be supposed when interest turns on general effects rather than those that are personal, subjective and internal. For, if it is held to affect the instant recipient only, that can give no more than a partial indication of the nature of disturbance as it affects the whole, society at large. Furthermore, with that as the real concern in mind, it is plain that what is detected must be gathered in the form that it actually has without subjective interpretation, which would plainly render it unique to the individual. Such a matter as this, or rather what it involves, cannot be considered with any show of sufficiency in the present exposition. And thus, the possibility of developing *epochai*, to the end of excluding irrelevancies, now in a realistic as opposed to idealist terms,[43] is not fittingly discussed at the present juncture together with such conditions as must apply to their employment. A similar reservation applies to the question of quoral 'reference', when that term is used in the sense in which artists use it. Indeed, as we pass from rational to sensuous response, that is, from the subjective to the potentially general, so much new ground is broken that fresh thinking is required, which is more difficult to develop when the usages of the past, almost exclusively bound about cognitive reception, are present, if only verbally, to obscure the issue: that of direct relation to real or actual pressures and their effects considered generally.

Finally, the problem of disciplining discourse referred to such matters as these, in effect the finding of a more sensitive methodology than that devised to serve strictly cognitive ends, must receive consideration, if only superficially. The key, as has been said above, is to be found in negation, for the interest is not to elicit truth or to further explanation, it is to detect the forms of what is socially disturbing. In the last analysis discipline comprises the power to criticize statements which are either mistaken, thereby to generate confusion, or inadequate to the occasion. In fine, it is always negative and has its essential warrant, as Kant so shrewly observed "in guarding us against error".[44] And since error is more destructive in a social context where it has repercussive effects – *apūrva* in Pūrva Mīmāmsā – than in some verbal frame, where, with its exposure, falseness may be corrected, discipline in that sphere is more urgently required. Negation in formal logic, characterized by Bergson to delimit its application, as "asservation of the second order",[45] is, if that defines it correctly, brought into play only *after* a truth-claim has been made, it might fairly be described as 'logic of inconsistency'. And that is, of course, the traditional form of the logic of negation, which, despite the advice of Kant, has tended to be neglected or taken to be subsidiary to the more sublime attempt to establish absolute truth, notwithstanding that it is the motor of discipline in every field in which criticism is needed. It is admirable, then, is as far as it goes; but confined to the sphere of words, or rather of propositions, it scarcely goes far enough. If the interest then comprises communication referred to relations in actuality, its limitations are obvious. For the form of a sentence may be correct whilst its reference is questionable, as is so often the case when statements affect to be general.

Discounting at once that reference is always in some sense precarious when an ideal projection, for words do not exactly reflect conditions in actuality, it is to the point to remark that when they are suggestive and make no pretence to be truth-claims, they may have greater reach. But without developing that at once, or observing that suggestion is as subject to negation as is propositional statement, the problem is to devise an adequate means of checking statements that refer to external actualities, as exemplified in reaction to what is out of place. When as an expression 'external actualities' is introduced into discourse what it plainly refers to, though it may have other meanings, is some external complex and the effects that it produces. What then is out of place in the world is scarcely 'inconsistent', for that as a term appears to have sentential reference only. Rather is it 'incongruous', which is generally understood to mean 'not fitting into the place that it should properly occupy'. The interest is then to devise a 'logic of incongruity', which shall relate to externals, that is, to displacements and to their proper detection. This is not the occasion to discuss that proposal in depth and in terms of what it fully implies, for that is not simply done – though indices of what it involves have already been noticed with the mention of *epochai*, quoral reference and so on, and by implication training in sensitivity, rather like that to which artists are subjected. Sufficient, then, that although these points have not been discussed in detail, there could be an alternative which could be just as strict as those that are now deployed. For negation in whatever form is a very powerful instrument, as is seen in its

168

rational application, though in that of course it can only relate, as a check upon them, to factual findings and truth-claims, which it shows to be untenable. But they are not now the interest, which is rather deeper. Such a proposal as this may not be very convincing when so summarily expressed. But that is not a reason for rejecting it out of hand as mere irrationality, if the principle that informs it could ground its fuller development. Indeed, the attempt to develop it is justified as a task, a task that falls to philosophy, if only in the thought that discourse referred to realities, dynamic and unobservable, must ultimately find better and more sensitive procedures than those that are merely cognitive and powerless therefore to engage the problem that is presented in general evaluation.

*

This represents an attempt, preliminary though it may be, to deal with the problem of discipline, which is plainly a very real problem if the extra-cognitive is fittingly to be studied. It cannot be disregarded and must be considered more fully, either by those who recognize that it represents a real challenge or, as one proposal, in a book that will follow. Meanwhile, to return to the meaning of 'understanding' considered as an alternative to cognition. First, then, it would be absurd to hold that even in the meaning sustained no knowledge would accrue. Any grasp of relationships presumes that as an outcome. But to suppose that that would be knowledge of similar form or status as that acquired by means of analytic procedures would be to confuse the meaning of such a term as this with what is acceptable cognitively, or rather to claim that in principle all knowledge has the same form. When, however, its gathering does not involve analysis – the introduction of which supposes subjectivity, as also some distortion, implicit necessarily in interpretation – its character must be different. This may not be wholly the case for understanding as an *end*, inasmuch as any end in systematic enquiry presumes a grasp of relationships, regardless of how what is acquired is at last attained. But considered as a means of deeper penetration, understanding seems to have a wider range and compass, and so a further meaning. It constitutes a means of grasping what is confronted – in aspects if no more – in the external world, in the complex of real relations as distinguished from those which are, since they must be objectified, that is, set

169

apart, phenomenal and no more. Nor is such grasping as this justly considered exceptional, since it is a common experience, from which disciplined understanding differs only in the degree of control that is exerted. Intuition, one of its forms, has already been mentioned, and that is certainly not confined to scientific studies, inasmuch as it is even widely employed in personal inter-relationships, with regard to strength or weakness, quality or its converse. The power implicit in this is certainly mysterious, which is a reason why it should not be equated with understanding seen in such a form as this, as a systematic means of comprehending at least aspects of reality, and acquiring through that perhaps a better, more sensitive idea of the general in actuality, which, because it is external, has received but little study. Knowledge does accrue from any responsive engagement;[46] but what it now comprises is something rather more subtle, something that refers to what is not in strict sense observable, clearly to be objectified, though undoubtedly influential.

Rather than with intuition, which is transient and personal, such that it can never ground a systematic entry, it is then with strict cognition that understanding should be contrasted, and so as something less inflexible, less restricted to clear perception. The very approach of the last, which must involve a freezing of the dynamic thrust of becoming, plainly limits enquiry, in that it confines it to a relatively narrow, a separated world. Strictly speaking, for instance, it cannot make use of suggestion, since that is not regarded as a legitimate means of entry controlled by rational procedures. Indeed, suggestion seems to have its roots in insight, a 'sensing' of what has meaning when what is presented is not precisely definable, a 'sense' which makes no pretence to be under rational regulation, of what might be appropriate in the conditions prevailing. That should not be confused with opinion, which is essentially personal and which claims, however precariously, to be based on factual evidence and even supported by logic. It is something much more subtle, which knows itself to be tenuous. Yet is it a potent instrument which, when subjected to check, check on the part of those who are sensitive to its suggestiveness as related to what is occurring, cannot simply be dismissed as a subjective involvement, as private, immune from critique. The aim is not to be precise, if that is taken to imply definitive expression; it is to penetrate more deeply into what bears

170

on response to living actualities. But perhaps the greatest difference resides in what is under review, in what is to be understood, using that term more generously than cognitivists normally do. In cognition there is, in principle, an exact relation between the observable and the definable, whereas in understanding no such relation obtains, since neither is applicable. The interest is simply a better grasp of what cannot be so comprehended because it is not observable in strict or objective sense. Reference is to states, or better perhaps relations when the presented is dynamic, operative below the level of clear consciousness, whether those are movements in the physical world or the effects of such movements on the subconscious psyche. And since it is known, as a factor in this, that nine tenths of our responses to external stimulation do not reach into consciousness, it is, when conscious response is all to which attention is given, commonly assumed that those have no effect. But it must plainly be accepted, unless prejudice resists the idea of their presence, that they do exert an influence, even on conscious response; and that that, as bearing on life, cannot be disregarded. As then a cognitive approach is powerless to reach beyond phenomenal presentations, or cannot at least make judgments independent of observation,[47] inference must take other forms if this influence is to be studied. It well may be the case that the only means of procedure in this is detection of what is 'non-fitting' – 'displaced' as might be said – leaving the nature or form of what constitutes the real interest protected as it were by a Socratic ring of negations against unwarranted ideas asserted in respect of it, such that suggestions made about what it actually comprises are not only tenuous, but projected with greater refinement, as provisional only. Any positive projection must then involve the thought that it indeed is speculative, but a tentative view of essence to be adopted with caution and willingly subjected to disciplined quoral critique.

That this defines the nature of 'understanding' adequately is not for a moment pretended; and indeed, that such a concept should be defined precisely, in rational terms that is, is an improper demand; for logical procedures are manifestly impotent precisely to define what lies outside their reach. It is in part defined by a *via negativa*, by showing what it is *not*, which might be regarded as a form of indirect knowledge. Although it must then remain, as compared with definable terms, a rather vague conception, that does not

171

exclude it from consideration. For that would simply be to reject a method of approach for which the need is evident if matters now neglected are to be studied more fully. It represents a means whereby deeper thought may be given to what bears directly on life, and plainly has a wider reach than any that is possible through cognitive procedures, so that, tenuous though it may be, it should certainly be exploited. Referring, in support of its adoption as an entry, to other meanings that it receives in a dictionary definitions, those of 'rapport', 'agreement', 'harmony of sentiment' – though, as that has emotional overtones, 'of attitude' would be better – it relates to communication with other sensitive persons on another plane than that of rational concurrence.[48] It presumes some unity of thought on the part of those concerned with relations in actuality, with what has real bearing on life, to the end that more refined ideas of what those may comprise may justly be developed. The aim in the present context, then, is simply to bring the power – recognized, if dimly, as differing from cognition – that it places at the disposal of interested thinkers under better control, as a systematic procedure for deeper penetration. This failure to be definitive may leave something to be desired; but it is deplorable only to dedicated cognitivists. And since what they demand, apparently to exclusion, is that which is being challenged in the present thesis, there is no obligation to comply with their requirements, which would merely trap us once again in their limitations. As response in the deepest sense is simply not explicable unless in the crudest terms, a better understanding must come from a more sensitive entry. And this is especially so when response is made in the complex of involvement and loses its real meaning when viewed in isolation, or rather in isolation generated consciously by acts of objectification. Men are sensuous beings enmeshed in the process of becoming, which clearly cannot be defined, as aspects of being may be. In more concrete form, it is not really known why we respond to artistic form, to rhythm and what sustains it, though it is evident that we do. And that is cited to show that there is a recognizable problem, which is also widely recognized as one that cannot be answered by rationalistic means. To confront such vital problems as these with greater finesse and delicacy is then the justification for an alternative entry which shall be no less disciplined, here distinguished as 'understanding' without pretence that what it presumes has as yet been developed adequately.

Conclusion

No point is served by writing an extensive conclusion as if there were need to repeat what has already been said in the form of a summary. Purpose should be broader, rather to show how issues discussed have effects on philosophy as it is currently practiced. For as long, it is then contended, as philosophy clings to idealist presuppositions, and with them to restrictive procedures, its contribution is minimal.[1] For it is as though it assumes that carried to extremes verbal precision is potent to find correct, conclusive answers to real or vital problems, which abstract terms are not suited to engage in an adequate manner. 'Fact', for an example, as used by empiricist thinkers – idealists whatever they call themselves – is employed restrictively, since its reference is only to phenomenal presentations, when *factum* means surely 'what is the case', 'what is or has been done, not in thought but in reality', 'what is out there', 'the given'. It refers to that which conditions life and is only in part cognizable. The expression 'the facts of life' illustrates this clearly, since those refer to what is basic and fundamental, placed upon us by nature and not simply a reflection of the phenomenal world, even if features of that are included in what it refers to, its meaning as an expression. 'Truth' again, as that term is employed by logocentrics, has a strictly verbal meaning and does not refer directly to underlying reality, to the complex which conditions all that we do and which, as has frequently been observed, is not in strict sense knowable. In other meanings truth may have, essentially in its absence, a recognizable nature with external reference; but, as used by logicians, its import is strictly internal, ideal that is to say.

No doubt, it is wholly proper that scientists should use the term 'fact' in a technical sense and logicians 'truth' in the special significance that they elect to give to it. But that permits no claim that either term refers, as if in these special meanings their bearings were universal, beyond those spheres of interest with which scientists and logicians are properly concerned, phenomenal presentations and abstract relations respectively. The point that then emerges is that philosophy is certainly not tied to formal logic, even though a long tradition in the West has constantly held that it should be despite persistent sceptical protest and the not infrequent recourse to more basic natural logic. It is tied to the latter, of course, as all disciplined discourse must be; but that is a very different restraint from compulsion to obey rules that are rigid and inflexible and in that way inhibit the flow of thought unduly. Philosophy has a role to perform, if it is prepared to accept it, which demands that it shakes off these even absurd limitations which disallow attention to what should really concern it, what man as a sentient being enmeshed in an interrelative complex confronts and with which he must come to terms. And that presumes that the terms it employs shall be understood in those meanings which relate to vital, evaluational problems, in realistic and not in idealistic senses.

The words that have been selected for attention in this work comprise but a few of those to which more thorough thought should be given once it is accepted that a rationalistic approach has serious limitations, in that it cannot properly deal with real or basic issues. For it should never be forgotten that reality is dynamic, not something objectifiable. That means devising another approach which shall be more flexible and take these subtler matters properly into account. If the problem that falls to philosophy is justly seen as that of general evaluation, of the values, more concretely, by which men most sensibly live,[2] as sensuous no less than as rationalizing beings, then philosophy is obliged to consider its assumptions with rather greater acumen and in all their implications. For to deal with questions of value, of priorities of importance, constitutes a task which is unique to that discipline, since it cannot be undertaken by science in any form, that is, by any cognitively oriented procedure. But such has been the dominant interest in the West, effectively since Parmenides elected for Being against the Becoming of Heraclitus, the stress has been exclusively on cognitive enquiry. This was much strengthened later by the determination of Christian theologians to establish absolute truth – in respect of the faith, of course, and not of the physical world, which was a later development. Effectively all terms in use relate to this primary interest and have cognitive meanings accordingly, as if there were no others. Those plainly exist and are revealed in ordinary language, to indicate that there are more than rational needs and requirements. If this is not entirely true of classical antiquity, in which scepticism arose whenever rational attitudes were too strongly asserted, it is certainly true of modern times when cognition and explanation afford the only conceivable ends, to the point where it is even believed that science has no limits and will in time leave nothing whatever unexplained.[3] That there is much beyond its reach must be plain to a little thought; and, as is more significant, that which has that character seems to have greater importance, since it bears directly on life, on man's relation to the world in and through which he acts. That such relations can be seen in an intellectual sense is sufficiently obvious, inasmuch as hitherto no other has been envisaged or has enjoyed a similar standing. That they are so seen, however, leads to misrepresentation, which on the surface seems to be plausible, is by contrast seldom noticed. For it seems that that set is pre-eminent, and so for two reasons is taken to be immune from serious questioning: one, that intellectual power is unique to man, or at least is assumed to be so; and two, it is with that that he aspires to dominion over nature, even other men. That is not the path, however, that leads to real fulfilment in life, since, as materialistic, it leaves many vital interests, broadly those called 'spiritual', largely out of account, and thus generates a malaise which tends to produce disturbing consequences. "The sheep look up and are not fed"; and though life becomes more comfortable, even more luxurious, something is missing when the last is in this way disregarded, as other than rationalizable.

Words are tools with which ideas are expressed. If then they are used insensitively, to serve a narrow interest – material, for all vaunted claims "to pierce the veil of truth"[4] – ideas themselves are insensitive and fail to engage real issues. To take the basic word 'meaning', basic because it refers to what really counts in life, even when it is given a cognitive significance, as if it referred to nothing more than explanatory findings or syntactical correlations, even that has been narrowed. 'Assertoric', 'informational', 'factual', 'descriptive' and 'declaratory' meanings – not to mention those applied in formal logic, 'apodeictic', 'extensional', 'connotative', and so on – all have such an import; although 'expressive meaning', as in poetry and rhetoric, permitted to cover that which the others cannot include, seems to afford an exception, if not necessarily so.[5] The word, however, basically means what signifies in life, as in the expression "what is the meaning of life?", which plainly poses a question that cannot be answered cognitively. Meaning in this basic sense, as apart from such vague questions, is not unrelated to *influence*, to what conditions life and gives it the forms that it has, to that which effects or better has affects upon us. Inasmuch as all action is purposive, and as counteraction it is undoubtedly so, to constitute adjustment to ever-changing conditions, influence determines everything we do, particularly in response to external stimulation. That is the very basis of life and is largely beyond our control, our conscious control that is, or at least our power of determining the forms that it may take, since external stimulation cannot as such be detected, for it only reaches consciousness after a filtering process. Influence is meaningful from whatever source is emanates, indeed is the essence of meaningfulness, since it carries consequences that cannot be disregarded if balance, psychic and physical, is to be sustained.

If meaning is understood in such a sense as this, all its cognitive imports fall into second place; and they in any case comprise a very small part of response, albeit it is that to which current thought is turned almost to exclusion as it has rational form. It is surely time, then, since it is so significant, that deeper thought be given to influence in this sense, if only for the reason that its bearing on life is so great. And once we grant that this is so, the whole vocabulary we employ in philosophical discourse, which has hitherto failed to relate the terms it commonly uses to this pervasive pressure, has to be subjected to re-examination. For that which stimulates response, change occurring externally, and the process which allows us to receive its effects in a form which is acceptable to consciousness, are not only the causes that lie behind our acts, they

176

are, seen realistically, conditions that oblige to see ourselves, our place in nature, at least a little more sensibly. We are beings, or modes of being, in the world of actuality, not independent of it, free from its ceaseless influence; and, as that is understood, its implications must follow. All terms in serious thought, or thought directed towards real problems, acquire their essential meanings only in as far as this salient point is grasped; for otherwise they are metaphors, metaphors unrecognized for what they really are. *Reality* must refer to that with which we are really confronted in the actual process of living, and as such it has little relation to verbal definitions, to what 'objective existence' is usually taken to mean. *Sensation* is wrongly regarded as a process which is cognizable, as "consciousness of perceiving" as it is quaintly defined, as if all response were conscious and so potentially knowable. In its basic meaning the *subject* is not the thinking self, as it is latterly taken to be, but the recipient of influences brought to bear upon him by external pressures, from which he cannot escape into a world fo abstractions fed by perceptions of phenomena, as if that were all he confronted. *Mind*, without elaboration, since it is active on more than one plane of response to external pressures, is certainly other than intellect and is confused with that at penalty, since that can only lead to blindness in respect of the nature of sensation as the impetus of action. As for *ethics* and *understanding*, their meanings must be distinguished from those which have so far obscured them that what they signify for life and its fuller understanding through a grasp of what informs it have largely been lost to view. In short, the reference of all terms that bear on serious thinking about fundamental problems must be clarified if those are to be given proper attention, by philosophers specifically, or those among them ready to grant that their role is one external to the province of cognitive science.

Though it may appear to be just that, the interest in this treatise is not in strict sense 'analytic', when analytic philosophy appears to be devoted to the idea that terms should have one, a definitive, meaning only. For there is no suggestion that the meanings here projected have universal reference, since that would be improper, indeed but a further form of analytic philosophy. Properly, words are only defined in terms of some declared interest; and, if that is the most important in a philosophical sense, it certainly does not authorize claims to universality. Thus, if logicians wish to use 'subject' in the sense of *hypokeīmenon* as employed by their founding father, that is as it may be. The only proviso then is that, just as any claim to universal bearing is relinquished here, so should it be abandoned in other fields of enquiry, formal logic in this case. As a technical usage, though that is a rather poor translation of what Aristotle meant – 'that of which something is to be said' – it is suitably retained, as is 'fact' in science. For, if it is extended to embrace the knower – redundantly, for 'the thinking self' was the expression employed for him prior to Kant and Fichte – unhappy ambiguity can be the only outcome. Other terms, conversely, 'sensation', 'mind' and 'ethics', which have hitherto been taken as more or less synonymous with 'perception', 'intellect', and 'moral philosophy' have rather different character, since their meanings are distinctive, in that they refer to distinctive spheres of interest. And plainly the last refers to a specific field of enquiry, which is of such importance that its neglect in its own terms even amounts to a scandal.

The criterion in discourse making any pretence to be disciplined is always apt definition, without which there must be confusion. But 'apt' itself must mean 'appropriate in conditions', given in effect by what is under study. If that is verbal precision, then 'truth', as noted above, is properly defined as the 'correct correlation of words',[6] and not, unless with deplorable looseness, as 'correspondence with external actuality'. If that is some form of cognition, though that is the province of science, then 'fact' must be referred to phenomenal presentations, in which case it is improperly used if it is assumed *in that sense* to refer to underlying reality. If that is evaluation, the problem unique to philosophy, then the terms employed in discourse must have appropriate meanings. And finally, if the last is to be regarded as the essential concern of philosophy, then the terms it uses must be seen in the meanings that such a study demands. For, as matters now stand, terminology is so far from being suited to the interest here sustained – general evaluation, which in practice means ethics – that it is in effect impossible to make any meaningful statement which is not ambiguous or, worse, misunderstood. Philosophy prides itself on securing precise definitions, without attending apparently, since they are essentially formal, to their bearing on vital discourse. Accordingly, it finds itself lost in a verbal forest, from which, without real purpose, that is, a clear sense of direction, it thrashes around in a vain attempt to see which way to turn, the path that is open to it if it stops to take its bearings. Or abandoning metaphor, which scarcely makes for clarity, the point is is it ready to give deeper thought to the manner in which it might contribute by studying certain problems that cry out for attention, attention that it is peculiarly qualified to give? Using words correctly is but a needed preliminary. In want of that, however, little can be done. For all remains in confusion, hopeless ambiguity, which inhibits any thinking directed towards real problems. It is then such problems as those that have to be tackled sensitively, equipped, as anglers are equipped with the appropriate lures, with a vocabulary which allows of serious thought on these matters.

Comment on the Text

A philosophical critic makes comment to the effect that I use standard terms of many meanings in philosophy without defining those in which I employ them. Whether this is wholly just and whether it would not involve me in complex definitions which would detract from the main theme, I will not discuss, electing rather to give brief definitions of how I use the terms he considered insufficiently defined. These terms are:

1) *Idealism*

   For me that means simply that approach which takes start from the knowing self and is primarily concerned with the nature or form of ideas present in the intellect, to the point of contending that reality is dependent for its existence on what is thought about it.

2) *Realism*

   I hold, though this is not the idea commonly held about it in a tradition which is as idealistic as that of the West, that it is that approach which gives priority to that which is confronted in life (or actuality), the reality in which we are enmeshed ('encompassed' in Jasper's language). Of course, we form ideas about it in the intellect, but those in the nature of the case can make no pretence to precision and are necessarily speculative.

3) *Rationalism*

   With this term I mean what Derrida so scornfully calls 'logocentrism', that is, a preoccupation with absolute truth, in which sense it is to be distinguished from 'reasoning', of which it is but a 'class'. It is an approach essentially disciplined by formal logic rather than by existential limitations, which may be interpreted as conditioning human needs.

4) *Materialism*

I regard this as a doctrine which in extreme form holds that nothing but matter in motion exists, and that that is potentially measurable. In that form it effectively denies the existence of undetectable psychical factors. In less extreme forms it is aligned – regardless of the etymon of that term – with the physical or, yet more crudely, with nature or the natural, which plainly comprises all that there is, not excluding psychical events. The final barbarism is to equate it with realism, thus to render that term unusable in any significant sense. It is the crudest of doctrines, which can only be held by those who believe that the only respectable pursuit is cognition, which will given time find answers to all presented problems.

5) *Determinism*

This is clearly related to materialism and could scarcely exist without it. That every effect has a cause (or rather causes) is doubtless correct. But from that it does not follow that every cause is material, and so potentially knowable. Indeed, the evidence now available seems to show that reality is more subtle and complex than this doctrine supposes and that many changes in it, particularly those that are psychical or sub-consciously mediated, are quite beyond determination.

6) *Atomism*

As apart from signifying that which is not divisible, atomism has had a number of different meanings throughout the course of history, culminating in that employed by chemists. As the atom can now be split, all ideas that take it to be ultimate are effectively outdated, logical atomism among them.

7) *Holism*

This term, which has two meanings, an earlier and a later, is frequently used in the text, which shows the earlier meaning to be a limited idea of it. It refers, as is now widely accepted (by scientists at least, if not by philosophers) to the indivisible, interrelative whole of dynamic becoming, which is not confined to organic structures, but embraces every aspect of nature.

Though this term was not mentioned by the critic, it is fittingly included.

8) *Spirituality*

Spirit, in this text, is taken to be immanent in nature (or vitality) and *not* transcendent of it, as traditional dichotomies have held it to be. It refers to all that, essentially responsiveness, which is extra-material and so resistant to cognitive engagement.

If these are not the commonly accepted definitions of these terms, the reason is that my earliest training in philosophy took place in China, so that my thought is conditioned by Chinese presuppositions, which may render it distinctive ("outside the mainstream of current thinking"). I do not pretend to be a sinologist, but I do believe that some point is served by bringing Chinese presuppositions – related to ethics rather than to cognition – to bear on Western thinking. Put crudely, should the criterion be truth – or for science reliable knowledge, which can only be material – or should it be human need, considered in its most basic or general sense? Of course, there is no absolute separation; but disciplined stress on the latter cannot be regarded as misplaced when it has tended to be neglected, or misunderstood with a rationalist, idealist approach, in modern philosophy. Inasmuch as we work with them we can scarcely detect the limitations imposed by our own presuppositions, so that to view them from outside may serve some purpose, if only as permitting a more flexible approach to real or vital problems, among them the criterion which really warrants philosophical or extra-cognitive thinking. And that, I repeat, is not irrefragable truth but human need in the deepest sense.

A Further Note

A common defensive stance adopted by rationalists is to argue that social conditions have actually improved – for instance, the indignity of poverty has been eliminated – and that that constitutes a spiritual advance with its causal base in rational procedures. This is irrefutable; but it fails to take account of the decay of sensitivity which has accompanied material advance. Moreover, that the weakening of or contempt for social norms, aided by rationalism, which disregards what cannot be rationalized, may have effects which threaten the future of society, is something to which it gives little thought. It is a question, then, of whether the values of rationalism are to be promoted at expense of social balance; in other words, whether the interests of relatively few should count for more than those of society at large. Materialism has a superficial attraction; spiritual needs are rather deeper and ultimately conduce to greater fulfilment.

Notes

Introduction

1. Chuang Chou, *Chuang Tzü* (tr. London, 1889), ch. XXVI.
2. The source of this comment has not been recovered as no note was taken at the time of reading.
3. Challenge in this form is strictly verbal and so rare as to have little bearing on vital interests. Hence the importance given to it by Russell and others is misplaced.
4. Searle, as reported in Magee, *Men of Ideas* (London, 1978), 187.
5. This is a fitting usage because the term 'assent', as used by Newman, carries quite a different meaning. One 'assents' to a logical proposition, one 'accepts' a faith, even blindly, as did Tertullian when he declared: "credo quia absurdum est".
6. Urban, *Beyond Realism and Idealism* (London, 1949), 241.
7. Russell, *Mysticism* and *Logic* (1918, 1954), 73.
8. Capra, *The Tao of Physics* (London, 1975, 1984), 318.
9. Bradley, *Appearance and Reality* (London, 1893), 363 ff.
10. Strictly speaking, 'rationalism' should be regarded as a subclass of the class 'reasoning'.

Chapter One

1. The Upanishads are said to have derived their name from a sage who propounded its doctrines about 800 BC. The word *māyā* does not refer to reality as opposed to appearance, but to the veil that hides the

former from us. *Tao*, as the power that lies behind appearances, may be an even earlier insight, long predating notice of it in writing, just as the notion of *māyā* may be older than this Upanishad.

2. Chuang Chou, op. cit. ch. II.

3. Bradley, *Principles of Logic* (Oxford, 1882, 1922), I, 114, in citing which it is important to note that that was not only that of which we are *conscious*.

4. Russell, op. cit. (1954), 80. Nor is there call for further comment unless it should be that these prejudices have been planted in the 'masses' in large part by idealist philosophers.

5. Kant, *Critique of Pure Reason* (1781, tr. London, 1929, 1933), 27.

6. This is said of Derrida in respect of his alleged 'literary pre-occupation'. But it did not result in the denial of a hearing; but then a prejudice in favour of logocentrism has never been so deep-seated in France as it has in England.

7. Quinton, *The Nature of Things* (London, 1973), 120.

8. Whilst it is evident that Parmenides developed the concept of Being in opposition to the Becoming of Heraclitus and claimed that to think at all we must postulate something which *is*, his idea of Being without differentiation as distinct from the particularity of individual appearances does not consort with later ideas of Being as knowable. He is doubtfully therefore the father of cognitivism, which deals with the phenomenal or 'factual' world. Kirk & Raven, *The Presocratic Philosophers* (Cambridge, 1971), 266.

9. It is not so much perhaps that it has been brushed aside as that, despite a vague recognition of it, there is a grim determination to maintain that all is in principle explicable. See Quine, *Philosophy of Logic* (New York, 1970), 68; Haack, *Philosophy of Logics* (Cambridge, 1978), 164 – with reason provided by Kagey, *The Growth of Bradley's Logic* (New York, 1931), 57, who questioned this approach.

10. Popper, *Open Society and its Enemies* (London, 1952), II, 352, where he properly distinguishes the two meanings of this term.

11. The confusion generated in the West with the claim that such Forms alone were real has been immense, since it has more than any other thesis rendered the intellect *sui generis*, as if above nature and has thus produced the mind-matter dichotomy with its pernicious progeny, idealist individualism.

12. *Natura naturans* is in effect the Chinese *tao* and the Heraclitan *logos*, neither of which presupposes a Godhead, though that creative power was divine in the sense that it was other than human. It was natural, that is to say, other than supernatural; and it could be that even some scholastics viewed it in that way, as did Bruno.

13. The verb *legein* has three distinct meanings: 1) to lie down; 2) to put

together, to gather with later derivatives, to count or to reckon; 3) to speak, to say, with several later kindred meanings. *Logos*, its nounal form, has at least twenty, one of which is *rapport*. How these different meanings arose, if *legein* was indeed one word, is obscure, but there is no doubt that, as used by Heraclitus, *logos* derives from the second meaning of *legein*. Nature acts to secure harmony in a continuous process. For Cusanus God was the harmoning power ("God makes a bond among them all") and the Stoic *logos spermātikos* seems to have similar associations. Therefore, to confine attention to the last of these three meanings is not only to misinterpret Heraclitus but even the Johannine Gospel, and to place the idea of creativity on an intellectual plane, as if that alone had significance. Kirk & Raven, op. cit (1971), 188, correct Kahn, *The Art and Thought of Heraclitus* (Cambridge, 1979), 130, on his interpretation of Fr. XXXVI.

14. It is possible to conceive of three spheres of interest: the supra-empiric, the empiric and the infra-empiric, of which the first concerns theology, the second science and the third a meaningful philosophy, making some attempt to deal with what science cannot.

15. Though a pragmatist, Peirce, *Collected Papers* (Cambridge, Mass, 1935), VI, 47 ff, did not scruple to take note of this factor, in an article "The Doctrine of Necessity", published in *The Monist* (1872).

16. Dubious generalization is instanced in formal logic's claim to have universal bearing on thought, as if that were always clearly conscious and had the characteristics of rationalistic thinking.

17. Nor is this remarkable when they can only be viewed in relative isolation by directing charges through slits or in static form by means of photographs when what is in fact confronted is a complex of interrelationships, "between elements whose meanings are wholly different from their relationships to the whole", Stapp, *Phys. Review* (1971), 1303.

18. That Honderich, *A Theory of Determinism* (Oxford, 1988), claims that that determinism applies at subatomic levels, still does not establish that determinism operates universally, since it depends on regularities which are not apparent at such levels.

19. That nature conforms to some sort of ordering and does not sink into chaos is sufficiently obvious. Indeed, it is fairly regarded as a structure constantly tending, through movements off-centre, to dynamic equipoise. That this process is so complex that it cannot be grasped by the categorizing intellect does not mean that that is not the case but simply that it cannot be known in the actual form that it has.

20. Carnap, *The Logical Structure of the World* (1928, tr. London, 1967), 290, affords the classic example of this over-confident stance.

21. An idealist ontology cannot be other than subjective, an intellectual or rationalized view of the world projected on to it so to say.

22. The term 'holism' was originally coined by Smuts in his *Holism and Evolution* (London, 1926), when its meaning was rather different from that accepted today. Tied to the cognitive tradition, his whole was regarded as a knowable 'object' rather than the whole which constitutes nature.

23. Many texts sustain this doctrine, but at once it is enough if two are cited: Bohm, *Wholeness and the Implicate Order* (London, 1981) and Lovelock, *Gaia* (Oxford, 1979). Inasmuch as findings in subatomic physics are highly speculative whereas those in biochemistry are tolerably well established, the second of these texts is more convincing.

24. Inasmuch as 90% of our responses to stimulation are mediated subconsciously, involvement is indeed the normal condition of life. Everyone has in this way to adjust to the environment simply to sustain his balance in it. Detachment by comparison is relatively rare and only maintained with considerable difficulty.

25. Harris, *The Foundations of Metaphysics in Science* (London, 1965), 17, 37, affords a sufficient comment on Russell's logical atomism.

26. The Unity of Science Movement, otherwise known as Logical Positivism, was one developed in Vienna from 1924. It enjoyed a wide influence for some twenty years but is now more or less defunct, since it was regarded by scientists as a philosophical imposition on something very much more complex.

27. Capra, op. cit (1975), 307.

28. Disdain for extra-European thought, because it is not rooted in logocentrism, has characterized Western thinking, dismissing it out of hand for that reason and leaving it to specialists, to whose studies philosophers pay little attention. Indeed, it is assumed to be exotic, poetic and undisciplined, though in fact different criteria are observed.

29. Whyte, *The Unitary Principle* (London, 1949), 28 et passim, develops this theme in a sadly neglected text.

30. 'Proposal' is not a true translation of Leibniz's *hypothèse* as used in his correspondence with Arnauld (30 April 1687), but that is what it amounts to: "an idea that is at least possible". It does not pretend to state a truth. Hypotheses seem to be all that are available when interest is referred to what cannot in strictness be proven.

31. Hegel, *The Phenomenology of Spirit* (1807, tr. New York, 1975), exact citation not recovered, but the idea is echoed throughout the work.

32. Brown, *Laws of Form* (London, 1969), 105, expresses man's predicament as he aspires to *know* what he confronts when he himself is a mode of it.

33. Reference is to the cult of the autonomous self, which, though in principle it sustains self-discipline, in practice leads to self-assertion,

aggression, romanticism in artistry and a number of other pernicious notions.

34. Marcel, in the title of his book, *Positions et approches concrètes du mystère ontologique* (Paris, 1949), in which its implications are developed.

35. Though science may and indeed must evaluate its own findings, as to whether they are just, it cannot by reason of the approach it adopts, if only in claiming value-neutrality, enter the field of general evaluation. The effects of its discoveries on the body social must be judged externally and by wholly different procedures. This responsibility properly falls to philosophy, working with a distinctive pre-suppositional set.

36. The problem this presumes will be considered in Chapter VI.

37. The last of these three concerns, which is a fitting subject for philosophical attention, is considered by Scheler, *The Nature of Sympathy* (1923, tr. London, 1954).

Chapter Two

1. Though *perceptio* was used for 'perception' in classical Latin, the word used for 'sensation' was *sensus*, with both physical and psychical meanings. Lucretius introduced the term *sensilis*, meaning 'sensitive', much as Milton introduced 'sensuous', to avoid the associations of 'sensual'. Whether by this he referred to subconscious response, since 'sensual' plainly refers to consciousness of concupiscent character, is uncertain. But 'sensuous' can fairly be taken to have that more sensitive import, in which sense it will be understood in this text.

2. It need scarcely be noted that the Latin *factum* means 'what is done', 'what is the case', not primarily in respect of what is thought, discerned by the intellect, but in actuality. Empiricism has purloined this term to the point where its use refers only to what is phenomenally presented. In common and legal use, however, it rather refers to realities. Broad, *Science: Its Method and Philosophy* (London, 1950), 38.

3. Since this notion was first projected with the James-Lange theory (1884–1886) and modified by the Cannon-Bard theory (1919–1924), it has been much refined by a series of thinkers, Young, Arnold, Hebb, Plutchik, and others.

4. Wundt. *Principles of Psychology* (1874, tr. London, 1904), 244 ff., though in fairness the ambiguity of the term 'sense', and so 'sensation' as referring to the organs through which we become aware of stimulant pressures, in part excuses this. For Wundt was not an

idealist.

5. Organisms such as protozoans or even multi-cellular forms such as porifera have such elementary nervous systems that eyes and other organs of perception are not given to them. Thus it was not until more fully developed animals emerged that perception played a role in their lives. Tropism cannot be regarded as perceptual, if that means 'having the power to seize thoroughly'.

6. Gregory, *Concepts and Mechanisms of Perceptions* (London, 1974), 585, and elsewhere in his writings.

7. This is now well recognized; but it is of interest to note that Brentano, *Psychology from an Empiricist Standpoint* (1874, tr. London, 1973), 104 n, holds that the first 'might be' the case.

8. This matter is dealt with at some length in Chapter III, with base in projections made many years ago, by Lewis, *The Physical Basis of Mind* (New York, 1897), 365, and is now widely accepted.

9. An inference from observed data is, of course, possible and has logical status. An inference in respect of what is not in strictness observable may also be made, though it cannot claim that status. To this it might be added that such inferences are not without grounding in experimentation, as those which are drawn in Gestalt psychology, by Wertheimer, Kohler, Koffka and others, whose works are readily available. The idea of *Gestaltqualität* goes back to Ehrenfels (1897).

10. Hirst, *The Problems of Perception* (London, 1959), 56.

11. McCullough, in private conversation (1954), cited because of his influence on my thinking, promulgating a finding since confirmed by many neurologists.

12. It is now widely recognized that response to stimulation, even on subconscious levels, involves the psyche, which is certainly not limited to conscious response. Indeed, preconscious response takes most subtle and delicate forms and is implicit in courtesy, response to rhythmic presentations, and so on.

13. Koestler, *The Act of Creation* (London, 1964), 552 et passim.

14. Kekulé's sudden insight did not come to him without prior mulling over his problem. But anyone who writes has similar experiences which seem to come out of the blue, whilst waking, whilst walking, whilst in one's bath (e.g., Archimedes); and the problem is to catch them in the forms in which they present themselves.

15. Accepting that 90% of our responses to stimuli are mediated subconsciously, that means that 10% are received consciously. That all of those presume clear consciousness is a mistaken idea, since only a small proportion of that 10%, supposing partial detachment from the process of becoming, has that character. As we, though aware, are normally involved in that process, our responses tend to be dim rather than clear, in that we must respond continuously.

16. This view is now almost archaic, a remnant of the mind-matter dichotomy, and no longer tenable. But inasmuch as men have developed keener psychical powers, such that their sensuous responses have become more delicate and richer, to ground not only courtesy and artistry but to allow of a generalized culture when they are not inhibited by intellectualism, effectively replacing sensitivity.

17. With so strong a bias in favour of intellectuality, as that alone which is meaningful, other aspects of response have tended to be neglected (or intellectualized). One of the more vicious effects of this has been to generate a division between those with intellectual powers and those in whom they are less developed, which a cult of democracy, the pretence that all are equally endowed, does not resolve but rather aggravates. Sensitivity is potentially universal, intellectualism is not.

18. If we consider earlier Egyptian thinking – later thought was highly personalized – we see that its tone was essentially ethical. Nor is this remarkable when, with the formation of larger groups calling for the exercise of authority, questions of justice and responsibility arose. This was also the case in ancient China. Nor should the Code of Hammurabi or the Laws of Manu be forgotten. See Simpson, *The Literature of Ancient Egypt* (New Haven (1972), Chêng Wing-tsit, Radhakrishnan and Frankfurt.

19. Whether, using the expression a 'rational animal', Aristotle placed the stress on rationality or animality is a point of some interest. The first is the usual interpretation, to give ground to intellectuality. But Aristotle was as much a naturalist as a metaphysician, and that must carry some weight when this question is raised.

20. Marco Polo, James Cook, David Livingstone, Arthur Grimble and Wilfred Thesiger, seem to confirm this in their memoirs.

21. Stankiewicz, *Aspects of Political Theory* (London, 1976), 124, makes the significant point that laws are based on norms and do not create them. This book merits greater attention than it is normally given.

22. Notwithstanding its political implication, *T'ien-ming* (The Mandate of Heaven) imposed a discipline on the governing classes in China. Its Taoist form, *T'ien-li*, might render it more acceptable to modern man, in that Nature rather than Heaven is the disciplining force, as advocated by Wang Pi.

23. Stirner, *The Ego and its Own* (1845) represents, under idealism in its extreme form, that doctrine carried to its limits.

24. Inasmuch as the standards or norms of the higher classes were sensuous and potentially generalizable, as contrasted with intellectual ideas of value, they were a refining force on society, promoting refinement, courtesy, honour and taste. To replace them with implicit subjective self-aggrandizement is to destroy the goose that lays the golden egg, to delimit the growth of culture when possibilities have never been

greater in economic and other senses.

25. All ideas of human potentiality are not quite so starry-eyed as those of liberal idealists. Said Hsün Ch'ing, *Hsün Tzu* (tr. New York, 1967), ch. 23: "Left to himself man works for evil; not because he desires evil, but because his passions are stronger than his powers of controlling them... Therefore..." That the power to think produces evil no less than good is often forgotten by idealists urging the doctrine of the autonomous individual.

26. That acceptance of responsibility presumes a deliberative act is a limited idea, since its exercise is largely impersonal. The difference between the ideas of Romero and Bowne is interesting in showing the difference of attitude prevalent in their respective cultural heritages.

27. 'Rational' and 'reasonable' have a common root in *ratio*, which originally meant 'proportion'. Initially, no doubt, this was sensed, and only later recorded and analysed. The word retains its earlier meaning when related to 'prudence', 'balance', 'fairness' or 'common sense', a 'sense of proportion apt to the occasion'.

28. Jaspers, *Way of Wisdom* (New Haven, 1951, 1975), 59, uses this expression.

29. A sense datum is quite plainly a percept, for otherwise it could not be registered consciously, designated 'red' or whatever is predicated of it. Sense data theorists, steeped in a cognitive tradition, could only interpret 'sensing' in this way, as conscious response, in effect exploiting its ambiguity, though in fact even conscious impression is initially complex and interrelative.

30. Liebniz, *Nouveaux Essais* (1701, 1765, 1916), 529 ff, 552 ff, promulgated this theory, though he had used the term in an untitled manuscript as early as 1680. This conception undoubtedly influenced Popper, although he did not acknowledge it in any of his published works.

31. Very broadly, these may be distinguished as knowing and acting, as involvement with thought and involvement with action, which is precise in quite a different sense.

32. Husserl, *Ideas* (1913, tr. London, 1931), by dismissing psychologism in favour of pure thought, effectively limits philosophy to metaphysics, the study of essences, and thereby deprives it of any pragmatic or ethical meaning, though Heidegger and Merleau-Ponty later developed phenomenology in rather different forms.

33. Artistic creativity constitutes a trial-and-error process, in which the trial must be spontaneous and in which the error involves a critical standing back. Both involve the broad envisaging of an ultimate compositional whole, though the second plainly supposes a clearer idea of what it should be.

34. Merleau-Ponty, *La Phénoménologie de la Perception* (Paris, 1945), 69, speaks of 'unconceptualized perception', which is certainly a more precise expression, adding that the prereflective world must not be equated with the subconscious sphere of response.

35. As with many Greek words, *epistēmē* underwent some changes of meaning in later classical times, such that when Ferrier introduced the term into modern philosophy (1854) he applied its later meaning, which had in effect replaced that of *gnōsis*, which in a curious perversion came to refer to esoteric knowledge.

36. If philosophy aspires to be influential, then it must recognize that it carries a responsibility, not to philosophers as such but to society. Right thinking has precisely this meaning. Rorty, *Philosophy and the Mirror of Nature* (Princeton, 1980, 61, 262), speaks well on this question. But that hermeneutics is the answer is rather doubtful.

Chapter Three

1. This distinction goes back to Aristotle, whence it came through Arabic thinkers to the Scholastics, notably William d'Auvergne and subsequently Thomas Aquinas, who developed a Christian version of it in the *Summa Theologica*, Part I, Q LXXIX.

2. Criticism, often of a rather biassed character, arose even in Descartes' lifetime, notably in Holland. Later it became sharper with Leibniz, who (op. cit. (1701, 1765, 1916), IV, vii, 7) expressed profound disagreement with certain aspects of his thinking.

3. Hamilton, *Lectures on Metaphysics and Logic* (Edinburgh, 1866), I, 5.

4. *Hsing* is justly translated as 'nature', when it has, as in Western languages, a dual meaning. It refers at once to all that there is and to the characteristics of any species in it. Thus *ma-hsing* means 'horsiness', *jên-hsing* 'humanness' ('humanity' has a slightly different character). One of the characteristics of man is his power to think, which is a gift producing two effects. It is mentioned here as a doctrine that corrects Western dualism, in that duality lies in thought itself, productive both of good and evil. This doctrine, which runs through Chinese thinking, was first promulgated in the *Analects*, Ch. V, but in that case rather superficially.

5. Languages are differently constituted, as is shown by Whorf, *Language, Thought and Reality* (Boston, 1956), or as in Chinese. All, however, are potent to express any idea that appertains to living.

6. Notwithstanding the efforts of formal logicians to engage tensed or suggestive expression, as in Temporal or Fuzzy Logic, it is evident that that cannot be done without clumsy circumlocutions, which are never applied in ordinary language. Prior and Zadeh show this.

7. Russell, *Wisdom of the West* (London, 1959), 303.
8. A discussion at the Aristotelian Society (1988) lead to the conclusion that little could be said that did not depend on a posteriori thinking. That A is A and is not B is effectively its limit. Even Kant's Transcendental Analytic depends on prior experience of space and time.
9. Logic's claim to be a science clearly rests on the idea that it accords knowledge. But that is necessarily confined to abstract or verbal relations. For as soon as a word is referred to actualities it ceases to have a precise and unchanging meaning. Grass is only green under certain conditions and so on through innumerable examples.
10. Lichtheim, *Lukács* (London, 1970), 60.
11. What might be called the cult of the knowing self, as distinguished from that of the immortal soul, seems to have had its origin in Locke, who predated the Romantic Movement by almost a century, but whose philosophy in some sense grounded it. It is of interest then to remark that it was a divisive force which effectively separated the sheep from the goats, the knowledgeable and the highly emotive from the 'lumpen' mass. Classicism by its appeal in artistry to the senses, as opposed to intellectual powers, was conversely a uniting force in all of its value aspects. Baroque was not romantic, eclecticism was.
12. This relates to what was said in Note II. 14, to confirm that the application of rational powers comes after intuition. This point was clearly made by Kant, following Leibniz, if not in the terms projected here.
13. To classical thinking value in artistry properly resides in receptivity, wherein alone it is general and not confined to the artist, who is in this sense simply an instrument for its attainment. It is assumed that all men are potentially sensitive, whereas intellectual powers or excessive sensibility are gifts enjoyed by but few. Thus is romanticism a divisive force, which effectively undermines a culture. Focillon, *Vie des Formes* (Paris, 1943, 1955), 51, makes this point.
14. De Waelhens, *Diogenes V* (1954), 44, interpreting Kierkegaard's 'aesthetic', makes this superb statement: "There is no *me* in aesthetic existence, which is immersion and dispersion in the momentary immediate: there is no *me* in ethical existence, which is simply conformity with the universal of the law".
15. It seems that *man* (or *ma*) originally meant 'inwardness', the self as opposed to the world, from which it is not too far-fetched to suggest that the English word 'man' and its Teutonic equivalents are derived from a very early form of Aryan, which, for reasons unknown, became *gham, cham, ham* and *hom* in other later forms of it.
16. For instance, the Greek *menos* is translated 'spirit' and doubtless similar ideas attached to it in kindred forms. It is of interest that the Chinese *hsin* (Rad 61) has the meanings of 'heart', 'mind', 'will' and so

on, to suggest a similar character; and we ourselves speak of 'heart-ache', 'stout-heartedness', which are spiritual states.

17. It is evident that empiricist psychologists lack the power of exploring subconscious states, but all psychologists are not so trapped. Dixon, *Preconscious Processing* (New York, 1981), 187, even talks of methodological limitations that have to be overcome.

18. Berlin, *Against the Current* (London, 1979), 351.

19. Jaynes, *The Origin of Consciousness and the Breakdown of the Bicameral Mind* (Boston, 1976), may be speculative and rather refer to self-consciousness; but it tends to confirm that intellectuality was the product of an evolutionary process rather than something outside nature and in that sense divorced from it.

20. Apart from Chinese sources of this doctrine, it may be noted that it was not unknown in early Greek thinking, as with Anaximenes and Diogenes of Apollonia.

21. *Vāc* is a Sanskrit word, occuring in the Vedas as a goddess to whom praises were sung. Powers not unlike those attributed to *logos* were ascribed to her (or to it in impersonal meaning), as the force behind all action. "I hold together all existence". Curiously, it later came to mean the 'word' in a creative sense, as did another *logos*.

22. Bartalanffy, *Problems of Life* (1949, tr. London, 1952), 153.

23. Hartmann, *New Ways in Ontology* (1949, tr. Chicago, 1953), 80, though 'intellect' might in context be substituted for 'mind'.

24. This again is a word of Teutonic origin, clearly allied to 'wit'. That it has tended to become synonymous with knowledge under cognitive dominance, is indicated in Maxwell's *From Knowledge to Wisdom* (Oxford, 1984) in which it seems to mean extended or more refined knowledge. But no amount of knowledge is equivalent to wisdom. *Scientia* is not and can never be *sapientia*.

25. The author recalls an incident within his own experience. Before a Picasso in the Ashmolean, a woman said to him: "What ought I to think of Picasso?". "Madam, there is no ought; you haven't got to think but simply to react. If favourably, well and good; if not, not". There is no compulsion to comply with current intellectual fashions, though propaganda may be difficult to resist.

26. Mill, *On Liberty* (London, 1859), 30.

27. Bachelard, *La philosophie du non* (Paris, 1940). This 'sense', incidentally, should surely indicate the notion that ratiocination has less significance in vital terms than natural reasoning or good sense, which, from a functional standpoint are infinitely more valuable.

28. It cannot be too strongly stressed that intellectuality relates to personal or subjective interest whereas sensitivity relates to external inter-relationships with social connotations.

29. Since this idea is rooted in a myth – that of Adam's fall – required as

a belief in Tomline, *Elements of Christian Theology* (London, 1843), I, 115, it may be dismissed as without rational standing. The idea, however, is not unique to Christianity and is expressed elsewhere in more natural terms. See Note II. 25.

30. Leach, Reith Lecture (1967), who, in his idea that intellectuals are 'mortal gods', echoes Cicero, knowingly or not.

31. *Geist* in Hegel seems to have several meanings, but in so far as it is linked to rationalism, its relation to sensitivity is doubtful.

32. Polanyi, *Knowing and Being* (London, 1969), developed this idea, which seems to have been neglected because of its implicit challenge to formal logic.

33. An aspect of Cartesian dualism, related to the excluded middle, has been the neglect of what takes place between innervation (held to be physical) and mental action (held to be psychical), now recognized as the sphere of the psychosomatic. The first two are in principle knowable, the last is not; and since it is within that sphere that basic responsiveness resides, its neglect is regrettable. That consciousness is held to be the ground of responsibility may justify dualism (Hawkins, *Men and Words* (London, 1960)), but it also grounds materialism, as if the physical were devoid of spirituality. Bowie in *Structuralism and Since* (ed. Sturrock, Oxford, 1979), 138.

34. Verification may present difficulties, though it is a well established doctrine. But it is scarcely suited to evaluation, which deals neither with 'facts' nor with events in isolation. That subject is not within the scope of cognitive enquiry; for, as Habermas, *Knowledge and Human Interests* (1968, tr. London, 1972), 143: "Nature we explain; psychic life we understand".

Chapter Four

1. The Chinese doctrine known as *fa-li*, in which *fa* means statute law and *li* means ethical obligation, held in principle to be natural, as in parentage, exemplifies this. If a man cannot or will not comply with the norms of social behaviour, or positively affronts them, then law is evoked coercively to restrain him in the greater or social interest. This doctrine is exemplified in Han Fei, Liao, *The Complete Works of Han Fei Tzu* (London, 1939 and 1960).

2. In dichotomic form the heritary-environmental controversy is clearly limited, since both play a part in behaviour. If genes cannot be shown to carry what are called 'acquired' characteristics, a cultural heritage is certainly passed on and clearly related to the acceptance of social norms. A colleague at the University of Puerto Rico, Dr. Juan Rivero, studied animal behaviour as indicating certain human attitudes and

raised questions as to whether that was purely 'instinctive', particularly with respect to adaptation to the environments in which animals found themselves.

3. There is a beautiful Spanish custom, not yet extinct, called *su papel*, originally meaning one's paper or script, and thence one's role in life, one's responsibility. Thus, on retirement, an old street-cleaner, who has performed an important social function fully, is addressed by an honorific, as Don Jorge, or whatever his name may be.

4. That this runs counter to the idea of innate characteristics would be a mistaken view, since full powers only emerge with maturation, as is apparent in artistry. Training is an instrument to aid the child to attain to adult responsibility.

5. Hobbes, *The Lethiathan* (1651), Part I, ch. 12.

6. It is surely the case that what is natural is common at base, even though there are variations. Thus various forms of greeting, the hand shake and clasped hands both indicate that no weapon is held. Hierarchies exist in the jungle, in which the lower species give way to the higher. Other forms are shown in respect for age, official status and so on. The story of Dr. Johnson and the Archbishop of York instances this.

7. In the West we might distinguish between an ontic *tao*, as in the projection of a holistic ontology, and a moral *tao*, referring to behaviour that is natural and appropriate. But this is a division which the Chinese do not normally make, since both, so to say, are read together.

8. Deleuze, *Kant's Critical Philosophy* (Paris, 1963, tr. London, 1984), 36.

9. It may be said that these thinkers distinguished between the soul and the intellect, that is in modern terms between the subject involved with the world (and through faith with God) and the thinking self. Otherwise said, they distinguished a power which was potentially general, common to all men, from that of the intellect; though Gerson held that the last was part of the soul, with the rider that knowledge of God was general and *not* particular.

10. Coplestone, *The History of Philosophy* (London, 1960), VI, 438.

11. Kantian scholars could doubtless make mincemeat of this summary. But, without regretting that unduly, this comment might be made. That if philosophy can only recognize specialist scholarship, the power to develop thought more broadly is impoverished. Few persons are competent to read texts in every language that is philosophically significant, and are obliged to take translations on trust. Behind translations, however, lies the thought of the thinker, which may be 'sensed', as if reading between the lines. Nor are experts always to be relied on. That *ding an sich* and *noumenon* are interchangeable

terms is justly to be questioned. For it would seem that the first refers to what is out there and the second to thought about it, *nous-menon*. It is further open to question whether *ethikos* as used by Aristotle means what moral philosophers often take it to mean; for the tradition of *ĕthos* still survived in his time. Oates, *Aristotle and the Principle of Value* (Cambridge, 1963), 321, weighs the question of whether his thought was morally (personally) or ethically (socially) directed, as did the disciples of K'ung Fu-tzu immediately after his death.

12. 'Sense' has traditionally been used to refer to the sense organs, the action of which is detectable. It is also clearly related to sensation proper, as in the term 'sensorium'. In the first sense Baumgarten's use of the term 'sense perception', may have been justified, except in one important particular, that it does not apply to direct response to artistic form. To that he gave the name 'aesthetic', improperly because *aisthesis* in Greek means 'perception' as used in modern English (confirmed by Dodds, Private Communication, 1952). As a consequence rationalists have since his time failed to recognize that they are using an inappropriate word to describe what they purport to discuss. Whether that should be 'architectonics' (the study of structures of form) or simply 'artistry' is an interesting point. Enough that 'aesthetics' refers only to after-effects, which in part are rationalizable, as direct or sensuous response is not.

13. That intuitions (*Anschauungen*) had to be received before the transcendental ego could apply its categories and develop understanding (*Verstand*) is surely Kant's doctrine. Overt perceptions have to be interpreted, even at lower levels (dim perception) though there they scarcely involve strict knowledge.

14. Although it is almost heresy to say so today when the cognitive interest is pre-eminent, Kant had his priorities right. For, although the augmentation of knowledge doubtless conditions and even enriches life, it is its quality or social tone that is vital to society's balance and persistence.

15. Kant, *op. cit.* (1787, tr. 1929), 328 ff, especially 380 ff., where, from contending that "All thinking beings, as such, are substances", he holds that the 'I think' and the 'subject' are identical. This is scarcely what Aristotle meant by the term *hypokeimenon*. See Coplestone, *op. cit.* (London, 1960), VI, 285, on Kant's use of the term 'subject' for 'substratum'.

16. Hegel, *op. cit.* (1807, 1975), where, in a complicated argument, all this is contended.

17. Since Hegel, as the first thinker to distinguish ethics from morality, can scarcely be charged with failure to consider the general or social interest, it is to later thinkers that an almost exclusive stress on individualism must be attributed.

18. Since only phenomena are knowable, the extra-phenomenal is beyond the reach of cognition. But externality cannot be dismissed out of hand, as if attempts to think about it could be damned as "fishing in muddy waters", a clear instance of rationalistic prejudice.

19. James, *Principles of Psychology* (Boston, 1890), I, 485, holds the first view, which might be called an ontology, Heidegger, *Being and Time* (1927, tr. Oxford, 1962), the second. Although these views of externality appear to be very different, they are plainly both idealist, seeing the world from a subjective standpoint. Realists by contrast, take it to be a dynamic, interelative, indivisible complex, always tending towards harmony.

20. It is perhaps better exemplified by Teilhard de Chardin, *The Phenomenon of Man* (1955, tr. London, 1959), 283 ff., whose thought is teleological without reservation.

21. Buber, *I and Thou* (1937, tr. Edinburgh, 1970), affords an excellent instance of this.

22. When the subject is contraposed to the object a false dichotomy is projected, since the object is a creation of the subject, a construct made up of particulars bound in the intellect. Strictly speaking, there are no objects in the world, which is an interrelative whole.

23. Early Egyptian thinking was distinguished by its ethical tone, stressing the need for justice and responsibility, and it was not until the irruption of the Hyksos that it became personalized. In so far as can be determined that was true of Chinese thought, as is exemplified in the *Shu King*, notably in the story of Duke Sung at the Battle of the Rivers (in 638 BC), reported in Fitzgerald, *China; A Short Cultural History* (London, 1935, 1976), 62.

24. This tendency has always been latent in idealism, which, with intellectual arrogance, especially on the part of the second-rate, has had the effect of bringing élitism, obviously valuable in some sense, into discredit.

25. When this point was brought up in conversation recently, Canon Stanley Ruff, who was present, observed that this earlier meaning was stressed by St. François de Sales (*Introduction à la vie dévote*, 1604) as the core of Christianity. A generalized sense of our humanity (as burdened souls) was more to be valued than an exclusive love of those with whom one was in sympathy. This lesson has particular value today when bickering, religious, political, racial and sexual, characterizes society.

26. Hartmann, *Ethics* (1926, tr. London, 1950), II, 270.

27. It is a Chinese contention that ethics should not be confused with politics, since an ethic is a social requirement regardless of the form of a regime, whether it be tyrannical or democratic. Moreover, political systems are transient and never free from relation to power and the

exertion of legal control, finally exerted by but few, even in democracies, which has its warrant in checking abuse.

28. Scott, *The Architecture of Humanism* (London, 1924), 25, 143, shows that a potential to respond to artistic form is innate in the human make-up. But indeed, all societies, when not corrupted by intellectualism, have displayed an artistic 'sense', if only in the dance and personal adornment. Its decay, or overriding by a demand for 'meaning', may well be one of the causes of the present unrest.

29. Derrida, *Positions* (1972, tr. London, 1981), 151, 156.

30. On an intellectual plane, nothing is common unless in abstract or, less certainly, empiric form. If then we look for what is common in human nature, which grounds what is common in society, we must probe more deeply into the subtler reaches of nervous response – the need for harmonious relations for example.

31. This was positively stated in conversation with the author by a philosopher who said that it was for this very reason that ethics was not now studied.

32. It is naïve, even irresponsible, to contend that all scientific discoveries are necessarily beneficial, even from a materialistic standpoint. It is their repercussive effects on society that should be subjected to external judgment.

33. To concentrate on suffering or on pain, as philosophers do, is to think only in terms of extremes or exceptions, and thus to lose sight of what is basic or general in the human condition. Existentialism, by stressing the morbid, falls into the same error of failing to get to grips with the general, the persistent as opposed to the transient.

34. With the dominance of cognitivism only that which can be observed and measures is given attention. But plainly that is not all of what nature – with its roots in what is born or brought to being – means. Indeed, even *physis* means rather more than material or embodied matter, since it originally meant growing or unfolding (cf. Brahman). Heidegger, *An Introduction to Metaphysics* (1953, tr. New York, 1961), 52 ff.

35. Standard dictionaries invariably define 'sentient' as 'having the power of sense-perception', which is implicitly taken, under empiricist influence, to signify a conscious power. If that is its sole meaning, then no term is available for the power to respond subconsciously, in which sense, for want of another term, it is used in this essay.

36. Heidegger, op. cit. (1953, 1961), 21.

Chapter Five

1. Roe, *Ethical Issues* (London, 1990).

2. Horkheimer, *Eclipse of Reason* (New York, 1947), 180.
3. Under an idealist dispensation this is not well understood: that personal values, or values accruing uniquely to the individual, as to the artist or to the sophisticated recipient, are not philosophical concerns. If philosophy claims to deal with the general, it is value in general, which accrues in more subtle forms, to which it should attend. Croce's interest in 'expression' is not in this sense philosophical, and that is even truer of such later works, as Naum, *The Artist as Creator* (Baltimore (1956).
4. Colloquialisms are found in all languages as needed means of expressing ideas in a way that formal logic cannot. Even slang in certain forms fills a lacuna quite beyond its reach. Contempt for such verbal formations is misplaced if they serve a function in communication which relates to social requirements.
5. Schiller, *Logic for Use* (London, 1929), 4 ff.
6. Hegel, *Philosophy of Right* (1821, tr. Oxford, 1942), 105 ff.
7. To render this idea acceptable to modern idealists, it is suitably noted by Lawson-Tancred, *Aristotle: De Anima* (London, 1986), 12, that for Aristotle, *psyche* did not have its modern meaning, but rather meant 'principle of life or of animation', whence its relation to the Chinese idea of spirit as immanent in vitality can be better understood.
8. Since nature is a dynamic complex in constant process of change, so human responsiveness must adapt to that: not that the structure of the nervous system undergoes alterations in the same way – though it does change slightly with growth – but that there are no absolutes present in adaptation, which is always circumstantial.
9. If nothing else, a dealing with objects and a dealing with dynamic interrelationships clearly demands distinctive approaches.
10. This is fairly translated as "The ethics that nature implants in us". This citation is given in Pessonneaux, *Dictionnaire Grec-Français* (Paris, 1895), 435, without note of source. All attempts precisely to locate it have thus far failed, though it is clearly echoed in *Politics*, Book I, 2 (1253a 30), as in Leibniz, op. cit., (1765), I, ii, 9.
11. Among those who have given thought to ethical as distinct from moral issues Hampshire, *Morality and Conflict* (Oxford, 1980), should be mentioned; for, despite his title, those are his concern.
12. Curiously, for *morālis*, derived from Cicero's *philosophīa morālis*, his translation of the Greek *ethikōs*, which yet retained some relation to its etymon *ĕthos*, had, with its roots in *mores*, a slightly different meaning. It was rather related to law or rule in contrast to spontaneous acceptance of one's role, one's commitment to the whole, rather than with a quasi-conscious obedience, to modern thinking wholly personalized. *Morale* was internalized, as was *ĕthos*: *philosophīa morālis* was an entirely conscious involvement.

13. *Magna Moralia*, I, 6, 1186a, (of which the Greek form was *Ethikā Megāle*).

14. Bury, *The History of Greece* (London, 1959), II, 148. This echoes *tao-ching-hsin* (literally 'right-sincerity-disposition') in classical Chinese, which, so far from being a primitive idea, gave roots to a general culture in both these areas, in a way that intellectuality, confined to relatively small classes, could not do.

15. Since documentation reflects only the ideas of the literate classes, it is difficult to detect the persistence of older ideas among those who did not express them in writing. This is more readily discernible in the case of *logos*, since it re-emerges in the Stoic *logos spermātikos*, as also in the Fourth Gospel, where *logos* scarcely meant the word in the sense of a vocable. That *ĕthos* survived in its earlier meaning is shown in certain attitudes of Socrates and even of Aristotle.

16. Stoicism later became the philosophy adopted by the upper classes in Rome, much as *Bushido* (the knightly way) did in Japan. It is difficult to know how Epicurianism fared, but there is index in a recently discovered monument to Diogenes of Oenoanda that it had wider influence than is generally supposed for lack of documentary evidence, doubtless neglected or destroyed, as a dangerous heresy, by the Christians. But apart from that, that it gave no promise of a future life, but merely of balance in this one, scarcely allowed it to compete with messianic religions in the disturbed conditions of the time. Its revival in aristocratic Europe was due to a growing refinement, to which it gave countenance.

17. This contention of Polystratus is interestingly echoed by Stankiewicz, op cit. (1976), 153, as already noted.

18. But so deeply embedded is its influence, to confirm that it is innate, that it survives all batterings. A sense of honour and decency is present even in modern life and cannot be wholly eradicated however great the pressures, products of individualistic self-assertion, that militate against it.

19. The mysteries (Orphic, Eleusian, and so on), in as far as they are separable from the Olympic Pantheon (Kitto, *The Greeks* (London, 1951), 19 ff.), long predated the introduction of oriental religions. Of pre-Hellenic origin, they appealed to subject individuals, from which it might be contended that they answered a need not otherwise met. Zeller, *Outlines of the History of Greek Philosophy* (1883, tr. New York, 1967), 336 ff. summarized the movement from philosophy into religion admirably.

20. Hierarchies there must be and it is naïve to think that they can be replaced by egalitarianism without cultural and political damage. All depends upon their quality. For, if power is used irresponsibly, that is bound to lead to reaction in the form of rebellion, which often replaces

one tyranny with another. Delicacy of touch in the art of exercising authority is the key to social stability. *Noblesse oblige*, whatever its origin, is a very profound doctrine, discussed in this sense by Ortega, *La rebellión de las masas* (Madrid, 1930), VI.

21. Slavery was much more extensive in Rome than in Greece and was undoubtedly one of the causes of Rome's decline, since, apart from objection to it in itself, scarcely then much felt, the presence of alien attitudes slowly corroded the standards by which the older Romans had lived (Westermann, *Greek and Roman Slavery* (Philadelphia, 1955)). Whether this has modern bearing is not fitly discussed.

22. Aristotle so strongly objected to Alexander's policy of racial admixture (in this case with a highly civilized people) that he is said to have sent him a bottle of poisoned wine. Whether true or not, what is of interest is that Aristotle, a man of liberal mind, disliked this policy and feared for its consequences: the breakdown of the Hellenic *ĕthos*.

23. When the later term, *moralitas*, was introduced is not clear.

24. Kirk, *The Threshold of Ethics* (London, 1933) makes the interesting point that conscience is an idea more or less unique to Christianity. Although defined as a 'sense', its root *conscientia* simply meant 'with knowledge' and carried no necessary idea of guilt or self-consciousness.

25. Philosophers – or those whose works are not read outside their own circle – may be flattered to think so. But the real point of this statement is that, if so, they carry a heavy responsibility, the real justification for serious criticism. It is not now evident, with the persistent propagation of dubious and even dangerous doctrines, that this is very well understood.

26. Of all the classical schools, Stoicism is the most difficult to summarize, since during its life of some five hundred years it underwent many changes. Although it was characterized by a persistent 'pantheism', if that is the proper term for a doctrine which in its earlier form was not in any real sense theistic, its conception of *logos spermātikos* changed. Sometimes translated as 'Divine Reason', it seems earlier to have had a meaning closer to *tao*, as an animating force rather than as something transcendent or supernatural, as with the idea of immortality, the soul's return to God, as it later seems to have become.

27. Julianus Imperator was naturally condemned by Christians (who were not persecuted by him) for his opposition to their faith or his tolerance of others. In so far as can be determined he took his responsibilities seriously and considered, with greater sophistication than Constantinus, that social unity had priority over personal salvation.

28. Hegel, both in op. cit. (1821, tr. Oxford, 1942), 167, 392, and in his

Earliest Writings on Religion, Politics and Economics (ed. Dublin, 1979), 57, makes this point, criticizing Kant for his failure to do so.

29. The weakening of its influence confirms this, as did the weakening of Confucianism, since that releases egocentric tendencies. Unchecked freedom has its vices as well as its virtues, as Mme. Roland, so shrewdly observed. The dominance of materialism is one of these.

30. It is true that *Mo-che* and the earlier *Ming-chia* both made their appearance in China, to be rejected as without real meaning, and that *Nyāya* was developed in India, together with various forms of Buddhist logic, to show close associations with religion, so that they were rather directed towards salvation than cognition.

31. It is noteworthy that Frege insisted that formal logic was a strictly abstract discipline and that its scope had not been delimited precisely (Kneale & Kneale, *The Development of Logic* (Oxford, 1962), 724, and Tarski, *Concept of Truth in Formalized of Logic* (1935, tr. Oxford, 1956), 267, expressed a not dissimilar idea. For a rather harsher finding, Gomperz, *Greek Thinking* (1893, tr. London, 1901), IV, 45, might be cited.

32. Foucault, *Power/Knowledge: Selected Papers* (tr. New York, 1980), 238.

33. Beveridge, *The Art of Scientific Investigation* (London, 1959), has something to say on this matter.

34. Intentionality doubtless plays a part in all response and action, but it is not necessarily overt and so detectable, as strong as these words suggest. We are not normally driven in the usual run of life, nor are we invariably conditioned by conscious goals. We act in the main without conscious thought and so with the utmost delicacy.

35. This may be disputed, but to bring rationalism to bear on the mysteries of religion and the meaning of ritual is a dubious extension of philosophy's role, which its claims to be all-embracing do not justify if it insists on its rationality.

36. As has already been observed, 'aesthetics', introduced by rationalists, is a most unsuitable word to apply to artistic reception. Slutsky might be cited on this matter: "When it comes to that with which we are concerned, all metaphysicians (read rationalists) are charlatans, either conscious or unconscious". Private Conversation (1948).

37. In fairness, it should be noted that tastes differ, albeit more subtly, on a sensuous plane, as in preference for certain colours or colour combinations, or in keener response to linear, mass or arabesque formations. Special delights in certain arts, a more developed plastic or musical sense, which seldom go together, almost certainly have psychophysical roots. But, as authentic, these attitudes are sensuous and not intellectual.

38. Such matters as the effects of ugly surroundings, vulgar displays, as in

advertizing, or harsh noises, on the psyche, and so on social relations and stances, would constitute a valid philosophical study.

39. Architecture has been excluded from this list because it is indeed a public art and so inescapable, notwithstanding that, in tune with the tone of the times, criticism tends to be confined to individual buildings regardless of their settings. Moreover, those evoke interest largely in degree as they are 'exceptional', stand out instead of folding in; they shout as opposed to whispering.

40. Williams, *Morality: An Introduction to Ethics* (London, 1972), reveals in his title, and more so in the text, that he has no conception of what ethics means, since his only concern is with the motives of the individual.

41. It is a Chinese doctrine, propounded, among others, by Tung Chung-shu, that a man is always aware that he acts improperly and cannot disguise this knowledge from himself, though he may deceive others by means of what is significantly called 'rationalization'.

42. Hegel, op. cit. (1807, 1975), 629 ff. 'Dubious' may not be the happiest term when statesmanship is considered. For a statesman, acting in what he believes to be the long-term interest, may disguise his intention, since it would be unwise to expose it. Mere politicians, conversely, often act quite cynically to impress the public as preoccupied with their interests, when the real motive is personal advance.

43. Romero, *Filosofía de la persona* (Buenos Aires, 1944), makes this point superbly: that responsibility presumes loss of the self and acceptance of involvement with the whole. Moreover, it is normally subconscious, since otherwise it might involve subjective calculation.

44. Durkheim, *Moral Education* (1925, tr. New York, 1961). This text, though officially sociological, is in fact deeply philosophical, stressing the social character of education as its essential purpose.

45. With concentration on conscious response, which, as subjective, is highly variable, search for what is common in humanity and underlies its deeper needs is bound to be abortive. Absolute similarity cannot, of course, be sustained and certainly cannot be proven. But, if there are common characteristics in the human make-up, regardless of culture, race and other external factors, it is on subconscious levels that these reside.

46. Academic prejudice is not unrelated to fashion, as has been evident in the last fifty years, such that, until recently, any other idea of the role of philosophy than that then in vogue was dismissed as 'unphilo-sophical' or, to cite a publisher's editor: "not within the mainstream of current philosophical thinking". No doubt, this has happened before, but seldom with so strong a bias as to constitute a form of censorship, against which, as unorthodox, a thinker has little redress.

47. For as long as the curious idea that all study which is not objective – when objectivity itself is subjective – reigns, the study of dynamic interrelationships is effectively blocked. Ethics is not amenable to rationalization, as Hegel himself observed. It follows that another approach than that of objectification is required.

Chapter Six

1. Scepticism has no virtue when it is merely destructive, as certain forms of it are. Its justification resides in clearing the ground for deeper thought on given problems. This was at times its purpose, if not with Gorgias, certainly with Carneades. In such sense, it is not to be dismissed as a threat to entrenched ideas, which are suitably challenged. Deconstruction, if it has more than a heuristic interest, presupposes reconstruction, but it is not yet apparent that this is being undertaken in the form that it should be.
2. That artists and musicians express themselves through symbols is improperly evoked in this context, since their appeal is to the senses, not to the intellect, to the real, that is, and not to the ideal, notwithstanding that romantics urge the latter view. Gurney, *The Power of Sound* (London, 1880), 331, is suitably cited in this connection.
3. The history of idealist philosophy, particularly in modern times, as with the neo-realists and the logical atomists, might be characterized as turning precisely on this effort. Armstrong, *A Materialistic Theory of Mind* (London, 1968) represents a recent attempt to bridge this gap.
4. Nor is it necessary to evoke the Sceptics, since Habermas, op. cit. (1968, 1972), 23, 140, who is certainly not to be so ranked, says much the same thing. Incidentally, that realism is commonly aligned with materialism affords an example of misunderstanding about what realism properly means.
5. Fishler on 'Heraclitus' in *The Dictionary of Philosophy* (New York, ND), apparently citing Diels, *Fragmenti der Vorsokretiker* (1902, tr. Oxford, 1954), though there is no evidence that he perpetrated such an idea.
6. Hawking, *A Brief History of Time* (London, 1988), 144.
7. It is true, of course, that spiritual issues have been given intellectual attention continually in the West under the name of theology, which might be regarded as an attempt to rationalize the mystical. One hesitates to comment on this, since that discipline deals with things sacred and so has special status. Even so, the Scriptures themselves might be cited: "Who lives by the sword shall die by the sword". In other words, to appeal to rationalism is to invite rational attack, as

mystics have recognized. But what is pertinent here is that spiritual interests which are other than religious and just as resistant to rationalization have received but scant attention, certain distinguished thinkers excepted, of whom Marcel, *Le Déclin de la Sagesse* (Paris, 1954) affords an instance.

8. Though the interest in this chapter is to work towards an adequate methodology for *evaluative* discourse, the problem is deeper. For science, once it accepts a holistic ontology, is confronted with a parallel problem, in that induction does not operate in a world in which there are no particulars.

9. There is noted by Aristotle himself in the *Nichomachean Ethics*, VI, x, 1, where he distinguishes between understanding (*eusunesīa*) and knowledge (*epistēmē*).

10. Ayer, *Language, Truth and Logic* (London, 1948), 104, affords the classical instance of this, though in fairness it should be said that he repudiated that crudeness later in life.

11. Jung, *The Secret of the Golden Flower* (1931, tr. London, 1962), in which he describes a mystical discipline.

12. Marcel, *L'homme problematique* (Paris, 1955), 21, 175, criticizing Sartre for his individualism and effective blindness to the real basis of human life, which presupposes involvement with others.

13. Gallie, *Peirce and Pragmatism* (London, 1952), 59.

14. It was once remarked, not entirely unjustly, that "The Oxford English Dictionary was a monument to empiricism".

15. Russell, *Problems of Philosophy* (London, 1912), Ch. V.

16. The term 'epistemology' was coined by Ferrier (1854), who based his use of it on later classical usage, notwithstanding that its earlier meaning was 'habitude', the sense required when riding a horse.

17. Koestler, op. cit. (London, 1964), 547, in which reference is to 'sensing', a term that is seldom used in philosophy.

18. Whitehead's 'prehension' (*Process and Reality* (Cambridge, 1929), Part III) has been omitted from this list, since it seems to refer to an immediate grasping of relationships, or rather an instant awareness of them.

19. Without citing well recorded instances, it is enough to quote Poincaré, *La Science et l'Hypothèse* (Paris, 1902), 41.

20. Angeles, *A Dictionary of Philosophy* (London, 1981), 39.

21. Käsher, *Max Weber* (1974, tr. London, 1988), 181 ff.

22. Lipps, *Asthetik* (Munich, 1903-1906), though the idea was first projected as early as 1885. Of this theory one critic (Hauser) observed: "The empathic act is not simply kinesthetic but has objective reference". That empathy is taken to be perceptual, and so intellectualizable rather than sensuous, is characteristic of a rationalistic approach to artistry.

23. Understanding undoubtedly plays some part in discovery, which itself culminates in knowledge, later confirmed by verification. Hence tacit knowledge, which is not itself consciously recorded and is in that sense subconsciously received, seems to contribute to understanding considered as a form of immediate grasping and is rather aligned with Kant's *Anschauung* than with his *Verstand*, though Polanyi himself might dissent from this (op. cit. (1969), 194).

24. This citation is from Lorenz, "The Role of Perception in Animal and Human Behaviour" in *Aspects of Form* (ed. Whyte, London, 1951), 176. Whyte's own ideas are to be found in *The Unconscious* (London, 1959).

25. Driesch, *The Possibility of Metaphysics* (London, 1924), for example, or Bergson, Whitehead, Merleau-Ponty, not to mention others.

26. It was not until Bolzano published his *Wissenschaftslehre* in 1837, to be followed immediately by Trendelenburg (1840), Mill (1843), De Morgan and Boole (1847) that interest in formal logic revived after many years of neglect, to be followed later in the century by a galaxy of prominent logicians, who grounded the modern interest in this discipline and realized that, as formal, logic had grave limitations.

27. Nagel, *What does it all mean?* (New York, 1989), and he might well raise the question in the present state of philosophy.

28. Even this example is far from absolute, since the collapse of stars and the creation of novae suggest that celestial movements are far from regular. But change must be more deeply considered. Bergson, *L'évolution creatrice* (Paris, 1903) shows, with *l'élan vital*, that what applies in inanimate bodies does not apply to living bodies organisms, or indeed to the forces behind movement. This has yet to be learned by rationalists who are too concerned with regularities.

29. Whether Moore, who was both a moralist and an epistemological intuitionist, ever put this idea so baldly is doubtful. But it was certainly the view of Spinoza (*Ethica* II, Prop. XL ff), echoed by a number of distinguished thinkers, and some who were less so, Parker in a sermon (1841).

30. Jaspers, *Reason and Existence* (1935, tr. London, 1956), 37, 138. Hui Shih, a contemporary of Aristotle, propounded a similar doctrine, *ming-shih*, which influenced Chinese thinking as much as Aristotle's *Analytikē* influenced that of the West.

31. If *logos*, as used by Heraclitus, is taken to mean *ratio*, that is surely to be understood as active in nature and not, as it was later taken to mean, quantitative relationships established intellectually, as is exemplified in the expression 'ratiocination'.

32. Angeles, op. cit. (1981) defines 'inference' as 'the logical or conceptual process of deriving a statement from one, or more, statements', or as 'deriving a conclusion from premises that are true', to imply that

wider meanings of it are out of order.

33. Although there is no famous incident, such as that recorded of Kekulé, in the history of philosophy, it is scarcely to be doubted that original ideas are not wholly the product of rational thought. Socrates' *daimon* suggests that intuition played some part in his critical thinking, and it might be asked what woke Kant from his dogmatic slumbers if not a sudden recognition that he had taken the wrong direction.

34. Under influence of an exclusively cognitive tradition, epistemology has given little or no attention to this means of grasping relationships, notwithstanding the pristine meaning of *epistēmē*. That requires that it should, if only in awareness of its etymon, give some thought to such matters as these.

35. Roe, *Logical Issues*, in preparation.

36. Much science is clearly negativistic, as the expression 'Preventive Medicine' indicates. From a philosophical standpoint, Popper's 'fallibilism' is plainly a negativistic doctrine, holding that science advances by falsifying prior discoveries, by continual emendation.

37. It could be argued that some of the commandments are expressed in positive form: "Thou shalt honour thy father and mother...". But that could as well be stated negatively: "Thou shalt *not* dishonour thy parents..." And it is wisely so understood because behind all prescriptions lies a reason: that to fail to do what is required would generate disturbance, in the family or in society at large.

38. The Chinese doctrine of *fa-li* is of interest in this context; for, briefly stated, its burden is this. If you cannot behave in a civilized way, comply with the norms, fulfil your natural responsibilities – for *li* means roughly 'ethical principle' – then *fa*, 'statute law', is properly evoked and force is applied in the public interest.

39. That Socrates aspired to positive answers and "repeatedly failed to produce the desired definitions" (Bambrough, Introduction to Lindsay's *Republic*), *aporīa* intervening, may not be a just interpretation. He rather realized that conslusive answers were not available in respect of the ethical questions he discussed, such that the proper end was to ensure that no false answers were allowed to stand. The essential interest was to form a ring of negations, and the more tightly it was drawn, the more refined or less inept, was thinking on these questions, themselves permitting of no final answers.

40. Spinoza, *Epis. L.* (1674), reproduced in Van Vloten & Land *Benedicti de Spinoza: Opera.* (The Hague, 1914), III, 173.

41. When stimuli can be mediated subconsciously, as they can be in the vast majority of reactions, the intellect is not called upon to intervene. It is only when some threat to the system is great enough to evoke consciousness that greater powers have to be brought into play. In nature that is the primary function of perception.

42. That earthquakes and floods, accidents or terrorism, are disturbing is sufficiently obvious. What generates subtler psychical disturbance, which has social repercussions, may not be so obvious or so readily detectable; but that comprises the real concern of ethics.

43. If Husserl found it possible to form an *epochē* on an ideal plane, it is not unreasonable to suggest that one might be formed on a real plane. In both cases the interest is to exclude irrelevances, that is, subjective factors in response to what is presented, in that case when response is immediate. However, this cannot properly be discussed unless all that it presumes is taken into account, as it will be in a further book, *Logical Issues*. Kolakouski, *Husserl and the Search for Certitude* (New Haven, 1975), 83, shows that certitude is not attainable on an ideal plane. But if that is not the end in view, which is quite other, forming *epochai* may yet serve some purposes.

44. Kant, op. cit. (1787, 1929), 574, a comment that might be said to echo Socrates' negativism, commonly called the Socratic Method.

45. Bergson, op. cit. (1907), 160, reluctantly quoted against him, who was otherwise a realist, though here projecting an idealist view.

46. If we suppose that knowledge can only be scientific (*scientia*, *epistēmē*), we blind ourselves to any further meaning that it may have. If a fly settles on one's cheek, one is aware of it, and has to be so in order to take appropriate counteraction; but that is scarcely scientific knowledge, as that it is disease-bearing might be. Used in a wider sense, knowledge refers to any form of awareness and need not, as related to memory, be original. It is the normal consequence of stronger stimulation.

47. An a priori judgment might be said to be independent of external stimulation. But behind it lie mnemonic influences, which give it its meaning. Even A is A presumes prior knowledge gathered by means of experience of what 'equals' means, indeed of what a symbol is intended to convey. As for reaching behind phenomenal presentations, that is no more than with the aid of instruments going beyond *naked* perception to what is yet presented phenomenally. Medawar, *The Limits of Science* (Oxford, 1985), 75, though he is more concerned with the limits of reasoning.

48. Though it may be difficult for rationalists to acknowledge this, they themselves, as when they 'fall in love', or simply act with courtesy, indulge rapport wholly without calculation.

Conclusion

1. And so because it is intrinsically subjective and cannot as a consequence properly engage external or vital issues.

2. However inadequately its problems are dealt with when they are personalized, axiology is a recognized philosophical discipline, dependent in effect on ideas projected by ontology. That has then a certain responsibility. But it too is limited if it is enmeshed in a cognitive approach, and adopts the dangerous idea that nature is 'knowable', something to be dominated and exploited in the material interest. If such a view is placed before simple men – and high-flown talk of being and causality sustains it, as does a tie to epistemology – then that their relation to the world is crude and insensitive is scarcely surprising. In sum, it is to ontology to promote a deeper understanding of what is actually confronted and given the names of 'nature' or 'reality'. Until men have the wisdom to learn to attune to that in which they are inextricably enmeshed, there can be no adequate ethics or no real understanding of spiritual issues, regarded under the present dispensation as transcendent in contrast to natural, to nature viewed itself as material. That man is a mode of nature, with which he must come to terms, is an idea that necessitates a more profound ontology, in want of which the blind drive to increasing wealth and mastery – exploitation of resources, and so on – can only lead to ultimate disaster, rivalry, discontent and a general malaise, because the nature of man's involvement with reality is so grossly misunderstood.

3. Scientists, when not under the influence of philosophers, tend to be more modest. The excesses of the latter, represented by Carnap, already cited, and by Mises (*Positivism*, Cambridge, Mass, 1951), 74), may be balanced by Bartalanffy and Medawar, both already cited. But scientists tend to hold saner views and now recognize that what is confronted is far from simply explicable with the techniques which they are obliged to employ.

4. This absurd remark, made by a starry-eyed lecturer, who was old enough to know better, many years ago, has never been forgotten, as representing a view of science for which idealist philosophers bear some responsibility.

5. For even expression, it seems, is to be rationalized, as if nothing were beyond the reach of the categorizing intellect. But then, as aestheticians concern themselves with perceptual response and with after-effects exclusively, blind to any other aspect of response, that is not surprising. Intellectuality cannot acknowledge limits. Croce, *Aesthetics as the Science of Expression* (1901, tr. London, 1922) and his followers, Collingwood, *Principles of Art* (Oxford, 1938) and Carritt, *Introduction to Aesthetics* (Oxford, 1949), all illustrate this.

6. When truth is defined by Baylis (*Dictionary of Philosophy*) as "a characteristic of some propositional meanings, namely those that are

true", no one can quibble, though that definition amounts to a *petitio principii*. It has the virtue, however, of restricting the term to logocentric discourse, unless 'true' purports to refer externally. But Strawson, *Introduction to Logical Theory* (London, 1952), 212 et passim, shows that truth in logic does not entail external commitment.

Index Rerum

212

214

Mind, 60f, 112; its etymon, 70; its function, 40; a universal endowment, 76; meanings given questioned, 177
Mind-independent, the, 17
Misinterpretation, 7, 105, 175
Moderation, advocated, 100
Modes, social corroded, 137; *agens & possibilis*, 21; Spinozean sense, 108
Moralis, 120, 123
Morality, 111f, 121, 124, 131, 134; its etymon, 131, as rationalizable, 115, 125
Mōres, pristine meaning, 121
Motivation, 132, 138; not a concern of ethics, 132, 147
Mystère ontologique, le, 32
Mystics, 67, 147

Natura naturans, 18
Nature, 96, 129, 142; attunement to, 34; man as a mode of, 34, 177
Nature, human, 47, 104
Needs, 5, 11, 45, 87, 116, 129, 135, 139; as the essential concern, 4, 11
Negation, 59, 166; as the key, 168, 171
Nemēsis, probable, 112
Noēsis & intellectus, 74
Non-fitting, the, 166, 168, 171
Norms, 87, 116, 135, 142
Noumenon, the, & nous, 75
Nous & mind, 74

Object, 83, 106, its etymon, 107; not antithesis of subject, 106
Objectification, 53, 66, 108, 149, 155, 161
Obligation, 86, 88; network of, 134
Observation, its limits, 144
Ockham's razor, applied, 105
Ontology, 19, 22, 30, 97, 127, 158; need of a more adequate, 19

Organisms, study of, 143
Out of place, the, 168

Pain, as sensation, 38
Pantheism, 125
Paradox, the Liar's, 5
Particulars, rooted in the general, 138
Perception, 35f, 46, 54, 108; its etymon, 37; as dim & clear, 54
Phenomenology, its influence, 155
Philosophīa, its meaning, 127
Philosophy, 11, 33, 89, 101, 109, 127, 147, 176; its concern, 22, 73, 86, 137, 174; its responsibility, 29, 57, 160, 179
Physical & Psychical, play between, 46
Planes, intellectual & sub-conscious, 80
Polis, the, collapse of, 120
Potentiality, human, 52, 58, 63, 124, 137
Powers, of early man, 73; rational & intuitive, 96
Precision, verbal, demanded, 128, 173
Pressures, subjection to, 85, 92, 167
Presuppositions, 129, 157
Pretensions, rationalistic, 140f
Problems, their forms, 27, 57, 100, 126, 152, 164; basic, 100
Procedures, 54, 166; ethical not universalizable, 166
Processes, mental, 159
Proposals, tentative, 103
Propriety, sense of, 50, 58
Proscriptions. interdictive, 165
Purusha, its character, 74

Quoral 'reference', 167, 171

Rapport, 99
Ratio, in nature & thought, 160

Index Nominum

Works of the Author

Letter to a Patron (1961)

Letters from Afar (1975)

Unacceptable Essays (1984)

Ethical Issues (1991)

> Introduction; I. Ethics as the Core of Philosophy; II. Ethics as a distinctive concern; III. Ethics developed in its own terms; IV. Ethics as promoting a potential; V. Ethics in its wider implications; VI. Ethics as disciplined discourse; Conclusion.

Semantic Issues (1993)

> Introduction; I. Reality and Appearance; II. Sensation and Perception; III. Mind and Intellect; IV. Subject and Object; V. Ethics and Morality; VI. Understanding and Knowledge; Conclusion.

Logical Issues (In preparation)

> Introduction; I. The complicated history of the word 'Logic' (*Logos* and *Logica*); The two basic forms of logic (Formal and Natural Logic); III. The two further forms of logic (Positive or Alethic Logic and Negative or Critical Logic); IV. The latent powers of Negation (interpreted as Responsive Rejection); V. The Logic of Incongruity; Conclusion.

In mind is a further work, to be entitled *Artistic Issues*, to complete the Issues Series. In addition there are a number of unpublished works leading up to the Issues Series, together with a translation of Romero's *Filosofía de la Persona*, *Comparative Thinking* (Chinese, Indian, Western) and *Res Architectonica*, related to *Artistic Issues*.